I0010416

Mastering Cross-Platform Development with Xamarin

Master the skills required to steer cross-platform applications from drawing board to app store(s) using Xamarin

Can Bilgin

PUBLISHING

BIRMINGHAM - MUMBAI

Mastering Cross-Platform Development with Xamarin

Copyright © 2016 Packt Publishing

All rights reserved. No part of this book may be reproduced, stored in a retrieval system, or transmitted in any form or by any means, without the prior written permission of the publisher, except in the case of brief quotations embedded in critical articles or reviews.

Every effort has been made in the preparation of this book to ensure the accuracy of the information presented. However, the information contained in this book is sold without warranty, either express or implied. Neither the author, nor Packt Publishing, and its dealers and distributors will be held liable for any damages caused or alleged to be caused directly or indirectly by this book.

Packt Publishing has endeavored to provide trademark information about all of the companies and products mentioned in this book by the appropriate use of capitals. However, Packt Publishing cannot guarantee the accuracy of this information.

First published: March 2016

Production reference: 1280316

Published by Packt Publishing Ltd.
Livery Place
35 Livery Street
Birmingham B3 2PB, UK.

ISBN 978-1-78528-568-4

www.packtpub.com

Credits

Author
Can Bilgin

Reviewers
Engin Polat

Lance McCarthy

Toni Petrina

Commissioning Editor
Veena Pagare

Acquisition Editors
Vinay Argekar

Meeta Rajani

Content Development Editor
Siddhesh Salvi

Technical Editors
Pramod Kumavat

Siddhi Rane

Copy Editor
Roshni Banerjee

Project Coordinator
Nidhi Joshi

Proofreader
Safis Editing

Indexer
Hemangini Bari

Graphics
Kirk D'Penha

Production Coordinator
Shantanu N. Zagade

Cover Work
Shantanu N. Zagade

About the Authors

Can Bilgin currently works for Authority Partners Inc. as a program architect. He has been working in the software industry, primarily with Microsoft technologies, for over a decade and has been recognized as a Microsoft Most Valuable Professional (MVP) for his technical contributions. In this period, he played key roles in projects for high profile clients using technologies such as BizTalk, SharePoint, Dynamics CRM, Xamarin, WCF, and other web technologies.

His main passion lies in mobile and IoT development using the modern toolset available for developers.

He tries to share his experience on his blog (http://canbilgin.wordpress.com), social media (@can_bilgin), and through speaking engagements at both local and international conferences and community events in the Balkans region.

This book is dedicated to three girls who shaped my life and still are doing so: my best friend and beloved wife, Sanja Grebovic Bilgin, our little daughter, Dilara Bilgin, and my loving mother, Turkan Bilgin.

About the Reviewers

Engin Polat has been involved in many large and medium-scale projects on .NET technologies as a developer, architect, and consultant, and has won many awards since 1999.

Since 2008, he has been giving training to many large enterprises in Turkey about Windows development, web development, distributed application development, software architecture, mobile development, cloud development, and so on.

Apart from this, he organizes seminars and events in many universities in Turkey about .NET technologies, Windows platform development, cloud development, web development, game development, and so on.

He shares his experiences on his personal blog (http://www.enginpolat.com).

He has MCP, MCAD, MCSD, MCDBA, and MCT certifications.

In 2012, he was recognized as a Windows Platform Development MVP (Most Valuable Professional) by Microsoft.

Between 2013 and 2015, he was recognized as a Nokia Developer Champion; very few people in the world are given this award. In 2015, he was recognized as the Regional Director by Microsoft.

I'd like to thank my dear wife, Yeliz, and my beautiful daughter, Melis Ada, for all the support they gave me while I was working on this book project.

Lance McCarthy, Microsoft MVP, is a community leader with an acute expertise for all things, such as .NET and C#, especially on the XAML stack, including WPF, Silverlight, Windows Phone, and Windows Store apps. He is very helpful online and guides and answers questions from Microsoft developers on Twitter as `@lancewmccarthy`. In his free time, he writes his blog at `http://WinPlatform.wordpress.com`, which focuses on Windows Universal apps. He organizes and hosts events in the Boston area, such as user group nights, mini-code camps, and full hackathons.

During the day, he is a senior technical support engineer at Telerik where he supports developers with their Classic Windows, Universal Windows Platform, Web and Mobile application development (Xamarin, Android native, and iOS native). He is also a technical consultant for the Windows Developer social media team where he helps respond to development questions via the official `@WindowsDev` Twitter account.

Previously, he worked for Nokia/Microsoft as a developer ambassador where he sought out and engaged developers through outreach programs and provided them with technical support and resources to make them successful on the Windows Phone and Windows 8 platforms.

He was also an assistant professor at Harvard University for a short time where he helped students build, market, and publish successful Windows Phone apps. At Boston University, he was a guest professor for the Cloud computing course and would teach one class a semester.

He has also appeared on podcasts, such as the Windows Developer Show, has been a technical editor for publications and books, has won several app building contests and hackathons (including the first place in the Microsoft Build 2013 hackathon), and is a published developer with over a million downloads in the Windows Store.

I'd like to thank my wife Amy for her undying patience while I did "more work after I got home from work" and to Can Bilgin for the opportunity to review this.

www.PacktPub.com

eBooks, discount offers, and more

Did you know that Packt offers eBook versions of every book published, with PDF and ePub files available? You can upgrade to the eBook version at `www.PacktPub.com` and as a print book customer, you are entitled to a discount on the eBook copy. Get in touch with us at `customercare@packtpub.com` for more details.

At `www.PacktPub.com`, you can also read a collection of free technical articles, sign up for a range of free newsletters and receive exclusive discounts and offers on Packt books and eBooks.

`https://www2.packtpub.com/books/subscription/packtlib`

Do you need instant solutions to your IT questions? PacktLib is Packt's online digital book library. Here, you can search, access, and read Packt's entire library of books.

Why subscribe?

- Fully searchable across every book published by Packt
- Copy and paste, print, and bookmark content
- On demand and accessible via a web browser

Table of Contents

Preface

Although it was initially born as a community effort to port the .NET libraries and common language runtime compilers to various operating systems, the Xamarin product suite soon became the common ground to develop applications for Android and iOS operating systems using the .NET framework and the most popular CLR language, C#. The emergence of the Xamarin development platform created a new development niche, serving products to a variety of platforms at the same time while letting users adapt their existing .NET development skills to these new platforms and produce applications for a wider range of devices and operating systems. Thanks to Xamarin, developers are now enjoying a new era where development efforts don't target only a single application platform, but span multiple devices including smart phones, tablets, personal computers, and even wearable devices, creating highly efficient native applications.

What this book covers

Chapter 1, Developing with Xamarin, provides an insightful look at the Xamarin framework and architecture on target platforms. It also includes introductory information and tips on preparing the development environment for Xamarin.

Chapter 2, Memory Management, investigates how memory is managed on iOS and Android with Xamarin runtime. While drawing parallels with .NET platform, it provides examples of pitfalls, patterns, and best practices.

Chapter 3, Asynchronous Programming, dives deep into asynchronous and multi-threaded programming concepts. Platform-specific problems in various threading scenarios on different platforms are discussed.

Chapter 4, Local Data Management, provides useful patterns and techniques to efficiently use, manage, and roam data on mobile devices using Xamarin.

Chapter 5, Networking, contains a detailed look at the networking capabilities of Xamarin applications and various service integration scenarios. Networking implementations are illustrated with real-world examples, including the use of local storage for data caching.

Chapter 6, Platform Extras, concentrates on platform-specific APIs and features. It explains some of the peripherals that can be employed in Xamarin applications. A look at native libraries and how to include them in cross-platform Xamarin applications is also included in this chapter.

Chapter 7, View Elements, provides introductory information about UX (User Experience) and design concepts, and an explanation of the differences and similarities between design principles on Xamarin platforms.

Chapter 8, Xamarin.Forms, focuses on the various features and extensibility options of Xamarin. It also covers the forms extension module and how to use it to generate consistent user interfaces on multiple platforms.

Chapter 9, Reusable UI Patterns, discusses the strategies and patterns for reusing visual assets in cross-platform projects. Some advanced software architectural topics about MVC and MVVM patterns are also analyzed and demonstrated.

Chapter 10, ALM – Developers and QA, provides an introduction to Application Lifecycle Management and continuous integration methodologies for Xamarin cross-platform applications. As the part of the ALM process that is the most relevant to developers, unit testing strategies are discussed and demonstrated, as well as automated UI testing.

Chapter 11, ALM – Project and Release Management, explains the essentials of version control and automated continuous integration workflows. Source control options, as well as automated build strategies for Xamarin projects, are demonstrated.

Chapter 12, ALM – App Stores and Publishing, explains the processes related to app package preparation and release, which constitutes the last step of the application lifecycle.

What you need for this book

In order to build the sample project and make use of the code samples in this book, you will need a Xamarin.iOS and/or Xamarin.Android subscription, depending on the platform you want to target. Most of the diagnostic tools used are distributed as part of the development SDKs for the target platforms. As a development IDE, you will need Visual Studio 2013 (or higher) or Xamarin Studio if you are using or configuring a Windows based development environment, but only Xamarin Studio otherwise. For testing and diagnostics, real mobile devices or SDK-provided emulators can be used.

Who this book is for

This book is ideal for those who want to take their novice or intermediate-level Xamarin mobile development skills to the next level to become the go-to person within their organization. To fully understand the patterns and concepts described, you should possess a reasonable level of knowledge and an understanding of the core elements of cross-platform application development with Xamarin.

Conventions

In this book, you will find a number of text styles that distinguish between different kinds of information. Here are some examples of these styles and an explanation of their meaning.

Code words in text, database table names, folder names, filenames, file extensions, pathnames, dummy URLs, user input, and Twitter handles are shown as follows: "For instance, Objective-C types such as NSObject, NSString, NSArray are exposed in C# and provide binding to underlying types."

A block of code is set as follows:

```
namespace Master.Xamarin.Portable
{
    public class MyPhotoViewer
    {
        private readonly IStorageManager m_StorageManager;
```

Any command-line input or output is written as follows:

```
bcdedit /copy {current} /d "No Hyper-V"
bcdedit /set {<identifier from previous command>} hypervisorlaunchtype off
```

New terms and **important words** are shown in bold. Words that you see on the screen, for example, in menus or dialog boxes, appear in the text like this: "It can still be accessed using the **Run with Mono HeapShot** menu item under the **Project** menu in Xamarin Studio."

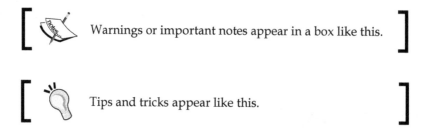

Warnings or important notes appear in a box like this.

Tips and tricks appear like this.

Reader feedback

Feedback from our readers is always welcome. Let us know what you think about this book—what you liked or disliked. Reader feedback is important for us as it helps us develop titles that you will really get the most out of.

To send us general feedback, simply e-mail feedback@packtpub.com, and mention the book's title in the subject of your message.

If there is a topic that you have expertise in and you are interested in either writing or contributing to a book, see our author guide at www.packtpub.com/authors.

Customer support

Now that you are the proud owner of a Packt book, we have a number of things to help you to get the most from your purchase.

Downloading the example code

You can download the example code files for this book from your account at http://www.packtpub.com. If you purchased this book elsewhere, you can visit http://www.packtpub.com/support and register to have the files e-mailed directly to you.

You can download the code files by following these steps:

1. Log in or register to our website using your e-mail address and password.
2. Hover the mouse pointer on the **SUPPORT** tab at the top.
3. Click on **Code Downloads & Errata**.
4. Enter the name of the book in the **Search** box.
5. Select the book for which you're looking to download the code files.
6. Choose from the drop-down menu where you purchased this book from.
7. Click on **Code Download**.

Once the file is downloaded, please make sure that you unzip or extract the folder using the latest version of:

- WinRAR / 7-Zip for Windows
- Zipeg / iZip / UnRarX for Mac
- 7-Zip / PeaZip for Linux

Errata

Although we have taken every care to ensure the accuracy of our content, mistakes do happen. If you find a mistake in one of our books — maybe a mistake in the text or the code — we would be grateful if you could report this to us. By doing so, you can save other readers from frustration and help us improve subsequent versions of this book. If you find any errata, please report them by visiting http://www.packtpub.com/submit-errata, selecting your book, clicking on the **Errata Submission Form** link, and entering the details of your errata. Once your errata are verified, your submission will be accepted and the errata will be uploaded to our website or added to any list of existing errata under the Errata section of that title.

To view the previously submitted errata, go to https://www.packtpub.com/books/content/support and enter the name of the book in the search field. The required information will appear under the **Errata** section.

Piracy

Piracy of copyrighted material on the Internet is an ongoing problem across all media. At Packt, we take the protection of our copyright and licenses very seriously. If you come across any illegal copies of our works in any form on the Internet, please provide us with the location address or website name immediately so that we can pursue a remedy.

Please contact us at copyright@packtpub.com with a link to the suspected pirated material.

We appreciate your help in protecting our authors and our ability to bring you valuable content.

Questions

If you have a problem with any aspect of this book, you can contact us at questions@packtpub.com, and we will do our best to address the problem.

1
Developing with Xamarin

This chapter examines the Xamarin framework and architecture on different target platforms and identifies the differences and similarities. It also includes introductory information and tips on preparing the development environment for Xamarin and covers some of the Xamarin development essentials. This chapter is divided into the following sections:

- Cross-platform projects with Xamarin
- Target platforms
- Setting up the development environment
- Emulator options
- A typical Xamarin solution structure
- Quality in cross-development

Cross-platform projects with Xamarin

Developers are enjoying a new era in which development is not restricted to one single application platform but spans across various media such as cellphones, tablets, personal computers, and even wearable devices. The shared code and assets between the development projects improves the elegance and the quality of the work. There is also a direct correlation between the robustness, the effort required for maintaining a multi-platform application, and the reusable modules.

Universal application is a term previously used to identify applications targeting devices running on the iOS operating system (the iPhone and iPad). However, the same term is now used to describe Windows Runtime applications (Windows Store and Windows Phone 8.1 - WinRT) and Android applications for phones and tablets. With the release of Xamarin, a truly universal application concept was born. When considering Xamarin applications, the term, universal, refers to applications that run on all three platforms and adapt to the system resources.

In this universal application context, developers are now finding it difficult to get the necessary solutions for common tasks on all three platforms. Moreover, taking on each platform as a separate development project results in wasted developer hours even though the main driving factors for such an application, namely data, business logic, and UI, are conceptually almost identical on all platforms.

Development strategies and patterns for the Xamarin platform, some of which are described in the rest of this book, try to resolve some of these problems and provide the developers with the tools and strategies necessary to produce cross-platform, manageable, and quality products.

Xamarin as a platform

Xamarin was initially born as a community effort to port the .NET libraries and common language runtime compilers to different operating systems. Initial attempts intended to create a set of binaries to develop, compile, and run applications written in C#, the indigenous language of .NET, on Unix-based platforms. This project, Mono, was later ported to many other operating systems, including iOS (Mono-Touch) and Android (Mono for Android).

The emergence of the Xamarin development platform created a new development niche creating products for three separate platforms at the same time, while allowing users to adapt their existing .NET development skills to these new platforms and produce applications for a wider range of devices and operating systems.

 Microsoft has been a strong supporter of Xamarin platform and toolset since the early phases. As you will see in the remainder of the chapter, Xamarin tools were fully integrated into Visual Studio and finally included in the Visual Studio 2015 setup. This partnership lasted until the eventual acquisition of Xamarin by Microsoft which was publicly announced in March 2016.

Xamarin provides compilers for each of the mentioned platforms so that the code written in the .NET framework (-alike) is compiled into native applications. This process provides highly efficient applications that differ greatly from interpreted mobile HTML applications.

As well as native compilation, Xamarin also provides access to strongly typed platform-specific features. These features are used in a robust manner with compile-time binding to the underlying platform. Platform-specific execution can also be extended with native invocations which is possible with the interop libraries.

Xamarin as a product

Xamarin, as a development suite, comes in different flavors. Developers with different sets of knowledge and experience can use these tools to set up their development environment according to their own needs. The Xamarin development environment can be configured on different operating systems. However, it is currently not possible to develop for all three platforms on the same operating system.

For developers who are looking to use the familiar interface of Visual Studio and leverage existing skills, Xamarin extensions for Visual Studio offer a suitable option. Once the extensions are installed, the environment is ready to develop Android and Windows Phone applications. This extension lets the developers take full advantage of Visual Studio, which includes designers for both of these platforms. In order to develop iOS applications, you need to go through the so-called pairing process of Visual Studio with an Apple OS X build machine. The build machine is used in return to visualize storyboards in the development environment (Visual Studio), compile iOS code, and debug applications.

The second option is to use Xamarin Studio. Xamarin Studio is a complete IDE with some of the features you are familiar with from Visual Studio, such as intellisense (smart code completion), code analysis, and code formatting. If you run Xamarin Studio on Apple OS X, you can develop for Android and iOS platforms with this IDE. However, with Xamarin Studio on Windows, you can only target the Android platform.

An important part of this development suite is the real-time monitoring tool called Xamarin Insights. Xamarin Insights lets developers monitor their live applications to help detect and diagnose performance issues and exceptions, and discover how the application is used. Xamarin Insights can also be connected to other applications so, for instance, application errors can be directly pushed into a bug tracking system.

Target platforms

As mentioned, Xamarin created a new platform in which the development efforts target multiple operating systems and a variety of devices. Most importantly, compiled applications do not run an interpreted sequence but have a native code base (such as Xamarin.iOS) or an integrated .NET application runtime (such as Xamarin.Android). In essence, Xamarin replaces the Common Language Runtime and IL for .NET applications with compiled binaries and an execution context, the so-called **mono runtime**.

Xamarin on Android

With Android applications, mono runtime is placed right on top of the Linux kernel. This creates a parallel execution context to the Android runtime. Xamarin code is then compiled into IL and accessed by mono runtime. On the other hand, Android runtime is accessed by the so-called **Managed Callable Wrappers (MCW)** which is a marshalling wrapper between the two runtimes. The MCW layer is responsible for converting managed types to Android runtime types and invoking Android code at execution time. Every time that .NET code needs to invoke Java code, this JNI (Java Interop) bridge is used. MCW provides a wide range of applications including inheriting Java types, overriding methods and implementing Java interfaces.

The following image shows the Xamarin.Android architecture:

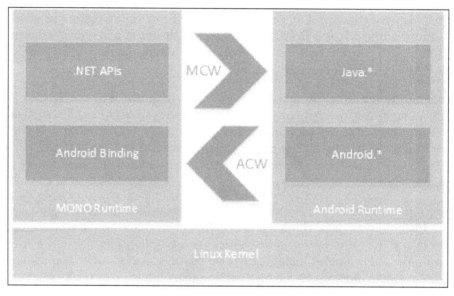

Figure 1: Xamarin.Android Architecture

`Android.*` and `Java.*` namespaces are used throughout the MCWs to access device- and platform-specific features in Android runtime and Java APIs such as facilities like audio, graphics, OpenGL, and telephony .

Using the interop libraries, it is also possible to load native libraries and execute native code in the execution context with Xamarin.Android. The reverse callback execution in this case is handled through **Android Callable Wrappers (ACW)**. ACW is a JNI bridge which allows the Android runtime to access the .NET domain. An ACW is generated at compile-time for each managed class that is directly or indirectly related to Java types (those that inherit `Java.Lang.Object`).

Xamarin on iOS

In iOS applications, the use of an integrated parallel runtime is (unfortunately) not permissible under the iOS SDK agreement. According to the iOS SDK agreement, interpreted code can only be used if all of the the scripts and code are downloaded and run by Apple's WebKit framework.

With this restriction in place, developers can still develop applications in .NET and share code over the other three platforms. At compile time, projects are first compiled into IL code and then (with the Mono Touch Ahead-Of-Time compiler – mtouch) into static native iOS bits. This means that iOS applications developed with Xamarin are completely native applications.

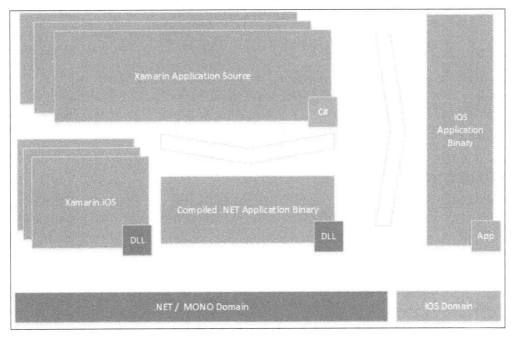

Figure 2: Xamarin.iOS Compilation

Xamarin.iOS, like Xamarin.Android, contains an interop engine that bridges the .NET world with the Objective-C world. Through this bridge, under the ObjCRuntime namespace, users are able to access iOS C-based APIs, as well as using the Foundation namespace, and can use and derive from native types and access Objective-C properties. For instance, Objective-C types like NSObject, NSString, and NSArray are exposed in C# and provide binding to underlying types. These types can be used either as memory references or as strongly-typed objects. This improves the development experience and also increases type-safety.

This static compilation is the main reason for using a build machine to develop iOS applications with Xamarin on the Windows platform. Therefore, there is no reverse-callback functionality in Xamarin.iOS where calls to native runtime from .NET code are supported but calls from native code back to .NET domain are not. There are other features that are disabled because of the way that Xamarin.iOS applications are compiled. For example, no generic types are allowed to inherit from NSObject. Another important limitation is the fact that no dynamic type creation is allowed at runtime which, in return, disables the use of dynamic keywords in Xamarin.iOS applications.

 Xamarin.iOS application packages, if built in a debug configuration, are much larger than their Release counterparts when compared to other platforms. These packages are instrumented and not optimized by the linker. Profiling of these packages is not allowed in Xamarin.iOS applications.

In a similar way to Xamarin.Android development, with Xamarin.iOS, it is also possible to re-use native code and libraries from managed code. To do this, Xamarin provides a project template called a **binding library**. A binding library helps developers create managed wrappers for native Objective-C code.

Windows Runtime apps

Even though Xamarin does not include Windows Runtime as a target platform nor provide specialized tools for it (other than Xamarin.Forms), cross-platform projects that involve Xamarin can and generally do include Windows Runtime projects. Since .NET and C# are indigenous to Windows Runtime, most of the shared projects (such as portable libraries, shared projects, and Xamarin.Forms projects) can be reused in Windows Runtime with no further modification.

With Windows Runtime, developers can create both Windows Phone 8.1 and Windows Store applications. Windows Phone 8 and Windows Phone 8.1 Silverlight can also be targeted and included in the PCL description.

Setting up the development environment

Xamarin projects can be carried out in various development environments. Since a number of platforms are involved in such projects, the operating system, the IDE selection, and the configuration are all crucial parts of the preparation.

Environment setup not only depends on the target application platforms but also on the Xamarin license. A comparison between different licensing options and pricing information can be found on the Xamarin website (`https://store.xamarin.com/`).

Choosing the right development OS

Android applications can be developed and compiled on Windows using both Xamarin Studio and Visual Studio with Xamarin extensions installed, as well as on an Apple OS X operating system with Xamarin Studio for Mac installed.

For iOS application development, whether using Visual Studio on Windows or Xamarin Studio on Apple OS X, an Apple Macintosh computer, running at least OS X Mountain Lion, is required. The build machine should have the Xcode development tools with iOS SDK together with the Xamarin.iOS suite installed.

On the other hand, Windows Store applications can only be developed on the Windows platform.

| | Apple OS X | Microsoft Windows | |
	Xamarin Studio	Xamarin Studio	Visual Studio
iOS Apps	Yes		Yes (with OS X Build Machine)
Android Apps	Yes	Yes	Yes
Windows Store Apps			Yes

Figure 3: Development IDEs on OS X and Windows

On the virtualization front, developers are also limited. OS X cannot be installed and run on a non-Apple branded machine nor can it be virtualized, according to the end user agreement. On the other hand, you can set up a virtual machine on an OS X development machine for Microsoft Windows and Visual Studio. However, in this case, the system should be running nested virtualization for Hyper-V to run Visual Studio for Windows Phone and Android emulators. Even though Parallels and VMWare Fusion support nested virtualization, Microsoft doesn't support nesting Hyper-V and, therefore, such machines may be unstable.

Xamarin Studio setup and configuration

Xamarin Studio can be set up on both the Windows and OS X operating systems. Developers can download it from www.xamarin.com and follow the installation instructions. Xamarin components for target platforms (for example, Xamarin.iOS, Xamarin.Android, and so on) together with the dependencies for these platforms (for example, Android SDK) should be downloaded and installed on the development machine. One required component for OS X, which has to be installed separately and configured, is the iOS SDK with the Xcode development environment.

Figure 4: Xamarin Setup on Mavericks (OS X 10.9)

On Microsoft Windows, it is important to mention that Xamarin Studio only supports the development of Android applications. Neither Windows Phone nor iOS application (even with the remote build machine) projects can be viewed, modified, or compiled with Xamarin Studio on Windows.

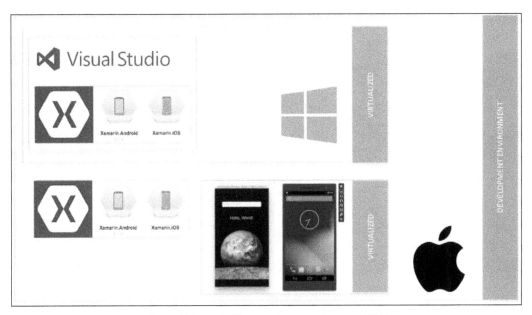

Figure 5: Xamarin Dev. Environment Setup on OS X

While developing on OS X, the only option for developing Windows Phone applications together with iOS and Android, is to use a Windows virtual machine and run Visual Studio in parallel with Xamarin Studio. This setup is also helpful for developers who use Team Foundation Server as the source control, since they can use the enhanced integration offered by Visual Studio Client rather than the standalone TFS Everywhere. It can also be set up so that the OS host machine can be paired with Visual Studio to become the build host for iOS applications.

Visual Studio setup and configuration

A typical Windows development platform configuration for Xamarin projects includes Visual Studio 2013 or 2015, an Apple OS X build host and Hyper-V and/or VirtualBox to be able to use Android and Windows Phone emulators. Xamarin.iOS applications are then compiled and emulated on the Apple OS X build host.

Figure 6: Windows Platform Xamarin Development Environment

In spite of the fact that it is technically possible to run OS X with a virtual machine in the Microsoft Windows environment, Apple's license agreement does not allow this:

"2.H. Other Use Restrictions: The grants set forth in this License do not permit you to, and you agree not to, install, use or run the Apple Software on any non-Apple-branded computer, or to enable others to do so."

On Microsoft Windows, the Xamarin installation is similar to the Xamarin Studio setup on Apple OS X. All of the prerequisites for Xamarin development are installed with the Xamarin for Windows package, together with the Visual Studio extension.

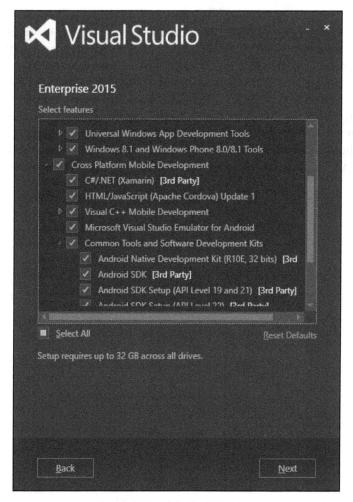

Figure 7: Visual Studio 2015 Setup

One of the key differences between OS X and Microsoft Windows is that Visual Studio 2015 now includes cross-platform development tools such as Android SDK, development kits, and Xamarin project templates. Therefore, the Xamarin installation is only responsible for installing the extensions for the requested platforms (that is, Xamarin.iOS and/or Xamarin.Android).

In order to develop and test iOS applications and visualize and edit storyboards with Visual Studio, an Apple OS X machine must be connected to Visual Studio as a build host. Xamarin 4.0 introduced the concept of Xamarin Mac Agent, which is a background process on the OS X machine providing the required SSH connection to Visual Studio (a secure connection over port 22). Prior to Xamarin 4.0, the build host machine needed to run the so-called Mac **build host** which was used to pair the Mac host with Visual Studio. The only prerequisites for Xamarin Mac Agent are to have Xamarin.iOS installed on both the Windows workstation and the OS X build host and the build host to have a remote login enabled for the current user. In Visual Studio, the **Find Xamarin Mac Agent** dialog helps establish the remote connection.

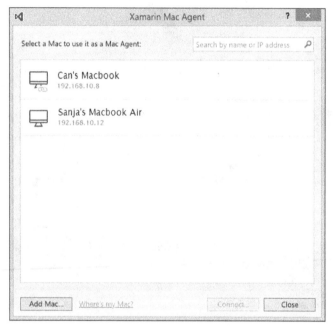

Figure 8: Xamarin.iOS Build Host

It is important to keep in mind that the Mac machine paired with Visual Studio has to have Xcode with iOS SDK installed. A developer account (either enrolled into the app developer program or not) must also be added to the accounts configuration section of Xcode.

If the account associated with Xcode does not have a paid subscription to the developer program, the platform for the iOS projects can only be set for simulator and debug selection to one of the simulator options, not an actual device. Otherwise, the user will be presented with an error message such as, **No valid iOS code signing keys found in keychain**.

Emulator options

There are a number of emulators for compiled Xamarin projects for the target platform and the development environment. Developers have most flexibility with the emulator for the Android platform, whereas the options for iOS and Windows Store Apps are limited to the SDK-provided emulators.

Emulators for Android

Android applications can be run and tested on a number of emulators on both Microsoft Windows and Apple OS X operating systems.

Android SDK comes with the default emulator that is installed on the development machine. This emulation option is available both on OS X and Windows operating systems.

Figure 9: AVD and Genymotion Emulators

This Android emulator uses the **Android Virtual Devices (AVD)** to emulate the Linux kernel and the Android runtime. It does not require any additional virtualization software to run, however, the lack of virtualization support makes AVD much less responsive and makes the startup time relatively longer. It also provides a wide range of emulation options for developers, from SMS and telephony to hardware, peripherals, and power events.

The Genymotion emulator (`https://www.genymotion.com/`) is one of the most popular emulation options for Xamarin and Android developers. Although it is available with a free license, the free version only allows for GPS and camera emulation. The Genymotion emulator runs on (and is installed with) VirtualBox virtualization software.

VirtualBox together with Hyper-V

Virtual Box software cannot be run alongside Hyper-V virtualization software, which is required for Windows Phone development and emulation on Windows operating systems. In order to use both the Windows Phone emulator and the Genymotion Android emulator, you can create a dual boot option to disable and enable Hyper-V on Windows start-up.

`bcdedit /copy {current} /d "No Hyper-V"`

`bcdedit /set {<identifier from previous command>} hypervisorlaunchtype off`

This would create a second boot option to start Windows without the Hyper-V feature so that the virtualization can be used by VirtualBox.

The last and the most recent Android emulation option is the Visual Studio Android emulator. This Android emulator runs on Hyper-V and provides various device API versions and emulation options for developers.

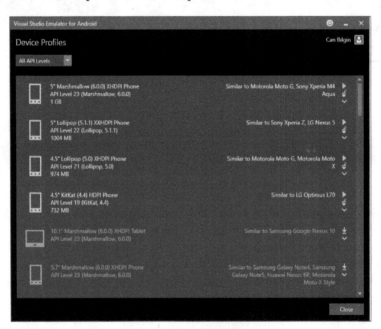

Figure 10: Visual Studio Android Emulator

The Visual Studio Android emulator is installed as part of the Visual Studio 2015 installation and can also be installed as an extension later. The emulator provides a similar experience to the Windows Phone emulator and allows developers and testers to use almost the same set of emulation options with different device profiles as well as different API levels.

iOS emulation

iOS emulation is only possible with the Xcode tools and iOS SDK. The iOS simulator can be started either directly on Apple OS X while developing with Xamarin Studio, or by pairing the build machine with the Visual Studio Xamarin extension running on Microsoft Windows. It also can be used to test both iPhone and iPad applications.

A typical Xamarin solution structure

A Xamarin solution can be composed of different types of projects. Some of these projects are platform-specific projects and the others are shared project types or modules that make it possible to reuse code across platforms.

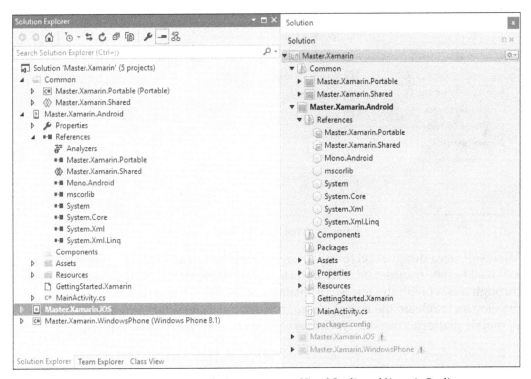

Figure 11: Xamarin project solution structure on Visual Studio and Xamarin Studio

Portable class libraries

Portable class libraries are the most common way of sharing code between cross-platform projects. PCLs provide a set of common reference assemblies that enable .NET libraries and binaries to be used on any .NET-based runtime or with Xamarin compilers—from phones to clients, to servers and clouds. PCL modules are designed to use only a specific subset of the .NET framework and can be set to target different platforms.

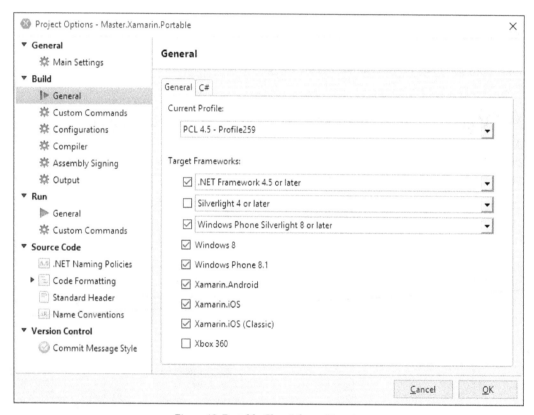

Figure 12: Portable Class Library Targets

Microsoft has a designation for each target combination and each profile also gets a NuGet target. A subset of .NET libraries for portable class libraries were released through NuGet with the release of Visual Studio 2013. This makes it possible for developers to release their work through NuGet packages, targeting a wide range of mobile platforms (see the *NuGet packages* section for more information).

The currently preferred profile and the greatest common subset for Xamarin projects is the so-called Profile 259. The Microsoft support designation for this profile is the .NET Portable Subset (.NET Framework 4.5, Windows 8, Windows Phone 8.1, Windows Phone Silverlight 8) and the NuGet target framework profile is `portable-net45+netcore45+wpa81+wp8`.

While creating a PCL, the biggest drawback is the fact that no platform-specific code can be included in or referenced by the project. This caveat is generally addressed by the abstraction of platform-specific requirements or by using dependency injection or similar methods to introduce the implementation in platform-specific projects.

For instance, in the device-specific peripheral example below, the common portable class library has a constructor that accepts two separate interfaces which can be injected with a dependency injection container or can be initialized with a device-specific implementation. The common library, in return, creates a business logic implementation, as shown:

```
namespace Master.Xamarin.Portable
{
    public class MyPhotoViewer
    {
        private readonly IStorageManager m_StorageManager;

        private readonly ICameraManager m_CameraManager;
        public MyPhotoViewer(IStorageManager storageManager,
          ICameraManager cameraManager)
        {
            m_StorageManager = storageManager;
            m_CameraManager = cameraManager;
        }

        public async Task TakePhotoAsync()
        {
            var photoFileIdentifier =
              await m_CameraManager.TakePhotoAndStoreAsync();

            var photoData =
              await m_StorageManager
              .RetrieveFileAsync(photoFileIdentifier);

            // TODO: Do something with the photo buffer
        }
    }

    /// <summary>
    /// Should be implemented in Platform Specific Library
```

```
    /// </summary>
    public interface IStorageManager
    {
        Task<string> StoreFileAsync(byte[] buffer);

        Task<byte[]> RetrieveFileAsync(string fileIdentifier);
    }

    /// <summary>
    /// Should be implemented in Platform Specific Library
    /// </summary>
    public interface ICameraManager
    {
        Task<string> TakePhotoAndStoreAsync();
    }
}
```

Shared projects

The term, shared project, was initially coined by the Microsoft team with the release of Universal Apps for Windows Phone and Windows Runtime (that is, Visual Studio 2013). With the arrival of Xamarin, shared projects can also be referenced by Android and iOS projects. These types of projects are essentially wrappers or containers for shared code and resource files that are linked to multiple projects and platforms. Shared file assets are included in the referencing projects later and compiled as part of these modules.

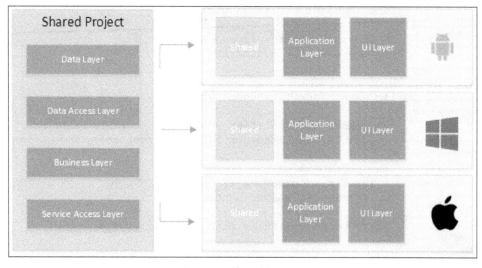

Figure 13: Shared Projects

While using shared projects, developers should be careful when including platform-specific code since the shared elements will be included in all the referencing projects and compiled. Compiler directives (for example, `#if __ANDROID__`) can be introduced in shared projects to denote that certain parts of the code are only for a specific platform.

Visualizing platform-specific code in shared projects

With Visual Studio (2013 or higher), it is possible to visualize different execution paths according to the combinations of conditional compilation constants.

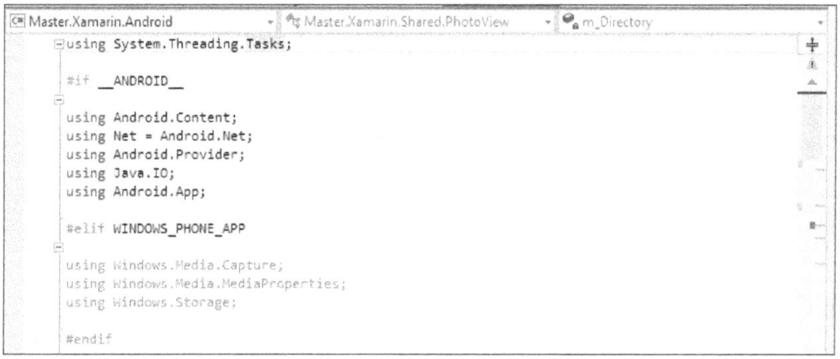

```
using System.Threading.Tasks;

#if __ANDROID__

using Android.Content;
using Net = Android.Net;
using Android.Provider;
using Java.IO;
using Android.App;

#elif WINDOWS_PHONE_APP

using Windows.Media.Capture;
using Windows.Media.MediaProperties;
using Windows.Storage;

#endif
```

Figure 14: Visual Studio shared project editor

Visual Studio provides a dropdown in the top corner of the editor window which determines the platform-specific projects that are referencing the shared project. By selecting the project, you can see the disabled sections of the code, according the target platform.

If we used the same example to take a photo, we would need to create two completely different implementations for the same action, as shown here:

```
private async Task<string> TakePhotoAsync()
{
    string resultingFilePath = "";

    var fileName = String.Format("testPhoto_{0}.jpg", Guid.NewGuid());

#if __ANDROID__

    Intent intent = new Intent(MediaStore.ActionImageCapture);
    var file = new File(m_Directory, fileName);
    intent.PutExtra(MediaStore.ExtraOutput, Net.Uri.FromFile(_file));
```

```
    // TODO: Need an event handler with TaskCompletionSource for
    // Intent's result
    m_CurrentActivity.StartActivityForResult(intent, 0);

    resultingFile = file.AbsolutePath;

#elif WINDOWS_PHONE_APP

    ImageEncodingProperties imgFormat = ImageEncodingProperties.
CreateJpeg();


    // create storage file in local app storage
    var file = await LocalStore.CreateFileAsync(fileName);

    resultingFilePath = file.Path;

    // take photo
    await capture.CapturePhotoToStorageFileAsync(imgFormat, file);

#endif

    return resultingFile;
}
```

Xamarin.Forms

Xamarin.Forms is the unified library for creating UI implementations for target platforms to be rendered with native controls. Xamarin.Forms projects are generally created as PCL projects and can be referenced by Xamarin.iOS, Xamarin.Android, and Windows Phone development projects. Xamarin.Forms components can also be included in shared projects and can utilize platform-specific features.

Developers can effectively create common UI implementations with these forms, either declaratively (with XAML), or by using the API provided. These views, which are constructed with Xamarin.Forms components, are then rendered at runtime with platform-specific controls.

Development projects can be realized with Xamarin.Forms by creating the data access model up until the UI components with a shared implementation, thus raising the amount of shared code between the platforms to as much as, or at times more than, 90%.

NuGet packages

NuGet, which was initially an open source Microsoft initiative to share code among developers, has now become a much larger ecosystem. While NuGet servers can be used as an open source library-sharing platform, many development teams use NuGet as a private company repository for compiled libraries.

NuGet packaging is a viable code-sharing and reuse strategy for Xamarin projects since it is supported by both Xamarin Studio and Visual Studio (with no further installation following Visual Studio 2012).

The NuGet target framework moniker for Xamarin projects is mono and there are further groupings such as MonoAndroid10, which refers to projects with a target framework of MonoAndroid version 1.0 or higher. Other platform targets are:

- MonoAndroid: Xamarin.Android
- Xamarin.iOS: Xamarin.iOS Unified API (supports 64-bit)
- Xamarin.Mac: Xamarin.Mac's mobile profile
- MonoTouch: iOS Classic API

Developers are free to either re-use publicly available NuGet packages or create their own repository to store compiled packages to include in Xamarin projects.

Creating NuGet packages in Visual Studio 2015

With the release of Visual Studio 2015, there is a new project template that should help developers to create and reuse NuGet packages.

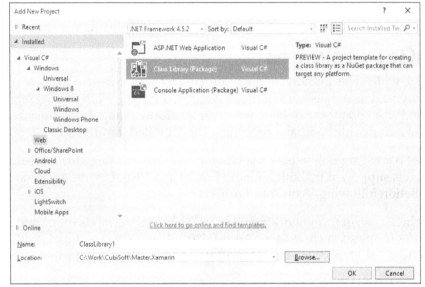

Figure 15: The Visual Studio NuGet package project template

More information on creating NuGet packages and publishing them can be found on the NuGet documentation hub: (http://docs.nuget.org/create/creating-and-publishing-a-package)

Components

Components are another approach to re-using compiled libraries and modules in Xamarin projects. The Component Store is built into both Xamarin Studio and Visual Studio and it has gathered a number of re-usable submissions from developers since its release in 2013. Components can be downloaded and installed into projects in the same way as for NuGet packages by using the Xamarin Component Store. The Xamarin Component Store can be found at `https://components.xamarin.com`.

Quality in cross-development

Some development terms help developers create robust, maintainable, high-quality code when developing for multiple platforms. These code descriptors help development teams identify architectural problems, software issues and random errors.

Reusability

"How much of the code can be reused throughout the project?"

Reusability is one of the key quality identifiers in cross-platform development projects. Xamarin, especially with the release of Xamarin.Forms, has provided developers with extensive resources to create platform-agnostic components that can decrease redundancy and reduce developer hours in complex projects. Code quality matrices generated by Visual Studio and unit test coverage results can convert this descriptor into a quantifiable measure.

Abstraction

"How much do the shared components know about the platform?"

It is almost unavoidable not to include platform-specific bits in cross-platform solutions. The level that these modules are abstracted to increases the robustness of the shared components and is closely related to how loosely the implemented logic is coupled with the underlying platform. In this way, the shared components can be tested easily with mock or fake libraries without having to create platform-specific test harnesses. Unit test code coverage results help determine the testability of the application.

Loose-coupling

"How easy is it to transpose the project into another platform?"

On top of the platform-specific abstracted implementation, an autonomous shared implementation layer creates flexible solutions which can easily be adapted to other platforms. Reducing the dependencies of the shared logic to the underlying platform not only inherently increases the reusability but also the agility of the development projects. The number of conditional compilation blocks or `if` or `else` loops for the underlying platform on shared projects identifies the amount of code executed according to the platform.

Nativity

"How much does your application blend into the platform?"

Even though the ultimate goal while developing with Xamarin is to create an application that can be easily compiled onto multiple targets, the applications created with Xamarin should look, feel and behave as if they were designed for that specific platform. The UI paradigms and user interaction mechanisms of each platform should be respected while creating a common foundation. Nativity is more of a nominal and subjective measure when compared to the aforementioned code descriptors.

Summary

In this chapter, we have discussed some of the key features of the Xamarin development suite and development on previously described platforms and looked at Xamarin essentials for developing mobile applications. The remaining chapters refer to these key features and the differences between the platforms to identify valuable patterns and strategies to create cross-platform applications with Xamarin.

The architectural overview of the target platforms and how Xamarin applications are developed and compiled on these platforms were also discussed. The most important difference between these platforms is that Xamarin.Android (and also Windows Phone) uses .NET binaries and mono (and .NET) runtime to execute code, whereas Xamarin.iOS applications have a completely different setup and double compilation (Ahead-of-Time) to make use of .NET binaries, but not to run them directly.

Whilst developing for Android and iOS platforms with Xamarin, developers are also forced to select between different OS platforms and development IDEs. The selection and configuration of the development environment depends on the targeted platforms. IDE features and emulator and simulator options play an important role in this selection. While providing a familiar interface and letting the developers transfer their .NET-related skills and know-how, the OS X operating system together with Xamarin Studio is currently a more viable option for developing iOS applications.

Another important refresher was for the Xamarin solution structure. We talked about how developers can share code between different platforms and re-use public or private stores to include shared modules. Shared projects make up the basis for most cross-platform development patterns and strategies together with portable class libraries.

Overall, when using the Xamarin specifications and features, the main objective of developers should be to create loosely coupled, platform-agnostic modules that increase productivity and improve the quality of cross-platform development projects.

2
Memory Management

This chapter investigates how memory is managed on iOS and Android with Xamarin runtime. Whilst drawing parallels to the .NET platform, it will provide examples of memory management problems and issues that can cause leaks, and also look at useful patterns that can help developers save valuable resources. This chapter is divided into the following sections:

- Application Component lifecycle
- Garbage collection
- Platform-specific concepts
- Troubleshooting and diagnosis
- Patterns and best practices

Application Component lifecycle

Each platform in the Xamarin ecosystem has certain processes and states that the applications go through during their execution lifetime. Developers can implement certain methods and subscribe to lifecycle events such as application start, suspension, termination, and backgrounding to handle much needed application state and release resources which are no longer required.

Activity lifecycle (Android)

In Android applications, contrary to the conventional application development model, any activity can be the access point to the application (as long as it is designated as such). Any activity in the application can be initialized at start-up or can be resumed directly when the application is resuming or restarting from a crash.

In order to manage the lifecycle of the activities, there are distinct states and events which help developers organize memory resources and program features.

Active/Running

An activity is said to be in the active state when an application is the application in focus and the activity is in the foreground. At this state, unless extraordinary measures are required by the operating system (for example, in case of system out of memory or application becoming unresponsive), the developer does not need to worry about the memory and resources, as the application has the highest priority.

In a creation cycle, OnCreate is the first method that is called by the application. This is the initialization step where the views are created, the variables are introduced, and static data resources are loaded.

OnStart or OnRestart (if the activity is restarting after it was backgrounded) is the second event method in a creation cycle. This method(s) can be overridden if specific data reload procedures need to be implemented. This is the last method called before the activity becomes visible.

The OnResume method is called after a successful launch of the activity. This method is the indication that the application is ready for user interaction. It can be used to (re)subscribe to external events, display alerts/user messages, and communicate with device peripherals.

Paused

An activity is paused when either the device goes to sleep having this activity in the foreground, or the activity is partially hidden by another dialog or activity. In this state, the activity is still "alive" but cannot interact with the user.

The OnPause event method is called right before the activity goes into the Paused state. This event method is the ideal place to unsubscribe from any external event providers, commit any unsaved changes and clean up any objects consuming memory resources since the user interaction is not possible in the Paused state. The activity will call only the OnResume method when once again the activity has the highest priority, it will not go through the full creation cycle.

Backgrounded

An activity goes into the Backgrounded state when the user presses the home button or uses the app switcher. In this state, it is not guaranteed that the activity will stay alive until the user "restarts" the application.

The OnStop method is called when the application is backgrounded or stopped. The difference between the Backgrounded and Stopped states is that the activity is in the Stopped state when it is being prepared for destruction and it will be followed by the OnDestroy method since the application is dismissed and will not be used by the user anymore. If the user resumes the application, the activity will call the OnRestart method and a full creation process will follow.

Stopped

The Stopped state represents the end of the lifecycle for the activity. The activity enters this state when the user presses the back button signifying that the application is not needed anymore. However, it is also possible that the activity is taken into this state because the system is starved of memory resources and it needs to take down activities that are on the lower priority states like paused or backgrounded.

The OnDestroy method follows the Stopped state and it is the last lifecycle event method that is called. It is the last chance for the application to stop long running processes that might cause leaks or clean up other persistent resources. It is advisable to implement most of the resource clean up in OnPause and OnStop methods, since OnDestroy can be called unexpectedly by the system contrary to the user initiated OnPause and OnStop methods.

Restarted

An activity is said to be "restarted" when it comes back to user interaction after it was backgrounded. Restarted activities can reload any saved state information and create an uninterrupted user experience. After going through the initialization steps, the application goes into the Running state again.

Application lifecycle (iOS)

On iOS, the application lifecycle is handled through UI application delegates. Once the delegate methods are implemented and registered, the methods will be invoked by the execution context.

```
public class Application
{
    static void Main(string[] args)
    {
        UIApplication.Main(args, null, "AppDelegate");
    }
}
```

```
[Register("AppDelegate")]
public partial class AppDelegate : UIApplicationDelegate
{
    //Implement required methods
}
```

Application events on iOS are a little more complicated than the top-down execution of events on Android. Developers can insert their methods into transitive states using the state-related methods implemented in the `AppDelegate`.

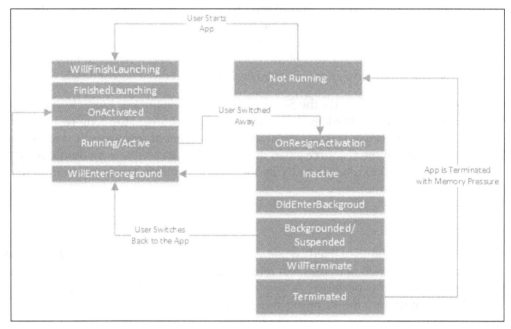

Figure 1: iOS Application State Transitions

The most important state-related methods are the following:

- `WillFinishLaunching` is the first chance of the application to execute code at launch time. It indicates the application has started to launch but the state has not yet been restored.

- `FinishedLaunching` is called once the state restoration occurs after the `WillFinishLaunching` is completed.

- `OnActivated` and `OnResignActivation` are similar to `OnPause` and `OnResume` event methods on the Android platform.

- `DidEnterBackground` is called when the application enters the Backgrounded state. It is similar to the `OnStop` method on Android but there is a time constriction on this method; the method should execute in less than 5 seconds, and the method exits without notification after the allocated time. If more time is needed to execute certain methods in this delegate, applications can start a background task to complete the execution.

- `WillEnterForeground` and `WillTerminate` can follow the `DidEnterBackground` execution. If the former method is called, the application is about to be brought back to foreground and active state, otherwise, the application is prepared to be terminated because the system needs more memory, or the user is closing a backgrounded application.

Garbage collection

Garbage collection (GC) is one of the most effective automated memory management techniques on modern application development platforms. In simple terms, with automated garbage collection, memory resources are allocated for objects used by the application and reclaimed for resources no longer needed by the application.

 In spite of the fact that garbage collection, as an automated process, takes over the burden of managing memory allocations, it can have a significant impact on performance. This performance handicap is one of the main reasons why there is no garbage collection mechanism on the iOS platform.

In theory, GC is responsible for reclaiming memory resources occupied by runtime elements that cannot be reached by the current executing application. However, this mechanism cannot always identify these unreachable resources correctly and/or have unexpected results while purging the identified memory pointers.

Memory leaks occur when an application fails to identify and/or free the resources occupied by unreachable code elements, which can lead to memory exhaustion problems.

Dangling pointers happen when a memory region is freed while references still exist in the execution context. These references are then removed and memory can be re-allocated for another use.

Double free bugs occur when a memory region is already reclaimed and the application or garbage collector tries to free this region once more.

GC on Xamarin projects

Managed code, as defined by the Common Language Runtime in the .NET framework, is application code where the memory resources are managed by the native garbage collector. GC, on initialization, allocates a segment of the memory to store and manage memory resources, which is called the "managed heap". The garbage collection in CLR happens on three different generations where objects with different lifespans live in the heap. Promotion between the generation and survival of objects depend on which generation they are placed in and how they survived prior GC cycles.

SGen garbage collector

SGen garbage collector is the generational garbage collector used in most Xamarin projects (both Xamarin.iOS and Xamarin.Android). SGen performs more frequent garbage collections over smaller sets of objects which makes it more efficient over the conservative Boehm GC.

SGen utilizes three heaps, namely The Nursery, Major Heap, and Large Object Space, to allocate memory segments for objects according to their memory requirements, and objects are promoted between the heaps when they survive through GC cycles. In this setup, The Nursery, similar to Generation 0 in CLR on .NET, is where most objects are created and destroyed and most of the GC cycles occur to release memory resources. Objects surviving the minor GC cycles can be promoted to the major heap. The major heap only has major GC passes in case the heap itself is running out of memory. The last heap is only for larger objects that have higher memory requirements, and does not accept promotion from other heaps.

 It is important to remember that during a garbage collection cycle all the threads registered with the runtime, including the main run loop thread are paused. One exception to this execution pause is the separate process that continues to run the iOS animations.

Boehm garbage collector (iOS only)

Boehm GC (aka Boehm-Demers-Weiser garbage collector) is an open-source garbage collector implementation that was initially created for C/C++ language implementations. As a conservative garbage collector, it still has procedures for leak detection, supports "finalized" semantics, and has limited support for generational implementations which makes it an attractive candidate for implementations and ports on various platforms.

An implementation of Boehm GC is only available for Xamarin.iOS applications using the Classic API, in which it is the default garbage collector.

Platform-specific concepts

In order to understand the memory management techniques and pitfalls, one must understand some platform-related concepts. Even though Xamarin provides an almost platform agnostic development experience, iOS and Android platforms deal with memory allocations and references slightly differently from .NET CLR and each other.

Object reference types

Referred objects can be classified according to application needs. This classification helps the garbage collector decide whether the memory allocation can be released for the referred objects.

A strong reference protects the object from being "garbage collected". A referred object is said to be strongly referenced/reachable when the class instance is directly used by the current execution context.

Weak references can be used for class instances when the need for the reference does not interfere with garbage collection. When the referred object is weakly reachable, the dependent section of code has to check whether the object is still alive before using the referenced object. Weak references have two types in CLR according to the dispose and finalization processes implemented by the declaring types: long and short weak references. Long weak references are types that can live on to be recreated and can be finalized by a destructor rather than being disposed or garbage collected.

Soft and phantom references are specific to Android runtime. Soft references, in simple terms, are a little more persistent than the weak references, and would only be cleared up by the garbage collector under memory pressure even though the object is no longer strongly reachable. Phantom references are the weakest reference in Android runtime. They are only used to implement specialized object finalization methods and have to be associated with a reference queue for processing.

Automatic Reference Counting (ARC)

Automatic Reference Counting is a compiler feature that was introduced in iOS 5. It is referred to as a compiler feature since it cannot be classified as a garbage collection implementation. It is a static analysis implementation where the compiler analyses the code execution tree and inserts retain and release messages according to the object persistence requirements.

With ARC, traditional memory management calls are not allowed to be inserted in the application to allocate memory and release memory addresses.

Troubleshooting and diagnosis

Profiling is the term used to describe the dynamic system analysis while the target application is running. Profilers generally collect data about metrics such as CPU utilization, framerate values, and most importantly data about memory allocations. Especially with Xamarin projects, since we are dealing with multiple platforms, profiling becomes an important part of testing and diagnostics.

There are numerous tools that one can use to profile memory usage on Xamarin projects, Xamarin Profiler being the only one that can be used both for Xamarin.iOS and Xamarin.Android applications.

Xamarin Profiler

Xamarin Profiler is the newest addition to the Xamarin Suite. This profiler has the advantage over other platform-specific applications since it can be run either on OS X or Windows targeting Xamarin.Android or Xamarin.iOS applications.

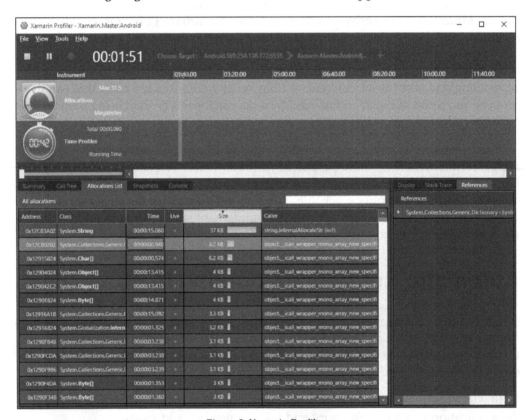

Figure 2: Xamarin Profiler

It was designed to give developers almost real time (depending on the sampling rate) information about the memory heaps for Xamarin applications. It can also save memory allocation snapshots which can later on be accessed and analyzed.

It can be started directly from Visual Studio or Xamarin Studio and can be used with both emulator and real device build/run configurations.

Currently there are two instruments you can select in the initial popup window.

Allocations instrument

The first instrument is the Allocations template which provides detailed information on the memory segments and allocations. In this view, developers can see a generalized list of allocations grouped by the class name under the **Summary** tab. The **Call Tree** tab gives a list of threads in the application and how they relate to the memory objects. Allocation list provides live data about the object allocations, and the **Snapshots** tab gives information about the memory snapshots stored.

Time Profiler

Time Profiler is the second instrument that can be used in Xamarin Profiler. It provides valuable information on how much time the application spent executing a certain method. Developers can see a whole stack trace on each method.

Device Monitor (Android only)

Android Device Monitor is hitherto the main diagnostic tool for Android development. And for Xamarin developers, when Android SDK is installed, device monitor can be accessed directly from a tool box item on Visual Studio and under the tools menu on Xamarin Studio.

On the main page of the device monitor there is a tree-view displaying each device or simulator that can be attached to with the device monitor.

 Only a single debugger can be attached to any device at a time, therefore other debuggers have to be detached before using the device monitor.

Once the device is selected, developers can get allocation information and the heap state using the graphical interface. It is also possible to trigger garbage collection cycles using the device monitor.

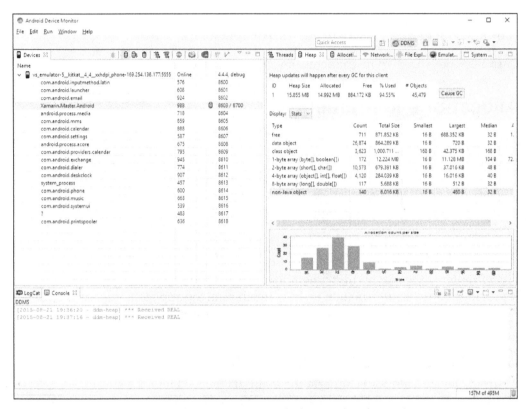

Figure 3: Android Device Monitor attached to Visual Studio Emulator

Instruments (iOS only)

Instruments is a valuable application that is installed together with the Xcode toolset. In this application developers are provided with a big set of diagnostic tools varying from energy consumption, graphic resources, to memory allocations.

The allocations instrument has a very similar interface to Xamarin Profiler, and gives almost real-time data about memory objects.

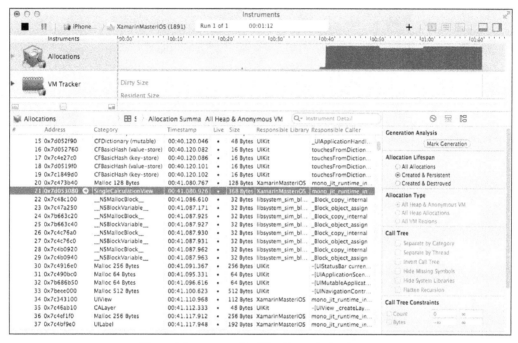

Figure 4: Instruments Profiling Xamarin Application

The Xcode Instruments tool can be used both together with an actual device or the iOS simulator. It can be started directly from Xamarin Studio. Once the application is started on the iOS simulator or on the actual device, it becomes available in the target selection window.

Figure 5: Instruments with iOS Simulator set as target

 If you are developing Xamarin.iOS applications on Microsoft Windows with an OS X build machine, you will not be able to access the Instruments directly from the development station. Once the application is either on the test device or the simulator, you can start the instruments on the build machine and choose the correct target to analyze.

Monotouch Profiler (iOS only)

Monotouch Profiler was the Xamarin tool used to diagnose memory issues with Xamarin.iOS applications before it was superseded by Xamarin Profiler. It can still be accessed using the **Run with Mono HeapShot** menu item under the **Project** menu in Xamarin Studio. While providing useful information about memory allocations and the heap, it currently does not go further than being a lightweight application to take memory snapshots.

Patterns and best practices

While dealing with managed runtime and garbage collection, there are certain patterns and anti-patterns developers must be careful with. If not handled properly, both managed and native objects can produce noncollectable traces, which in turn can cause memory leaks and unnecessary resource consumption.

Disposable objects

The resources managed by the garbage collector are generally limited to memory allocations. Other resources like network sockets, database handles, UI elements, and file/device descriptors need to have additional definitions or mechanisms.

In managed runtime, these object resources can be cleaned up in two different ways. The first, less efficient, unpredictable way is to implement a destructor/finalizer. With a finalizer implementation, once the garbage collector decides the object is no longer strongly reachable, the resources such as network sockets can be disposed. However, finalizable objects have to wait for the following GC cycle to be cleaned up and cannot be finalized with developers' initiatives.

Another way to clean-up application resources is to implement the IDisposable interface in the class that has the references to the resources. This interface requires only a single Dispose method implementation to get rid of managed resources. The garbage collector also offers a method (GC.SuppressFinalize) to avoid finalization since the object is going to be disposed using the IDisposable interface.

```
public class DisposableFinalizableClass : IDisposable
{

    private ManagedResource m_Resource; // reference to a resource

    public DisposableFinalizableClass()
    {
        m_Resource = new ManagedResource(); // allocates the resource
    }

    /// <summary>
    /// Destructor for the DisposableFinalizableClass
    /// <remarks>
    /// Note that we are not overriding the object.Finalize method
    /// but providing a destructor for the Finalize method to call
    /// </remarks>
```

```
/// </summary>
~DisposableFinalizableClass()
{
    Dispose(false);
}

/// <summary>
/// Implementing the Dispose method
/// </summary>
public void Dispose()
{
    Dispose(true);

    // Letting the GC know that there is no more need for
    // Finalization, the resources are already cleaned-up
    GC.SuppressFinalize(this);
}

protected virtual void Dispose(bool disposing)
{
    if (disposing)
    {
        if (m_Resource != null) m_Resource.Dispose();
    }
    else
    {
        // Called from Finalize
        // Clean-up any unmanaged resources
    }
}
}
```

The fact that disposable objects can be used together with using blocks, gives a deterministic way for developers to release associated resources as soon as the object is no longer needed.

The lapsed listener problem

One of the most common patterns used with UI elements or legacy API implementations is the observer pattern. As you might know, there are two stakeholders in this pattern, the observer and provider. The observer subscribes to the event provided by the provider to receive updates.

The lapsed listener problem occurs when the observer pattern is implemented incorrectly or better yet incompletely. In this pattern, after the subscription, the provider keeps a strong reference to the observer. If this subscription is not removed before the subscriber goes out of context, the application will leak the subscriber object since it cannot be garbage collected (for example, an Android activity, or a view model).

In order to demonstrate this problem, we will use a singleton implementation of Fibonacci sequence with asynchronous methods as the event provider.

```csharp
public event EventHandler<int> CalculationCompleted;

public event EventHandler<List<int>> RangeCalculationCompleted;

/// <summary>
/// Calculates n-th number in Fibonacci sequence
/// </summary>
/// <param name="ordinal">Ordinal of the number to calculate</param>
public void GetFibonacciNumberAsync(int ordinal)
{
    var task = Task.Run(() =>
    {
        var result = GetFibonacciNumberInternal(ordinal);
        if (CalculationCompleted != null) CalculationCompleted(this,
result);
    });

    // Avoiding Deadlocks on the UI thread
    task.ConfigureAwait(false);
}

/// <summary>
/// Calculates a range of numbers in Fibonnaci sequence
/// </summary>
/// <param name="firstOrdinal">Ordinal of the first number</param>
/// <param name="lastOrdinal">Ordinal of the last number</param>
public void GetFibonacciRangeAsync(int firstOrdinal, int lastOrdinal)
{
    var task = Task.Run(() =>
    {
        var result = GetFibonacciRangeInternal(firstOrdinal,
lastOrdinal);
```

```
        if (RangeCalculationCompleted != null)
    RangeCalculationCompleted(this, result);
        });

        task.ConfigureAwait(false);
}

public static FibonacciSource Instance
{
    get
    {
        return m_Instance ?? (m_Instance = new FibonacciSource());
    }
}
```

We will implement two separate view models using MvvmCross and use associated views to invoke the asynchronous methods, then navigate back to the main view using the Close method on the view models. In the constructor of each view model, we will be subscribing to the respective event on the FibonacciSource.

Figure 6: Fibonacci Calculator App

In order to investigate any memory leaks, we navigate back and forth between the main and the calculation views. After a couple of iterations on both of the views (that is, single and range), we have the results shown below on the Xamarin Profiler (just using the "Allocations" template.)

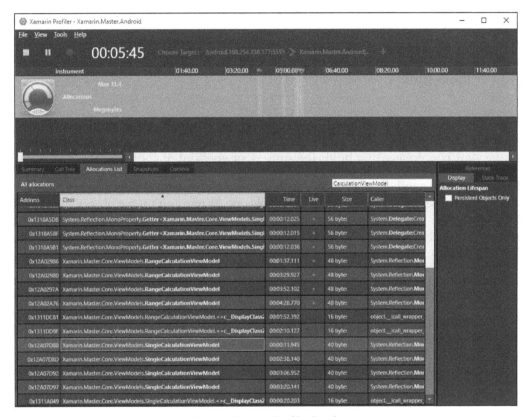

Figure 7: Xamarin Profiler Results

You will notice that none of the instances of `SingleCalculationViewModel` are alive after garbage collection (you can trigger a GC run with `GC.Collect()`), however `RangeCalculationViewModel` instances are persistent. The reason for this is the missing unsubscribe call in the close command of the `RangeCalculationViewModel`.

```
private MvxCommand m_CloseCommand;

public ICommand CloseCommand
{
    get
    {
```

```
            m_CloseCommand = m_CloseCommand ?? new MvxCommand(DoClose);
            return m_CloseCommand;
        }
    }

    private void DoClose()
    {
        // FibonacciSource.Instance.RangeCalculationCompleted -=
    OnCalculationCompleted;
        Close(this);
    }
```

We could have also used the OnPause event on this Android application or any other relevant event on other platforms to get rid of the subscription before the subscriber or the view component that holds the subscriber goes out of context.

In this scenario, another solution would be to use a TaskCompletionSource to convert the observable pattern to an awaitable one. Wrapping up the observable Fibonacci source would give you a better control over the subscription and the resulting asynchronous task would be better suited for mobile development and MVVM pattern.

```
    private Task<List<int>> CalculateFibonacciRangeAsync(int firstOrdinal,
    int secondOrdinal)
    {
        TaskCompletionSource<List<int>> taskCompletionSource = new TaskCom
    pletionSource<List<int>>();

        EventHandler<List<int>> calcCompletedEventHandler = null;

        calcCompletedEventHandler =
            (sender, e) =>
            {
                FibonacciSource.Instance.RangeCalculationCompleted -=
    calcCompletedEventHandler;
                taskCompletionSource.SetResult(e);
            };

        FibonacciSource.Instance.RangeCalculationCompleted +=
    calcCompletedEventHandler;

        FibonacciSource.Instance.GetFibonacciRangeAsync(firstOrdinal,
    secondOrdinal);

        return taskCompletionSource.Task;
    }
```

Finally, this async task would be called with a `ContinueWith` statement to set the result in the view model.

```
private void DoCalculate()
{
    if (!string.IsNullOrWhiteSpace(Input1) && !string.
IsNullOrWhiteSpace(Input2))
    {
        int numberOrdinal1, numberOrdinal2;

        if (int.TryParse(Input1, out numberOrdinal1) && int.
TryParse(Input2, out numberOrdinal2))
        {
            InfoText = "Calculating";

            var fibonacciTask = CalculateFibonacciRangeAsync(numberOrd
inal1, numberOrdinal2)
                .ContinueWith(task =>
                {
                    Result = string.Join(",", task.Result);
                    InfoText = "";
                });

            fibonacciTask.ConfigureAwait(false);

            return;
        }
    }

    InfoText = "Invalid Input";
}
```

Weak references

Weak references can be of great assistance while dealing with loosely coupled application layers. In these type of scenarios, where objects need to be managed outside the class domain, weak referencing can be used to remove these instances from the GC protection based on the notion of reachability because of the strong references they have to other layers of the application.

Let us assume in the previous example that the Fibonacci sequence items are handled as reference values with a class called `FibonacciItem`. This class carries the value calculated and the time it was calculated.

```
public class FibonacciItem
{
    public int Value { get; private set; }

    private readonly DateTime m_Calculated;

    public FibonacciItem(int value, DateTime calculatedTime)
    {
        Value = value;

        m_Calculated = calculatedTime;
    }
}
```

To decrease the processing time, we can now implement a caching mechanism which would force the source to recalculate the value according to the ordinal if it does not already exist in the cache or just does not sound right is disposed of in favor of memory resources. For this purpose we can use the `WeakReference` to cache Fibonacci items.

```
public class FibonacciCache
{
    // Dictionary to contain the cache.
    private static Dictionary<int, WeakReference> _cache;

    public FibonacciCache()
    {
        _cache = new Dictionary<int, WeakReference>();
    }

    /// <summary>
    /// Accessor to FibonacciItem references
    /// </summary>
    /// <param name="ordinal"></param>
    /// <returns>FibonacciItem if it is still alive</returns>
    public FibonacciItem this[int ordinal]
    {
        get
        {
            if (!_cache.ContainsKey(ordinal)) return null;
```

```
        if (_cache[ordinal].IsAlive)
        {
            // Object was obtained with the weak reference.
            FibonacciItem cachedItem = _cache[ordinal].Target as
FibonacciItem;
            return cachedItem;
        }
        else
        {
            // Object reference is already disposed of
            return null;
        }
    }
    set
    {
        _cache[ordinal] = new WeakReference(value);
    }
    }
}
```

Cross-domain objects

In Xamarin applications, one of the most common memory issues, cross-heap references, occur when there is a cross-over between the native runtime and mono runtime. This issue stems from the fact that mono runtime is almost handled as a separate domain and managed in a heap only with GC handles to the native domain.

In an Android scenario, where Java objects are referenced by managed C# objects or vice versa, the communication between the two runtimes becomes expensive. For instance, if we were implementing the Fibonacci calculator without using the ViewModel pattern, we would want to create a data adaptor to load the range calculation results into a list view.

```
private void OnFibonacciCalculationCompleted(object sender,
List<FibonacciItem> result)
{
    RunOnUiThread(() =>
    {
        var listView = FindViewById<ListView>(Resource.Id.lstResult);

        listView.Adapter = new ArrayAdapter<string>(this, Resource.
Layout.ListViewItem,
```

```
                    result.Select(val => val.Value.ToString()).ToArray());

        });
    }
```

This implementation has a higher cost of being garbage collected. It also has performance penalties considering the language crossing, not to mention the fact that objects from each world are effectively mirrored increasing the memory allocation costs.

The solution here would be to do as much work as possible in the managed world and let the runtime take care of the rest. So instead of using the native `ArrayAdapter`, we could implement a base adapter that would feed the `FibonacciItem` instances to the `ListView`.

```
public class FibonacciResultsAdapter : BaseAdapter<FibonacciItem>
{
    List<FibonacciItem> m_ResultItems;

    Activity m_Context;

    public FibonacciResultsAdapter(Activity context,
List<FibonacciItem> items)
    {
        m_Context = context;
        m_ResultItems = items;
    }

    public override long GetItemId(int position) { return position; }


    public override FibonacciItem this[int position]
    {
        get { return m_ResultItems[position]; }
    }

    public override int Count
    {
        get { return m_ResultItems.Count; }
    }

    public override View GetView(int position, View convertView,
ViewGroup parent)
```

```
    {
        View view = convertView;

        if (view == null)
            view = m_Context.LayoutInflater.Inflate(Resource.Layout.
ListViewItem, null);

        view.FindViewById<TextView>(Android.Resource.Id.txtOutput).
Text = m_ResultItems[position].Value.ToString();

        return view;
    }
}
```

By implementing the adapter we removed the usage of Java type `ArrayAdapter`, `ArrayList` and the Java references to the `FibonacciItem` instances.

The same applies to scenarios where native objects are being inherited in the managed domain. These, so-called, "special objects" are handled differently by the garbage collector. They have to be rescanned for all the references they carry with each garbage collection cycle.

Cyclic references (cycles)

Cyclic references occur, in general terms, when the underlying platform uses some type of reference counting as memory management strategy and the memory is cleaned up according to the number of references to that specific object instance.

Reference counting was abandoned by Microsoft with the release of .NET and the introduction of the generational tracing garbage collection. SGen in mono runtime on Android devices also uses some form of a mark and sweep algorithm. In both runtimes, the references are traced from so called "application roots". These objects are the ones that are "presumed" to be alive at the time of a garbage collection cycle.

The roots can be:

- References to global objects
- References to static objects
- References to static fields
- References on the stack to local objects
- References to objects waiting to be finalized
- References in CPU registers to objects on the managed heap

However, as mentioned before, on iOS, garbage collection was abandoned in favor of performance and yet ARC (automatic reference counting) fails to deal with what is called a retain cycle. Retain cycle occurs when the lower elements (aka children) in the creation hierarchy require references to the parent items. In this scenario, when the child or the parent sends a `release`, the `dealloc` methods never get to run since there is an extra reference keeping each of the items alive.

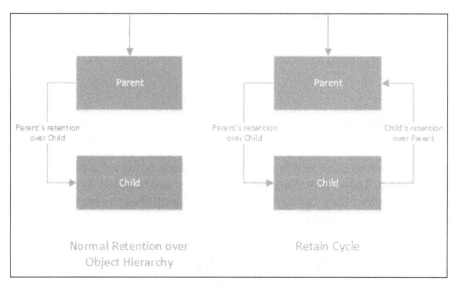

Figure 8: Retain Cycle

This native iOS problem becomes a problem in Xamarin applications when managed objects derive from native objects (that is, any object deriving from `NSObect`) such as UI controls. When managed classes are inheriting from native objects, in order to keep them from getting garbage collected, Xamarin.iOS creates a GCHandle. These GCHandles, together with the managed references between the objects, create the described (indirect) retain cycle.

If we were dealing with a parent `UIView` that holds an array of children and the child view objects that were retaining a reference to the parent object:

```
public class RetainingParentClass : UIView
{
    public RetainingParentClass()
    {

    }
}
```

```
public class RetainingChildClass : UIView
{
    private RetainingParentClass m_Parent;

    public RetainingChildClass(RetainingParentClass parent)
    {
        m_Parent = parent;
    }
}
```

The following piece of code would create a retain cycle and would cause memory leaks in the application:

```
var parent = new RetainingParentClass();

parent.Add(new RetainingChildClass(parent));
```

If we were to execute this code in the constructor of a view, every time the application navigates to this view, we would be creating a new parent object, never to be garbage collected.

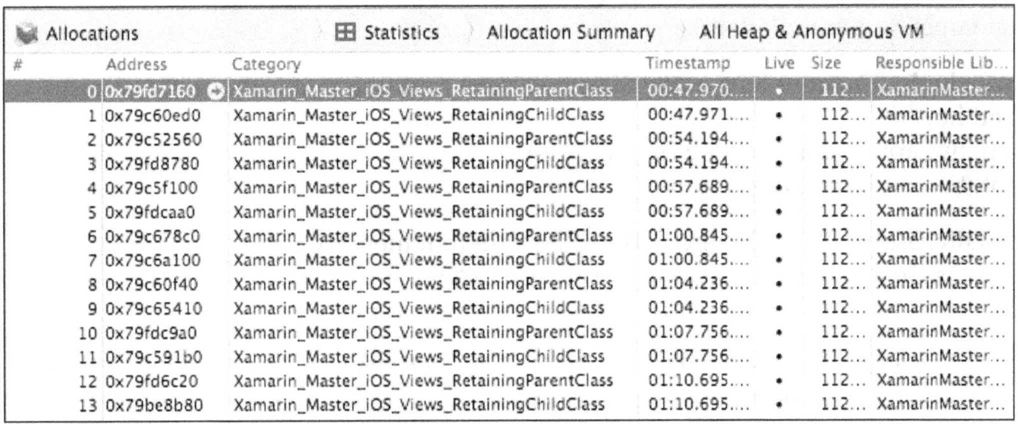

Allocations | Statistics | Allocation Summary | All Heap & Anonymous VM

#	Address	Category	Timestamp	Live	Size	Responsible Lib...
0	0x79fd7160	Xamarin_Master_iOS_Views_RetainingParentClass	00:47.970....	•	112...	XamarinMaster...
1	0x79c60ed0	Xamarin_Master_iOS_Views_RetainingChildClass	00:47.971....	•	112...	XamarinMaster...
2	0x79c52560	Xamarin_Master_iOS_Views_RetainingParentClass	00:54.194....	•	112...	XamarinMaster...
3	0x79fd8780	Xamarin_Master_iOS_Views_RetainingChildClass	00:54.194....	•	112...	XamarinMaster...
4	0x79c5f100	Xamarin_Master_iOS_Views_RetainingParentClass	00:57.689....	•	112...	XamarinMaster...
5	0x79fdcaa0	Xamarin_Master_iOS_Views_RetainingChildClass	00:57.689....	•	112...	XamarinMaster...
6	0x79c678c0	Xamarin_Master_iOS_Views_RetainingParentClass	01:00.845....	•	112...	XamarinMaster...
7	0x79c6a100	Xamarin_Master_iOS_Views_RetainingChildClass	01:00.845....	•	112...	XamarinMaster...
8	0x79c60f40	Xamarin_Master_iOS_Views_RetainingParentClass	01:04.236....	•	112...	XamarinMaster...
9	0x79c65410	Xamarin_Master_iOS_Views_RetainingChildClass	01:04.236....	•	112...	XamarinMaster...
10	0x79fdc9a0	Xamarin_Master_iOS_Views_RetainingParentClass	01:07.756....	•	112...	XamarinMaster...
11	0x79c591b0	Xamarin_Master_iOS_Views_RetainingChildClass	01:07.756....	•	112...	XamarinMaster...
12	0x79fd6c20	Xamarin_Master_iOS_Views_RetainingParentClass	01:10.695....	•	112...	XamarinMaster...
13	0x79be8b80	Xamarin_Master_iOS_Views_RetainingChildClass	01:10.695....	•	112...	XamarinMaster...

Figure 9: Instruments view for retained objects

In this case, the easiest fix would be to use a `WeakReference` while we are creating a reference to the parent object from the child one. Using the weak reference avoids the retain cycle situations and does not interfere with the garbage collection.

```
public class RetainingChildClass : UIView
{
    private WeakReference<RetainingParentClass> m_Parent;
```

```
public RetainingChildClass(RetainingParentClass parent)
{
    m_Parent = new WeakReference<RetainingParentClass>(parent);
}
```

Another option would be to implement `IDisposable` interface to remove the strong link between the objects by setting the references to null before GC.

Summary

In order to manage application resources, one must have a deeper understanding of the application lifecycle. Application lifecycle events, outlined in this chapter, are the main access points to underlying platform runtime on both iOS and Android. If used properly, the event delegates and event methods on both platforms can help developers save valuable resources and avoid memory problems.

Other concepts discussed were garbage collection, object references, and automatic reference counting. These concepts make up the foundation of memory management on target Xamarin platforms.

We also had a closer look at the diagnostic and profiling tools for target platforms and how they can be used effectively. While iOS and Android platforms each have a native app to analyze memory allocations, Xamarin Profiler provides a unified solution for both platforms.

Finally, useful patterns were outlined for different memory related issues and pitfalls. To analyze these patterns, Xamarin Profiler and Instruments were used for Android and iOS applications respectively.

In the next chapter, we will be looking at asynchronous implementation techniques and investigate various patterns of multi-threading and background execution.

Asynchronous Programming

3

This chapter deep-dives into the asynchronous and multithreaded programming concepts. We will discuss platform-specific problems and give an in-depth description of how threading scenarios are executed on different platforms. The chapter is divided into following sections:

- Multithreading on Xamarin
- Asynchronous methods
- Parallel execution
- Patterns and best practices
- Background tasks

Multithreading on Xamarin

Xamarin platforms together with Windows Runtime follow the basic principles of a single-threaded apartment model. In this model, in simple terms, a process is assigned a single thread which acts as the main trunk for all the other possible branches to be created from and yield back to.

While developers still have the ability to create and consume multiple threads, in modern applications on Xamarin target platforms, this model has been extended with concurrency implementations that delegate the responsibility of thread management to runtime and allow the developer only to define execution blocks which may or may not be executed on a separate thread.

Single thread model

In Android and iOS, each mobile application is started and run on a single thread that is generally referred to as the main or the UI thread. Most of the UI interaction and process lifecycle event handlers and delegates are executed on this thread.

In this model, developers' main concern should be keeping the main thread accessible to UI interaction as long as possible. If we were to execute a blocking call on this thread, it immediately would be reflected to the user as a screen freeze or an application nonresponsive error, which will inevitably get terminated by the so-called watch-dog implementation of the underlying platform. In addition to the platform-specific restrictions, users also expect a responsive UI at all times and cannot tolerate frozen screens even for a fraction of a second. If the screen freeze lasts any longer, they will try to forcefully terminate the application (see the *Feedback* section of *Chapter 7*, *View Elements*).

Developers can still create, consume, and monitor other threads from the main thread. It is possible to use background threads and invoke long running processes in the background. For this purpose, the System.Threading namespace and threading related classes are available on Xamarin.iOS and Xamarin.Android projects. Moreover, each platform has its own threading implementation under the hood.

For example, let's imagine we want to execute a long running process and we do not want this method to block the UI thread. With classic threading, the implementation would look similar to:

```
//var threadStart = new ThreadStart(MyLongRunningProcess);
//(new Thread(threadStart)).Start();

// Or simply
(new Thread(MyLongRunningProcess)).Start();
```

Each Thread can give information about the current execution state, and it can be canceled, started, interrupted, or even joined by another thread. Developers can use the threading model for throttling their application and/or executing their code more efficiently without committing the cardinal sin of blocking the UI thread.

It might get a little complicated when the process you are executing on a separate thread needs to update a UI component. This would be a cross-thread violation.

For instance, if we wanted to update a UI component from a separate thread in an Android activity, we would need to execute it on the activity as follows (using `Activity.RunOnUiThread`):

```
this.RunOnUiThread(() => { UpdateUIComponent(); });
```

The same execution on iOS would look similar to (using `NSObject.InvokeOnMainThread`):

```
this.InvokeOnMainThread(() => { UpdateUIComponent(); });
```

For reference, on Windows Runtime the same execution would look like this:

```
CoreApplication.MainView
    .CoreWindow.Dispatcher.RunAsync(CoreDispatcherPriority.Normal,
        () => { UpdateUIComponent(); });
```

The implementation in classic threading gets even more complex when there is an exception or the operation has to be canceled, not to mention the fact that synchronization between threads and thread-safe data flow is completely left to developers or third-party implementations.

Another important mishap of using the `System.Threading` namespace and the classic threading model in Xamarin, is that this namespace and thread-related classes cannot be used in PCLs.

Task-based Asynchronous Pattern

Since the introduction of the Tasks framework in .NET 4.0 and its later adoption by Mono, the **Task-based Asynchronous Pattern (TAP)** has become de-facto the main implementation strategy for mobile applications. While providing the required abstraction from the treading structure, it also gives the development teams the opportunity to create easily readable, manageable, and scalable application projects. As mentioned earlier, since each Xamarin target platform has the threading implemented according to the underlying runtime, this abstraction that the Tasks framework provides makes it the perfect candidate for asynchronous implementations in cross-platform projects and an invaluable part of portable class libraries.

In this pattern, each execution block is represented by a `Task` or a `Task<T>` according to the return value of the block (for example, if the block is returning void, it should be converted to return `Task` and if the block is returning an `int`, the method signature should be `Task<int>`). Tasks can be executed either synchronously or asynchronously, can be awaited for a result or executed as a promise with a callback on completion, can be pushed to another thread-pool or executed on the main thread taking processor time when available.

Tasks are especially suited for computationally intensive operations, since they provide excellent control over when and how the asynchronous method is executed. Cancellation and progress support on these methods makes long running processes easily manageable.

Concurrency model on iOS

Concurrency and operation blocks on iOS runtime are Apple's take on the same issues that the Tasks framework is trying to resolve. In essence, the Tasks framework and concurrency model on iOS are the solution to creating multitasking, robust, and easily scalable applications by creating an abstraction layer so that applications do not directly manage threads, but let the operating system decide on where and when to execute operations.

The iOS runtime uses operation or dispatch queues to asynchronously dispatch tasks in a **first-in-first-out** (**FIFO**) manner. This approach provides automatic thread-pool management as well as a simple programming interface.

While the iOS runtime constructs such as `NSOperation`, `NSBlockOperation`, and `NSOperationQueue` are implemented in the Xamarin.iOS framework and are ready to use, the implementations would only be targeting the iOS platform while Tasks can be used on all three platforms.

Asynchronous methods

The **Task Parallel Library** (**TPL**) constitutes the core part of parallel computing in the .NET framework and has inherently the same stature in Xamarin runtime(s).

Asynchronous method execution, together with the `async` and `await` keywords (introduced with C# 5.0), can make the apps more responsive and efficient and decrease the complexity of implementing multithreading and synchronization. Without having the need to implement a parameterized thread, start and push are delegated to a background thread, with so called "awaitables." You can convert your methods to async promises easily with `Task` or `Task<T>` as the return type. In return, the runtime chooses the best time to execute the code and returns the result to your execution context.

For instance, the previous thread creation example with Tasks would be as simple as:

```
Task.Run(() => MyLongRunningProcess());

// Or
Task.Factory.StartNew(MyLongRunningProcess, TaskCreationOptions.
LongRunning);
```

However, the Tasks framework is not only about creating threads or executing non-blocking methods, but also about coordinating and managing these asynchronous tasks in the easiest way possible. There are many static helper methods as well as methods implemented for Tasks that help developers to easily implement some of these coordination scenarios.

Continuation

The `ContinueWith` function on the `Task` class allows the developers to chain dependent Tasks together and execute them as one Task as a whole. The continuation delegate is executed once the result from the first task is posted back to the task scheduler. It is important to mention that the first task and the continuation methods are not necessarily executed on the same thread. The code is as follows:

```
Task.Run(() => MyLongRunningProcess())
    .ContinueWith(task => MySecondLongRunningProcess());
```

In case the second task was dependent on the result from the first task:

```
Task.Run(() => MyLongRunningProcess())
            .ContinueWith(task => MySecondLongRunningProcess(task.
Result));
```

Cancellation

`CancellationToken` and `CancellationTokenSource` are used as the remote token to control the execution lifetime of an async method, thread, or a number of threads and the event source that the token reflects the events of.

In simple terms, `CancellationTokenSource` is responsible for throwing either time-based or manual cancel events and these events can be retrieved through the token in the context of the asynchronous method.

You can create a cancellation source using the default constructor and time-based cancellation can be added to the token:

```
m_CancellationSource = new CancellationTokenSource();

var token = m_CancellationSource.Token;

// You can cancel it after a certain amount of time, which would
trigger an OperationCanceledException
// m_CancellationSource.CancelAfter(2000);
```

Once we are executing an async method, we can use the token from this source, or we can associate it with a `TaskFactory` to create a cooperating list of tasks:

```
Task.Run(() =>
{
    // Executing my long running method
    if (token.IsCancellationRequested)
    {
        token.ThrowIfCancellationRequested();
    }
}, token);
```

Or:

```
var taskFactory = new TaskFactory(m_CancellationSource.Token);
taskFactory.StartNew(() =>
    {
        // Executing my long running method
        if (Task.Factory.CancellationToken != CancellationToken.None
&& Task.Factory.CancellationToken.IsCancellationRequested)
        {
            Task.Factory.CancellationToken
                .ThrowIfCancellationRequested();
        }
    });
```

Finally, you can also cancel the thread or a group of threads using the `Cancel` or `CancelAfter` (with a time delay) methods of `CancellationTokenSource`.

Progress

Another asynchronous control feature that helps keep the user informed about the operations being invoked in the background is the progress callback implementation. Just like `CancellationToken`, we can supply the asynchronous tasks with an event handler for progress events that the asynchronous method can invoke to pass progress information back to the main thread.

For simple progress reporting, it is enough to expand asynchronous methods with an additional parameter that derives from the `IProgress<T>` interface.

For instance, if we were to implement a progress event handler in the `GetFibonacciRangeAsync` method, we could use the number of values to be calculated and the current ordinal being calculated to report an overall progress in percentages:

```
public async Task<List<int>> GetFibonacciRangeAsync(int firstOrdinal,
int lastOrdinal, IProgress<int> progress = null)
{
    var results = new List<int>();

    for (var i = firstOrdinal; i < lastOrdinal; i++)
    {
        results.Add(await GetFibonacciNumberAsync(i));

        decimal currentPercentage = (decimal) lastOrdinal - i/
(decimal) lastOrdinal - firstOrdinal;

        if (progress != null)
            progress.Report((int)(currentPercentage * 100);
    }

    return results;
}
```

In order to be able to use the progress value in our view model, we can make use of the `Progress<T>` class, which is the default implementation of `IProgress<T>`. The code is as follows:

```
Action<int> reportProgress = (value) =>
{
    InfoText = string.Format("{0}% Completed", value);
};

var progress = new Progress<int>(reportProgress);

m_SourceAsync.GetFibonacciRangeAsync(numberOrdinal1, numberOrdinal2,
progress)
    .ContinueWith(task =>
    {
        Result = string.Join(",", task.Result.Select(val=>val));
        InfoText = "";
    });
```

Task batches

In task-based asynchronous pattern, there are other ways than continuation to execute tasks in a batch, even in parallel. The example from the previous section was awaiting each number calculation separately and executing the next call. However, the manner in which the inner methods were implemented made them independent from each other. Hence, it is not actually necessary to wait for them one by one to return the result. The code is as follows:

```
List<Task<int>> calculations = new List<Task<int>>();

Mvx.Trace("Starting Calculations");

for (var i = firstOrdinal; i < lastOrdinal; i++)
{
    var currentOrdinal = i;
    calculations.Add(Task.Factory.StartNew(() =>
        GetFibonacciNumberInternal(currentOrdinal).Value,
TaskCreationOptions.LongRunning));
}

Mvx.Trace("Starting When All", DateTime.Now);
int[] results = await Task.WhenAll(calculations);
Mvx.Trace("Calculations Completed", DateTime.Now);

return results.OrderBy(value=>value).ToList();
```

The Mvx static class and the `Trace` method are provided by the MvvmCross library. It will be further discussed in later chapters.

Now, each Fibonacci number in the sequence is calculated in parallel and when the sequence range is complete, an array of result values is returned. Finally, we sort the array and return the list of values.

We can extend this implementation by adding a progress notifier with an interlocked (thread-safe) counter:

```
calculations.Add(Task.Factory.StartNew(() =>
    GetFibonacciNumberInternal(currentOrdinal).Value,
TaskCreationOptions.LongRunning)
    .ContinueWith(task =>
    {
        if (progress != null)
        {
            var currentTotal = Interlocked.Increment(ref
currentCount);
            decimal currentPercentage = (decimal) currentTotal/
(decimal) totalCount;
            progress.Report((int)(currentPercentage * 100));
        }
        return task.Result;
    }));
```

The resulting log traces from the calculations above are as follows:

```
09-07 21:18:29.232 I/mono-stdout( 3094): mvx:Diagnostic: 40.80
Starting Calculations
09-07 21:18:29.352 I/mono-stdout( 3094): mvx:Diagnostic: 40.92
Starting When All
09-07 21:18:30.432 I/mono-stdout( 3094): mvx:Diagnostic: 42.00
Calculations Completed
```

The total time for the calculations was about 1.2 seconds.

Repeating the same calculations with an `await` on each method would give the following output (calculating ordinal 4 until 11):

```
09-07 21:26:58.716 I/mono-stdout( 3281): mvx:Diagnostic: 10.60
Starting Calculations
09-07 21:26:58.724 I/mono-stdout( 3281): mvx:Diagnostic: 10.61
Starting calculating ordinal 4
...
```

```
09-07 21:27:03.900 I/mono-stdout( 3281): mvx:Diagnostic: 15.78
Starting calculating ordinal 11
09-07 21:27:05.028 I/mono-stdout( 3281): mvx:Diagnostic: 16.91
Calculations Completed
```

The same calculations took around 6.3 seconds overall.

On top of `WhenAll`, developers are also equipped with the `WhenAny`, `WaitAll`, `WaitAny` methods on the `Task` class and `ContinueWhenAll` and `ContinueWhenAny` on the `TaskFactory` class.

Parallel execution

In the previous section, the discussion was centered on the `System.Threading.Tasks` namespace and the `Task` class. Even though tasks are the cornerstone of the task-based asynchronous model and so-called Task Parallelism, the concurrent collections namespace makes up the Data Parallelism side of the async model and provides developers with tools to execute code most efficiently and in a thread-safe manner.

`BlockingCollection<T>` is one of the concurrent collection implementations that encapsulates the core synchronization and coordination between threads and provides a thread-safe data storage to implement a provider-consumer model in Xamarin applications.

Using `BlockingCollection<T>`, we can easily implement a new method that makes use of the parallel execution from the previous example. In this implementation, our view model will be the consumer and the Fibonacci source and the range calculation tasks will be the provider.

If we were to rewrite the range calculation method using a blocking collection, our method signature would be similar to:

```
public async Task GetFibonacciRangeAsync(int firstOrdinal, int
lastOrdinal, BlockingCollection<int> blockingCollection)
```

So in a way, the consumer is going to create the blocking collection and will pass it to the provider to fill it up with the calculated values. The provider in return will need to push each calculated value from the parallel tasks with the `TryAdd` or `Add` methods. The code is as follows:

```
for (var i = firstOrdinal; i < lastOrdinal; i++)
{
    var currentOrdinal = i;
```

```
        calculations.Add(Task.Factory.StartNew(() =>
            GetFibonacciNumberInternal(currentOrdinal).Value,
    TaskCreationOptions.LongRunning)
            .ContinueWith(task =>
            {
                blockingCollection.Add(task.Result);
                return task.Result;
            }));
    }
```

Finally, once all the calculations are completed, the provider needs to mark the collection as add-completed. The code is as follows:

```
//
// Collection is filled completely
await Task.WhenAll(calculations).ContinueWith(task =>
{
    blockingCollection.CompleteAdding();
});
```

While these tasks are being executed on the provider side, we can create the consumer in our view model with a `while` loop, checking on certain intervals if there is a new item with `TryTake` until it is completed. However, there is already an implemented method on the concurrent collection for this purpose: `GetConsumingEnumerable`. Using this method makes the execution on the consumer thread as simple as a `foreach` block. The code is as follows:

```
var blockingCollection = new BlockingCollection<int>();

var fibonacciTask = (new FibonacciSourceAsync())
    .GetFibonacciRangeAsync(numberOrdinal1,
        numberOrdinal2, blockingCollection);

fibonacciTask.ConfigureAwait(false);

//
// Starting the Consumer thread
Task.Factory.StartNew(() =>
{
    foreach (var item in blockingCollection.GetConsumingEnumerable())
    {
        var currentItem = item;
        if (Result != string.Empty) Result += ",";
```

```
        Result += currentItem;
    }

    InfoText = "Done";

}, TaskCreationOptions.LongRunning);
```

In this model, the provider thread (together with each parallel task being executed) and the consumer thread are executed almost instantaneously and the results are reflected to the UI almost immediately through the view model.

In the previous implementation, even though possibly multiple values are added to the blocking collection and the blocking collection's support for multiple consumers, the `foreach` loop follows a more linear execution. We can extend this model by adding multiple consumers using the `Parallel.ForEach` extension method from the `System.Threading.Tasks.Parallel` namespace. The code is as follows:

```
Task.Factory.StartNew(() =>
{
    var result = Parallel.ForEach(blockingCollection.
GetConsumingEnumerable(), item =>
    {
        UpdateUIWithItem(item);
    }).IsCompleted;

    if (result) InfoText = "Done";
}, TaskCreationOptions.LongRunning);
```

There are other constructs and implementation patterns that developers can use and adapt on concurrent scenarios such as `Partitioner`, `ActionBlock`, `ConcurrentScheduler`, among others. However, these concepts are beyond the scope of this book.

Patterns and best practices

It is possible to draw parallels with and even convert from the classic threading and eventing patterns while implementing asynchronous tasks. However, async methods have to be implemented with caution to avoid deadlocks and uncaught exceptions.

Async pattern conversions

The Observer pattern—also known as the **Event-based Asynchronous Pattern (EAP)**—used to be the main development tool for long running processes and service/remote application APIs. Events and delegates still make up a considerable amount of UI-related implementation in modern applications.

However, asynchronous tasks and awaitables provide a much more convenient way to deal with long running processes and chain completion methods.

Fortunately, it is possible to implement conversion patterns from other async patterns to task-based implementations. These types of scenarios involve using the `TaskCompletionSource` class.

In order to demonstrate this, we will be using a simplified version of the Fibonacci source implementation from previous examples:

```csharp
public event EventHandler<int> CalculationCompleted;

public event EventHandler<string> CalculationFailed;

/// <summary>
/// Calculates n-th number in Fibonacci sequence
/// </summary>
/// <param name="ordinal">Ordinal of the number to calculate</param>
public void GetFibonacciNumber(int ordinal)
{
    try
    {
        var result = GetFibonacciNumberInternal(ordinal);

        if (CalculationCompleted != null)
          CalculationCompleted(this, result);
    }
    catch (Exception ex)
    {
        if (CalculationFailed != null) CalculationFailed(this,
          ex.Message);
    }
}
```

In this example, we have an event handler for successful calculations and another one for failed calculations (for example, if the ordinal is less than 0, it should throw an `ArgumentOutOfRangeException`).

Our aim here is to implement an asynchronous method, which we can execute and yield the result to the UI without having to subscribe to the event every time a new `FibonacciSource` is created.

For this purpose, we can implement a new version of `FibonacciSource` and expose only async methods instead of event-based methods. The code is as follows:

```
public class FibonacciSourceAsync : FibonacciSource
{
    public new Task<int> GetFibonacciNumberAsync(int ordinal)
    {
        var myTaskSource = new TaskCompletionSource<int>();

        EventHandler<FibonacciItem> onCalculationCompleted = null;
        EventHandler<string> onCalculationFailed = null;

        //
        // Subscribe to TaskCompleted: When the CalculationCompleted
event is fired, set result.
        onCalculationCompleted = (sender, args) =>
        {
            // Not forgetting to release the event handler
            CalculationCompleted -= onCalculationCompleted;
            myTaskSource.SetResult(args.Value);
        };

        //
        // Subscribe to TaskFailed: If there is an error in the
execution, set error.
        onCalculationFailed = (sender, args) =>
        {
            CalculationFailed -= onCalculationFailed;
            myTaskSource.SetException(new Exception(args));
        };

        CalculationCompleted += onCalculationCompleted;

        CalculationFailed += onCalculationFailed;
```

```
        // Finally execute the task and return the associated Task
promise.
        base.GetFibonacciNumberAsync(ordinal);

        return myTaskSource.Task;

    }
}
```

Now calls to calculate Fibonacci numbers would look similar to:

```
public async Task<int> CalculateFibonacciValueAsync(int ordinal)
{
    var fibonacciSource =  new FibonacciSourceAsync();

    try
    {
        return (await fibonacciSource.GetFibonacciNumberAsync(ordin
al));
    }
    catch (Exception ex)
    {
        // TODO: Do something with exception
    }
}
```

This implementation can be further extended with progress and cancellation token implementations.

Multi-threading with tasks

One important thing to realize about asynchronous calls is that they don't necessarily run on a separate thread. As a matter of fact, calls are "scheduled" to run in a so-called Synchronization Context on the main thread unless they are instructed otherwise. Synchronization Context is the message queue that takes care of the scheduling of the async calls that need to be awaited. Once the async method (or `Task` in most of the cases) is successfully executed, the result is posted back onto the Synchronization Context (that is, the main UI thread).

For demonstration purposes, we will be using the async implementation (EAP conversion) from the previous example with some additional diagnostic calls to get additional information about the threads and synchronization contexts being used.

The `TraceThreadInfo` method and the associated `ThreadInfo` class used in the examples here is a custom implementation used through dependency injection. The reason for this is that threading namespace only contains task-related classes in PCLs and the only way to actually get the current thread ID is to use platform-specific implementation. Platform-specific implementation patterns will be discussed in detail in later chapters.

In the tracing method, we will be logging the current thread ID and the current synchronization context:

```
public IThreadInfo ThreadInfo
{
    get { return Mvx.GetSingleton<IThreadInfo>(); }
}

private void TraceThreadInfo(string message)
{
    Debug.WriteLine("{0} on Thread '{1}'", message,
        ThreadInfo.CurrentThreadId);
    Debug.WriteLine("Current Synchronization Context is {0}",
        SynchronizationContext.Current);
}
```

The calculation command attached to the calculate button is:

```
TraceThreadInfo("Begin DoCalculate");

if (!string.IsNullOrWhiteSpace(Input))
{
    int numberOrdinal;

    if (int.TryParse(Input, out numberOrdinal))
    {
        InfoText = "Calculating";

        TraceThreadInfo("Calling GetFibonacciNumberAsync");

        var result = await GetFibonacciNumberAsync(numberOrdinal);

        TraceThreadInfo("Response from GetFibonacciNumberAsync");

        Result = result.ToString();
```

```
        InfoText = string.Empty;

        TraceThreadInfo("End DoCalculate");

        return;
    }
}

InfoText = "Invalid Input";
```

The associated trace log will look like this:

Time		PID	Tag	Message
5:07 AM	I	1796	mono-stdout	Begin DoCalculate on Thread '1'
5:07 AM	I	1796	mono-stdout	Current Syncronization Context is Android.App.SyncContext
5:07 AM	I	1796	mono-stdout	Calling GetFibonacciNumberAsync on Thread '1'
5:07 AM	I	1796	mono-stdout	Current Syncronization Context is Android.App.SyncContext
5:07 AM	I	1796	mono-stdout	Begin GetFibonacciNumberAsync on Thread '1'
5:07 AM	I	1796	mono-stdout	Current Syncronization Context is Android.App.SyncContext
5:07 AM	I	1796	mono-stdout	Calling FibonacciSource.GetFibonacciNumberAsync on Thread '1'
5:07 AM	I	1796	mono-stdout	Current Syncronization Context is Android.App.SyncContext
5:07 AM	I	1796	mono-stdout	Begin FibonacciSource.GetFibonacciNumberAsync on Thread '1'
5:07 AM	I	1796	mono-stdout	Current Syncronization Context is Android.App.SyncContext
5:07 AM	I	1796	mono-stdout	End FibonacciSource.GetFibonacciNumberAsync on Thread '1'
5:07 AM	I	1796	mono-stdout	Current Syncronization Context is Android.App.SyncContext
5:07 AM	I	1796	mono-stdout	End GetFibonacciNumberAsync on Thread '1'
5:07 AM	I	1796	mono-stdout	Current Syncronization Context is Android.App.SyncContext
5:07 AM	I	1796	mono-stdout	Begin FibonacciSource.GetFibonacciNumberInternal on Thread '106'
5:07 AM	I	1796	mono-stdout	Current Syncronization Context is
5:07 AM	I	1796	mono-stdout	End FibonacciSource.GetFibonacciNumberInternal on Thread '106'
5:07 AM	I	1796	mono-stdout	Current Syncronization Context is
5:07 AM	I	1796	mono-stdout	Response from GetFibonacciNumberAsync on Thread '1'
5:07 AM	I	1796	mono-stdout	Current Syncronization Context is Android.App.SyncContext
5:07 AM	I	1796	mono-stdout	End DoCalculate on Thread '1'
5:07 AM	I	1796	mono-stdout	Current Syncronization Context is Android.App.SyncContext

Trace for in-line execution of tasks

Looking at the trace messages of the execution stack above, one can easily see that in spite of the fact we are dealing with async tasks, the whole execution takes place on the main thread except for the actual call for the internal method of the source (that is, it is executed on Thread 106). The rest of the method calls have `Android.App.SyncContext` as the synchronization context and the execution order is no different than the call sequence that is implemented.

Changing the implementation a little bit and using the `ContinueWith` function of the `Task` item, we get slightly different results. The code is as follows:

```
TraceThreadInfo("Calling GetFibonacciNumberAsync");


await GetFibonacciNumberAsync(numberOrdinal).ContinueWith(task =>
{
    TraceThreadInfo("Response from GetFibonacciNumberAsync");

    Result = task.Result.ToString();

    InfoText = string.Empty;
});


TraceThreadInfo("End DoCalculate");
```

The trace log for this implementation looks like this:

Time	PID	Tag	Message
5:42 AM I	2177	mono-stdout	Begin DoCalculate on Thread '1'
5:42 AM I	2177	mono-stdout	Current Syncronization Context is Android.App.SyncContext
5:42 AM I	2177	mono-stdout	Calling GetFibonacciNumberAsync on Thread '1'
5:42 AM I	2177	mono-stdout	Current Syncronization Context is Android.App.SyncContext
5:42 AM I	2177	mono-stdout	Begin GetFibonacciNumberAsync on Thread '1'
5:42 AM I	2177	mono-stdout	Current Syncronization Context is Android.App.SyncContext
5:42 AM I	2177	mono-stdout	Calling FibonacciSource.GetFibonacciNumberAsync on Thread '1'
5:42 AM I	2177	mono-stdout	Current Syncronization Context is Android.App.SyncContext
5:42 AM I	2177	mono-stdout	Begin FibonacciSource.GetFibonacciNumberAsync on Thread '1'
5:42 AM I	2177	mono-stdout	Current Syncronization Context is Android.App.SyncContext
5:42 AM I	2177	mono-stdout	End FibonacciSource.GetFibonacciNumberAsync on Thread '1'
5:42 AM I	2177	mono-stdout	Current Syncronization Context is Android.App.SyncContext
5:42 AM I	2177	mono-stdout	Begin FibonacciSource.GetFibonacciNumberInternal on Thread '113'
5:42 AM I	2177	mono-stdout	End GetFibonacciNumberAsync on Thread '1'
5:42 AM I	2177	mono-stdout	Current Syncronization Context is Android.App.SyncContext
5:42 AM I	2177	mono-stdout	Current Syncronization Context is
5:42 AM I	2177	mono-stdout	End FibonacciSource.GetFibonacciNumberInternal on Thread '113'
5:42 AM I	2177	mono-stdout	Current Syncronization Context is
5:42 AM I	2177	mono-stdout	Response from GetFibonacciNumberAsync on Thread '104'
5:42 AM I	2177	mono-stdout	Current Syncronization Context is
5:42 AM I	2177	mono-stdout	End DoCalculate on Thread '1'
5:42 AM I	2177	mono-stdout	Current Syncronization Context is Android.App.SyncContext

Async execution of Tasks

As the trace log suggests, `ContinueWith` lambda is executed on a separate thread but the execution is still sequential.

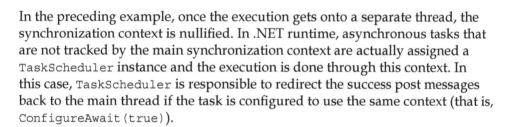

> An important note here is that we are assigning the results back to the ViewModel on a separate thread. In this example, the cross-thread invocation is handled by the MvvmCross framework. If we were to deal with this assignment, the call would look similar to:
>
> ```
> await GetFibonacciNumberAsync(numberOrdinal).
> ContinueWith(task =>
> {
>     TraceThreadInfo("Response from
> GetFibonacciNumberAsync");
>
>     this.RunOnUiThread(() =>
>     {
>         txtResult.Text = task.Result.ToString();
>     });
>
>     txtInfo.Text = "";
> });
> ```

In the preceding example, once the execution gets onto a separate thread, the synchronization context is nullified. In .NET runtime, asynchronous tasks that are not tracked by the main synchronization context are actually assigned a `TaskScheduler` instance and the execution is done through this context. In this case, `TaskScheduler` is responsible to redirect the success post messages back to the main thread if the task is configured to use the same context (that is, `ConfigureAwait(true)`).

However, the way synchronization context works in .NET and the configured task invocations yield back to the main thread can cause deadlocks if the asynchronous tasks are called synchronously (that is, with `Task.Result` or `Task.Wait()`) on the main thread. In such a scenario, once the async call finishes executing and tries to yield back into the main context, the main context will still not be accessible since it is actually waiting for the async task itself to complete.

`ConfigureAwait(false)` informs the scheduler not to look for and post back the result to the same execution context where the task was invoked, but rather just execute and run to completion on the execution context. This avoids the deadlock scenario.

This deadlock scenario is specific for .NET runtime and because of the way mono runtime on Android and Mono.Touch compiler deal with the task executions; the deadlocks currently do not happen on these platforms. However, it is important to follow the coding conventions associated with asynchronous tasks and awaitables to avoid any unexpected behavior.

In order to execute the whole task on a separate thread we can use `Task.Run` (which will push the task to the ThreadPool) or `Task.Factory.StartNew`. Using the `StartNew` method would let you define which type of a method you are about to execute in this task and let the runtime make an informed decision about using a different thread. The code is as follows:

```
var task = Task.Factory.StartNew(async () =>
{
    TraceThreadInfo("Calling GetFibonacciNumberAsync");

    var result = await GetFibonacciNumberAsync(numberOrdinal);

    TraceThreadInfo("Response from GetFibonacciNumberAsync");

    Result = result.ToString();

    InfoText = string.Empty;

}, TaskCreationOptions.LongRunning);

task.ConfigureAwait(false);
```

In the trace below, the biggest difference with the previous examples is that the `DoCalculate` method exits before even the execution starts for the task we created for the calculations. This type of execution would eloquently fit with the MVVM pattern applied on a cross platform mobile app project. It would avoid any UI blocking issues and create a sense of continuity for the user.

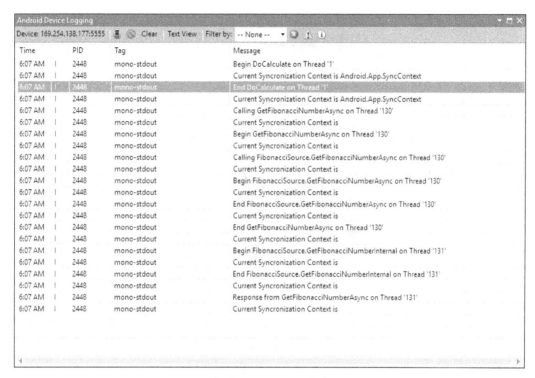

Starting a new async task

If we want to analyze the same execution on the iOS application (that is, calculate the number on the Fibonacci sequence on a certain ordinal), we can easily identify the threading pattern with the Xcode Instruments "System Trace" template.

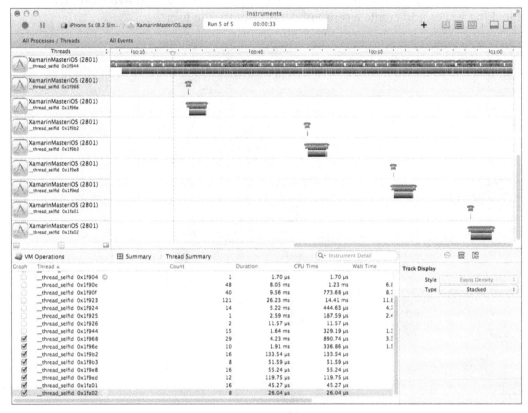

Calculating four different Fibonacci numbers

Exception handling

Handling exceptions can become cumbersome if correct asynchronous paths are not followed in multithreaded implementations. However, in most cases, the async/await language constructs take the load of the developers. If the async chain is not broken and calls are implemented correctly, catching exceptions in asynchronous context is no different than catching them with linear code.

Using our example from previous sections:

```
try
{
    var result = await GetFibonacciNumberAsync(numberOrdinal);

    Result = result.ToString();

    InfoText = "";
}
catch (Exception ex)
{
    Debug.WriteLine("Error:" + ex.Message);
    InfoText = "EX:" + ex.Message;
}
```

In this example, if the ordinal we pass in as a parameter is a negative number, it would throw an exception with the message **Cannot calculate Fibonacci number for a negative number** and we would be displaying the error message in the info textbox.

However, if we were to use the ContinueWith construct to execute the same code the outcome would have been a little different:

```
try
{
    await GetFibonacciNumberAsync(numberOrdinal).ContinueWith(result
=>
    {
        Result = result.Result.ToString();

        InfoText = string.Empty;
    });
}
catch (Exception ex)
{
    Debug.WriteLine("Error:" + ex.Message);
    InfoText = "EX:" + ex.Message;
}
```

In this example, the exception message we would receive would be **One or more errors occurred**. The reason for this is that the exception thrown in the second scenario is an `AggregateException` because of the async chain we created.

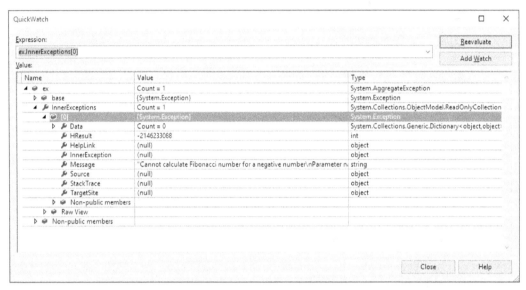

AggregateException in async chain

The result would have been the same if we were using the `.Result` or `.Wait()` calls on the task itself.

The important part of this implementation is where we are calling `await` on the asynchronous method. The catch block would never have been called if this was not the case. Without the `await` keyword, the try/catch block would have been just checking if the preparation of the Task went as expected, not the actual execution.

Another type of async execution that cannot be caught with a try/catch block is the type of async methods that return `void` instead of a `Task` or `Task<T>`. Similar to having an exception thrown in an event handler, the only two places they would be caught are the `AppDomain.UnhandledException` or `Application.ThreadException` events. It is always a better practice for asynchronous methods to return `Task` and then return void.

However, in the `ContinueWith` implementation, with the reference to the `Task` at hand, we can also check for the status of the task once it runs to completion before we make the result assignment. This assignment is what actually causes the exception to bubble-up to upper layers. In this case, we do not need a try/catch block. The code is as follows:

```
await GetFibonacciNumberAsync(numberOrdinal).ContinueWith(result =>
{
    TraceThreadInfo("Response from GetFibonacciNumberAsync");

    if (result.IsFaulted)
    {
        Result = string.Empty;

        InfoText = string.Join("\r\n", result.Exception
            .InnerExceptions.Select(exception => exception.Message));
    }
    else
    {
        Result = result.Result.ToString();

        InfoText = string.Empty;
    }
});
```

Initialization pattern

Especially in scenarios where a service is involved, a common requirement is to have an initialization function that would prepare the communication channel and/or make a "ping" or an authentication call. When developers are confronted with this type of a scenario, the biggest mistake they can make is to call the asynchronous initialization function in the constructor with a `.Result` and/or `.Wait()` statement (making it a synchronous call).

For this scenario, let's assume we have a service that implements an interface with two simple async method implementations.

```
public interface IService
{
    Task<string> AuthenticateAsync(string username, string password);

    Task<int> ServiceMethodAsync(string myParameter);
}
```

In order to be able to call `ServiceMethodAsync`, we first need to make an `AuthenticateAsync` call and receive the authentication token from the service. The code is as follows:

```
public MyService(string username, string password)
{
    //
    // Following call would block the constructor
    // IMPORTANT: If it was being called from the main UI thread, it might cause a deadlock
    // Blocking Call Example 1:
    // AuthenticateAsync(username, password).Wait();
    // Blocking Call Example 2:
    m_Token = AuthenticateAsync(username, password).Result;
}
```

In this example, we implemented the call for authentication in the constructor of the service. Even though the implementation might work in some cases, if the service constructor is called from the main UI thread, the thread would go into a deadlock as it was described in the previous section.

The easiest solution would be to either expose the initialization function to outer layers or have the service call initialization before each service call. For this purpose we can wrap the authentication call in an initialization method. The code is as follows:

```
public MyService(string username, string password)
{
    m_Username = username;
    m_Password = password;
}

private async Task EnsureInitializationAsync()
{
    if (string.IsNullOrEmpty(m_Token))
    {
        m_Token = await AuthenticateAsync(m_Username, m_Password);
    }
}
```

The service method call would look similar to this:

```
public async Task<int> ServiceMethodAsync(string myParameter)
{
    await EnsureInitializationAsync();
```

```
    try
    {
        int result = await InternalServiceMethodAsync(myParameter);

        return result;
    }
    catch (Exception ex)
    {
        // TODO:
        throw;
    }
}
```

As mentioned, we can also expose the initialization through an interface:

```
/// <summary>
/// Describes the service as requiring async initialization
/// </summary>
public interface IAsyncInitialization
{
    /// <summary>
    /// The result of the asynchronous initialization.
    /// </summary>
    Task Initialization { get; }
}

public class MyService : IService, IAsyncInitialization
{
...

    public Task Initialization { get; private set; }

    public MyService(string username, string password)
    {
        m_Username = username;
        m_Password = password;

        Initialization = EnsureInitializationAsync();
    }

    private async Task EnsureInitializationAsync()
    {
        if (string.IsNullOrEmpty(m_Token))
        {
```

```
        m_Token = await AuthenticateAsync(m_Username, m_Password);
    }
  }

  ...
}
```

In this case, the caller method needs to check if the service needs async initialization and check for the required task results. The code is as follows:

```
if (serviceInstance is IAsyncInitialization)
{
    /// Wait for the results of the initialization
    await serviceInstance.Initialization;
}

await serviceInstance.ServiceMethodAsync("param");
```

Semaphores

Synchronization and throttling methodology on the asynchronous context is a little different than the classic .NET runtime implementations. For instance, lock blocks are not allowed on async calls and you will not be able to use Mutex for synchronization. Mutex is inapplicable as a mutex can only be owned by a single thread and async executions are not guaranteed to complete on the same thread as they started. The code is as follows:

```
//
// Error: The 'await' operator cannot be used in the body of a lock
statement
//lock (m_FibonacciSource)
//{
//    var result = await GetFibonacciNumberAsync(numberOrdinal);
//}

//
// Warning: Might work but not guaranteed
m_Mutex.WaitOne(200);

await GetFibonacciNumberAsync(numberOrdinal).ContinueWith((task) =>
{
    TraceThreadInfo("Response from GetFibonacciNumberAsync");

    Result = task.Result.ToString();
```

```
    InfoText = string.Empty;
});
```

```
m_Mutex.ReleaseMutex();
```

In order to handle the non-deterministic execution and threading model of asynchronous tasks, a new construct was added to .NET: Semaphore. Semaphore (implementation of WaitHandle) and SemaphoreSlim (lightweight version of Semaphore that is implemented with monitors) types do not enforce thread identity on the Wait and Release calls and can be asynchronously awaited.

For instance, let's execute a number of parallel calculations orchestrated with a semaphore that allows 3 access count (SemaphoreSlim(3) or SemaphoreSlim(3,3)) such as:

```
var semaphoreSlim = new SemaphoreSlim(3);

int count = 11;

for (var i = 0; i < 7; i++)
{
    Task.Factory.StartNew(() =>
    {
        return semaphoreSlim.WaitAsync().ContinueWith((waitTask) =>
        {
            return Task.Factory.StartNew(() =>
            {
                return GetFibonacciNumberAsync(count = Interlocked
                    .Increment(ref count)).ContinueWith(
                    (calculateTask) =>
                    {
                        TraceThreadInfo(string.Format(
                            "Current count on Semaphore: {0}",
                            semaphoreSlim.Release() + 1));
                    });
            }, TaskCreationOptions.LongRunning);
        });
    }, TaskCreationOptions.LongRunning);
```

This parallel execution can be easily spotted on the average system time view of Instruments' System Trace template. This is shown in the screenshot below where each ordinal calculation would give the exact number of peaks on the selected calculation threads):

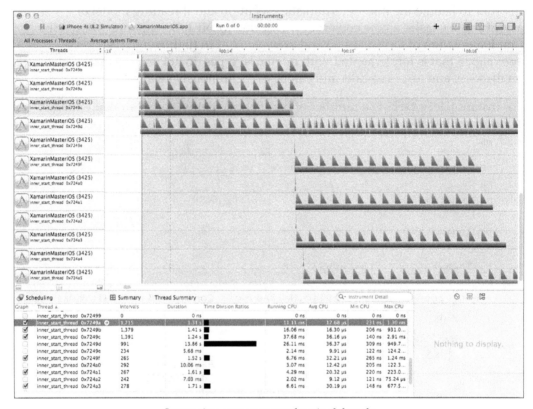

System time average on synchronized threads

Background tasks

Threading and task solutions are not the only option when there is a need to execute a not time-bound, long running process. Moreover, both of these options are for executing code when your application is in the foreground or in an active state. When the application is entering the backgrounded or suspended state, the application might still require the execution of some longer method before the volatile data is lost, or it might require a process to be running in the background when the application is not in an interactive state.

For these types of scenarios, both iOS and Android offer backgrounding and background operation options.

Background tasks on iOS

Background tasks on iOS are the easiest way for your application to execute processing tasks without the need for the UI thread or having to respond to lifecycle delegates.

There are three types of background tasks that can be executed for different needs:

- **Background-safe tasks**: These tasks are the ones that can be executed at any stage of the process lifetime. They are not affected and/or interrupted by the application going into the background. The code is as follows:

```
nint taskId = UIApplication.SharedApplication
    .BeginBackgroundTask(() =>
{
    // TODO: Do something if the allotted time runs out
});

// TODO: Implement the processing logic

if (taskId != UIApplication.BackgroundTaskInvalid)
{
    UIApplication.SharedApplication.EndBackgroundTask(taskId);
}
```

- **DidEnterBackground tasks**: Another type of background task is executed to pass the state-save or clean-up logic to a background process. The `DidEnterBackground` lifetime delegate is used to initialize these tasks and continue processing even after the application goes into the background state. The creation of these tasks is similar to the background-safe tasks. The only difference is that the `EndBackgroundTask` method has to be called inside the execution block rather than the calling thread, since the calling process might have already returned not waiting for the execution of the background task. The code is as follows:

```
public override void DidEnterBackground (UIApplication
application)
{
    nint taskId = UIApplication.SharedApplication
        .BeginBackgroundTask(() =>
    {
        // TODO: Do something if the allotted time runs out
    });

    Task.Run(() =>
    {
```

```
        // TODO: Implement the processing logic
        UIApplication.SharedApplication.EndBackgroundTask(taskId);
    });
}
```

- **Background transfers**: These tasks are specific to iOS 7+ and provide a longer processing time (a strict limit on other background tasks is 600 seconds, while background transfers can last up to 10,000 seconds). Background transfer tasks are used to perform long lasting network operations and upload/download large files over the wire.

Services (Android only)

On the Android platform, once the activities enter the backgrounded state, they cannot perform tasks and are usually stopped soon after entering the background. Services are application components introduced to provide an interface for developers to start and stop long running processes in the background.

Even though services are created as part of an application, they have their own separate lifecycle and can run even if the application and activity that started them was stopped or destroyed.

A service can take one or both of two forms:

- **Started**: A service is "started" when an activity explicitly starts it by calling the `StartService` method using an intent. A started service is generally used as a `BackgroundWorker` and once the processing operation is finished, the service itself or the activity stops it.

- **Bound**: A "bound" service generally acts as the provider to clients in the activities of the application or even other applications. A bound service is kept alive as long as another component is bound to it.

Both of these initialization patterns use the callback methods similar but not limited to `OnStartCommand`, `OnBind`, `OnCreate`, and `OnDestroy` to start background processing and deal with its lifetime.

There are various base classes implemented in the Android namespace and according to the requirements, these base classes can be implemented and started or bound.

In order to implement a started service to do some background processing, the first step of the implementation process would be to create the IntentService class:

```
[Service]
[IntentFilter(new String[] { "com.xamarin.MyDemoService" })]
public class MyDemoService : IntentService
{
    public MyDemoService()
        : base("MyDemoService")
    {
    }

    protected override void OnHandleIntent(Intent intent)
    {
        var myParameter = intent.GetStringExtra("parameter");

        // Invoke long running process
        DoWork(myParameter);
    }
}
```

The IntentService base class already deals with lifecycle events such as OnStart, so all we have to implement is the OnHandleIntent method to respond to intent requests from activities. The two attributes of the class, Service and IntentFilter, are used by Xamarin compiler to generate the entries in the application manifest. The debug build for this implementation gives out the following service entry in the application manifest. The code is as follows:

```
<service android:name="md5d06a1058f86cf8319abb1555c0b54fbf.
MyDemoService">
    <intent-filter>
        <action android:name="com.xamarin.MyDemoService" />
    </intent-filter>
</service>
```

With this implementation in an activity, the intent service can be started by either using the intent filter entry or using the type of the service.

```
//StartService (new Intent (this, typeof(MyDemoService)));
StartService(new Intent("com.xamarin.MyDemoService"));
```

Summary

Overall, asynchronous/concurrent implementation patterns and background tasks allow the developers to push the heavy-lifting away from the UI thread and create responsive applications in the single-threaded paradigm of modern mobile applications.

The Task-based Asynchronous Pattern provides an efficient and scalable way to implement asynchronous operations with ease. Moreover, progress, cancellation, and concurrent collections help monitor, scale, and manage the execution of these asynchronous blocks while providing a way to cooperate between each other. Implementing these blocks, developers do not need to carry the burden of threads, synchronization, and scaling the threads according to the hardware resources.

After analyzing memory and CPU-related topics so far in this book, in the next chapter we will discuss local storage and how to use it efficiently.

4

Local Data Management

In this chapter, you will find patterns and techniques to efficiently use, manage, and roam data on mobile devices. It also investigates SQLite database creation and usage strategies. The chapter is divided into the following sections:

- Data in mobile applications
- Application data
- Local filesystem
- Data roaming
- SQLite
- Patterns and best practices
- Backup/roaming

Data in mobile applications

The term "data" can refer to different types of information and storage locations in mobile app development. It can be used to describe a volatile state that is created and destroyed each time a view in the application is used, or it might refer to persisted settings and configuration information that are required to run the application, or even the data stored in the local filesystem. Each type of data is created and persisted or destroyed throughout the lifecycle of the application or a view in the application. We can talk about four distinct groups for this discussion.

Each data type is stored and accessed from different locations and each location has its own unique restriction and access models.

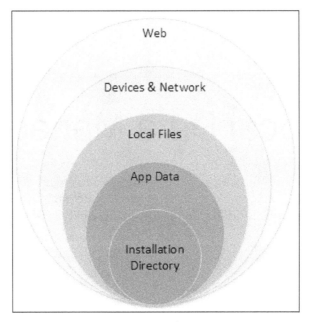

Data type storage locations

State

Mobile applications are generally *stateful*. Transient data that is used to visualize items on the UI or the data created by the user of the application falls into this category. The purpose of state is to maintain a consistent app experience across sessions, devices, and/or process lifecycle. Application settings or the current state of the view is a good example for this category.

App data

App data generally refers to the data that is essential for the execution of the application. This data is created, stored, and managed by the application itself. It can be structured data storage or it might be the cached version of online application resources. This type of data can be raw, in the form of a SQLite database, or stored by other facilities on the current device by the current application.

App data stored in different locations can survive through different stages of an application lifecycle.

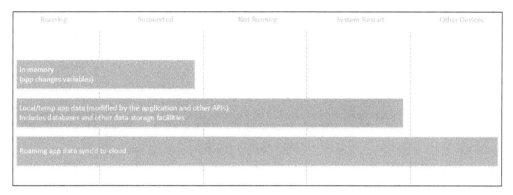

App data lifecycle

Local files

Local files are the stored items in the local filesystem. These files are generally created outside the lifecycle and/or scope of the application and are only made use of by the application. For instance, a photo taken by the user can later on be used by the mail client app as an attachment item.

External data

External data can be described as the combination of all the other data sources that are used by the application during runtime. This can include network or web resources.

Application data

Application data makes up the core of the data storage on Xamarin platforms and Windows Runtime. This data is specific to your application. It lives and eventually dies with it, and in most cases it is not relevant or even accessible by other applications running on the same device or even by the user who is using the application (at least directly).

The application has unrestricted access to application data, or so-called isolated storage, without having to ask for permission from the user or add a declaration and can (in most cases) write, read, and query items in this storage according to the type of the application data location.

Installation directory

The installation directory is the innermost part of the accessible data storages and is the most intimate location for the application. Access to this location by the application is unrestricted but read-only. The access models on iOS, Android, and Windows Runtime vary greatly.

Android

For Xamarin.Android applications, the installation directory essentially refers to the compressed Android package (the .apk file), and the defined subdivisions are just abstractions of folders packaged and added to the manifest during the compilation. The installation directory and subfolders can be accessed in various ways.

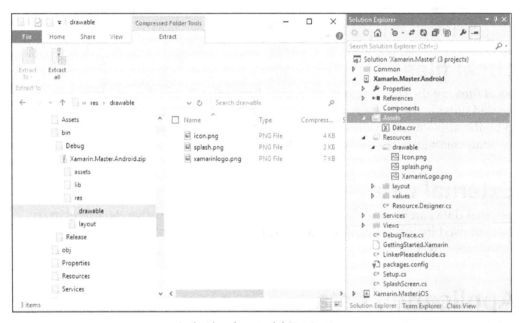

Android package and the project tree

The most important location in the installation directory for Android apps is the Resources folder. Resources can be generalized as the UI-related items that will be used to render the views of the application. One of the resource types that can be included in the application package is the drawable type. Drawable resources are image resources and can exist in alternate flavors for different conditions and devices that the application runs on (see *Chapter 9, Reusable UI Patterns*). In order for the compiler to include the resources in the application package, the build action of each item in this folder has to be set to AndroidResource.

It is important to mention that Android packages do not allow filenames to contain uppercase characters, and yet Xamarin developers can include these types of files in their projects. Xamarin.Android deals with this by renaming the resources during compilation (for example, see the `XamarinLogo.png` file in the `drawable` folder).

Programmatically, they can be accessed using the generated `Resource` class to get the assigned resource ID and the `Resources` static class that provides access methods, or by using the `android.resource://` protocol and the resource identifier (or the package name together with the resource name). However, in most scenarios, using only the assigned ID to use the resources with UI controls will suffice. The code is as follows:

```
var myImageResourceId = Resource.Drawable.XamarinLogo;

var myImageView = (ImageView)
  FindViewById(Resource.Id.MyImageView);

// Set the Image resource using the id.
myImageView.SetImageResource(myImageResourceId);

// OR:

// Retrieving the resource itself and then assigning it.
Drawable myImageResource =
  Resources.GetDrawable(myImageResourceId);
myImageView.SetImageDrawable(myImageResource);
```

In the declarative UI (layouts), the drawable resources folder can be accessed with the alias `@drawable`. Similarly, string resources can be accessed with `@string`. The code is as follows:

```
<ImageView android:src="@drawable/xamarinlogo"
           android:layout_width="wrap_content"
           android:layout_height="match_parent" />
```

Another important location in the installation directory is the `Assets` folder. The `Assets` folder is used for any raw assets that you want deployed together with your application (other than the `Resources` folder) and not to be processed by the compiler or the runtime. Assets can be retrieved with the `AssetManager` class, and the `Assets` property in the `Activity` class can be used to access the `AssetManager` class. The code is as follows:

```
Task.Run(async () =>
{
    using (var dataPackageStream = Assets.Open("Data.csv"))
    using (var streamReader = new StreamReader(dataPackageStream))
    {
        var content = await streamReader.ReadToEndAsync();
        // TODO: Do something with the comma separated content.
    }
});
```

Other resource types in the installation location, such as layouts, raw, and string resources can also be accessed in the described manner using the abstraction provided by Android runtime.

iOS

The building units of an iOS application, such as executable code and associated resources, are contained in a so-called **bundle**. A bundle is part of the application sandbox and the path to the bundle is determined by the operating system during installation.

Similar to Android applications, iOS application projects can also include compiled image resources (bundle resources). These items are then accessed using the abstraction layer provided by the runtime.

For instance, in order to access an image resource from the bundle directory, you would need to call the `FromFile` method on the `UIImage` class:

```
var image = UIImage.FromFile("XamarinLogo.png");

//
// OR making a roundtrip (get the path, read the file, create
// image
// Similar to /data/Containers/Bundle/Application/<id>/
XamarinMasteriOS.app/
   XamarinLogo.png
```

```
var imagePath = NSBundle.MainBundle.
    GetUrlForResource("XamarinLogo", "png").Path;
var fileContent = System.IO.File.ReadAllBytes(imagePath);

var secondImage = UIImage.
    LoadFromData(NSData.FromArray(fileContent));
```

Similar to the access model in Android applications, the bundle container is read-only and should not be modified. The simple reason for this is that iOS application bundles are signed by the publisher key and any change in the bundle container would invalidate the package signature.

Local storage

There is a both in the second part as well. Android and iOS runtimes provide different storage facilities for application data both in the form of structured data and raw content files.

Android

On the Android platform, **Shared Preferences** and **Internal Storage** are the two local storage options. Both of these options have different access models and your applications have read/write access to these locations.

Using `SharedPreferences` is the most basic way of storing data on the Android platform. This class provides a simple persistent dictionary implementation that allows the application to create, modify, and retrieve primitive data types (that is, `boolean`, `float`, `int`, `long`, `string`, and `string_array`) and their associated key. The size on these values is only restricted by the data type itself.

As the name suggests, `SharedPreferences` is generally used to store configuration options selected by the user and is persisted across user sessions. There is also a base activity implementation, `PreferenceActivity`, to easily create and reuse a view for user preferences that makes use of the `SharedPreferences` for the application.

The usage pattern for SharedPreferences class is straightforward. In order to use the default preferences for the activity or a custom preference file, the Activity class provides specialized methods:

```
// Retrieve an object for accessing private to this activity
ISharedPreferences myPreferences =
  GetPreferences(FileCreationMode.Private);

// Retrieve and hold the contents of the preference file
'MyCustomPreferences'
ISharedPreferences myCustomPreferences =
  GetSharedPreferences("MyCustomPreferences",
  FileCreationMode.Private);
```

After the retrieve call, the preference file is created according to the FileCreationMode class selected if it did not exist already. To get the value of a preference entry, you can use one of the get methods provided by the class. The code is as follows:

```
var myStringValue = myCustomPreferences.GetString("MyStringValue",
    string.Empty);
var myIntValue = myCustomPreferences.GetInt("MyIntValue",
    default(int));
```

To edit the values, the Editor class for the SharedPreferences class can be used. The code is as follows:

```
ISharedPreferencesEditor myEditor = myCustomPreferences.Edit();
myEditor.PutString("MyStringValue", myStringValue);
myEditor.PutInt("MyIntValue", myIntValue);

// Apply the current changes from the editor back
// to the Singleton SharedPreferences class
myEditor.Apply();

// OR
// Commit the changes to the singleton instance
// AND the disk immediately
myEditor.Commit();
```

Internal Storage is the dedicated storage for your application. The application is free to create and retrieve any type of file (and folder) in this directory.

FileCreationMode is an access modifier used in Android runtime to define the access type and permission levels of a file.

- **Append**: If the file already exists, then write data to the end of the existing file instead of erasing. This is to be used with `Android.Content.Context.OpenFileOutput`.
- **EnableWriteAheadLogging**: When this database's open flag is set, the database is opened with write-ahead logging enabled by default.
- **MultiProcess**: legacy behavior in and before Gingerbread (Android 2.3) and is implied when targeting such releases. For applications targeting higher SDK versions, it must be set explicitly. When used together with `SharedPreferences`, the file on disk will be checked for modifications even if the shared preferences instance is already loaded in this process. This behavior is desired when the application has multiple processes accessing the same file.
- **Private**: This is the default file creation mode where the created file can only be accessed by the calling application (or all applications sharing the same user ID).
- **WorldReadable/WorldWritable**: Both deprecated in API level 17 for security vulnerabilities, they can pose to enable file access to application files.

Files in this folder, without any manifest declaration, can be accessed with the designated methods on the application context or by using the Xamarin/Mono implementation of IO methods. The code is as follows:

```
// Creating a file in the application internal storage root
using(var fileStreamInRootPath =
    this.OpenFileOutput("FileInRootPath", FileCreationMode.Private))
using (var streamWriter = new StreamWriter(fileStreamInRootPath))
{
    streamWriter.Write("Hello World!");
}

//
// Reading the contents of the file
using(var fileStreamInRootPath =
    this.OpenFileInput("FileInRootPath"))
```

```
using (var streamReader = new StreamReader(fileStreamInRootPath))
{
    var stringContent = streamReader.ReadToEnd();
}


// Getting the file path.
// e.g.: /data/data/Xamarin.Master.Android/files/FileInRootPath
var filePath = FilesDir.AbsolutePath + "/" + "FileInRootPath";

// Using the Xamarin (Mono) implementation.
System.IO.File.AppendAllText(filePath, "\r\nAdditional Content");
var allText = System.IO.File.ReadAllText(filePath);
```

In addition to basic CRUD operations, you can also create additional folders and enumerate files and folders.

iOS

The simplest data storage option on iOS applications are the property lists. (the .plist files). These files are designed to be used for relatively small amounts of data that can be represented with primitive data types. They can be defined as dictionaries or arrays that are serialized and persisted in XML format.

You can read and write to a property list directly using the associated classes (NSArray and NSDictionary). For instance, a simple implementation that creates and reads a property list would look similar to the following code (with additional diagnostic entries):

```
myNSDictionary.WriteToFile(dictionaryPath, true);

Debug.WriteLine("File Contents:");
var fileContents = System.IO.File.ReadAllText(dictionaryPath);
Debug.WriteLine(fileContents);

var myNewNSDictionary = NSDictionary.FromFile(dictionaryPath);

Debug.WriteLine("Values read from plist:");
foreach (var key in myNewNSDictionary.Keys)
{
    var keyValue = myNewNSDictionary[key];
    Debug.WriteLine(string.Format("Value for the key '{0}' is
        '{1}'", key, keyValue));
}
```

The output from the preceding implementation would look like this:

```
File Contents:
<?xml version="1.0" encoding="UTF-8"?>
<!DOCTYPE plist PUBLIC "-//Apple//DTD PLIST 1.0//EN" "http://www.apple.
com/DTDs/PropertyList-1.0.dtd">
<plist version="1.0">
<dict>
        <key>firstKey</key>
        <string>firstValue</string>
        <key>secondKey</key>
        <string>secondValue</string>
        <key>thirdKey</key>
        <integer>8</integer>
</dict>
</plist>
Values read from plist:
Value for the key 'firstKey' is 'firstValue'
Value for the key 'secondKey' is 'secondValue'
Value for the key 'thirdKey' is '8'
```

When it comes to the local file storage, the iOS filesystem reserves several locations for applications; each of these locations have a specific purpose from the application's perspective.

- `Documents/`: The `Documents` library is generally designated for user-generated content. This folder should be used if the contents of the files are to be exposed to the user. Contents of this folder are backed up by iTunes.

- `Documents/Inbox`: The `Inbox` folder is where files that are requested to be opened by the application are kept. An application can read and delete these files; it does not have privileges to modify these documents.

- `Library/`: The `Library` folder is the root directory for the files that you don't want to expose to the user. Applications can create files and additional folders in this directory.

- `Library/Application Support`: This subdirectory in the library folder is generally used to contain files managed by your application, such as configuration files, templates, saved data, and purchases. Contents destined for this folder should be placed in a custom subdirectory with the bundle identifier or company ID of your app.

- `Library/Caches`: The `Caches` folder is used for non-essential, application created files.
- `Library/Preferences`: App-specific preferences are stored in this folder. However, access to this folder should be done through the preferences API.
- `tmp/`: The `tmp` folder is another location for non-essential temporary files.

Access to these library locations is possible using the `System.IO` namespace and associated classes.

Temporary storage

Temporary storage and/or the cache directory is another location that the application does not need any specific permission. This is where non-essential files can be saved by the application to decrease network or processing time. The persistence of these folders is not guaranteed by the operating system.

In both Android and iOS systems, designated cache and/or temp locations are accessed through the context properties and the CRUD operations can be performed using the `System.IO` namespace and the related classes.

On Android, the cache directory can be accessed with the `CacheDir` property on the context:

```
// Path similar to /data/data/Xamarin.Master.Android/cache
var cacheFilePath = this.CacheDir.AbsolutePath + "/" +
  "CacheFile";

// Writing to the file
System.IO.File.AppendAllLines(cacheFilePath, new[] { "Cached
  Content" });

// Reading the file
var cachedContent = System.IO.File.ReadAllText(cacheFilePath);
```

On iOS, there are two separate locations for temporary files (`/temp/`) and cache files (`Library/Caches/`). Cache files are persisted for longer than the temporary data, but they still might be deleted by the system to free up disk space. The code is as follows:

```
// getting the root application sandbox path
var documents = Environment.GetFolderPath (Environment.SpecialFolder.
MyDocuments);
// paths to caches and temporary files directories.var cache = Path.
Combine(documents, "..", "Library", "Caches");
var tmp = Path.Combine(documents, "..", "tmp");
```

Neither of these directories are backed up or synchronized to iCloud.

Local filesystem

On iOS, applications cannot programmatically access files external to the application sandbox (for example, an iOS application cannot programmatically navigate to the user's picture directory and pick a file). The bridge between the local filesystem and the iOS app's sandbox was limited to the image picker controller until iOS 8. iOS 8 introduces the new document picker controller and document provider API. In this interaction model, the application implementing the document provider extension creates the document picker UI and the host application uses this provided UI to let the user select the documents to be used in the host application execution (similar to the file open picker and provider capability on the Windows Runtime platform).

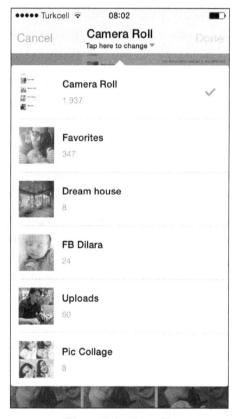

UIImagePickerController

For Android, on top of the local file storage that is only app-specific, applications have access to two other locations: public and private external storage (depending on the hardware). External storage in this context refers to SD card storage, which is not available on iOS systems. On Android runtime, applications can have access to the root path (OS root path) and iterate through public folders.

Let's have a look at the returned paths for some of the internal and external paths on an Android filesystem:

```
Trace.WriteLine(Environment.RootDirectory, "FileSystem");
Trace.WriteLine(Environment.DataDirectory, "FileSystem");

Trace.WriteLine(this.GetExternalFilesDir(Environment.
    DirectoryDownloads).AbsolutePath, "FileSystem");
Trace.WriteLine(this.GetExternalFilesDir(Environment.
    DirectoryDocuments).AbsolutePath, "FileSystem");

// Call with GetExternalFilesDir
Trace.WriteLine(this.GetExternalFilesDir(Environment.
    DirectoryMovies).AbsolutePath, "FileSystem");
Trace.WriteLine(this.GetExternalFilesDir(Environment.
    DirectoryMusic).AbsolutePath, "FileSystem");
Trace.WriteLine(this.GetExternalFilesDir(Environment.
    DirectoryPictures).AbsolutePath, "FileSystem");

Trace.WriteLine(Environment.GetExternalStoragePublicDirectory
    (Environment.DirectoryMovies).AbsolutePath, "FileSystem");
Trace.WriteLine(Environment.GetExternalStoragePublicDirectory
    (Environment.DirectoryMusic).AbsolutePath, "FileSystem");
Trace.WriteLine(Environment.GetExternalStoragePublicDirectory
    (Environment.DirectoryPictures).AbsolutePath, "FileSystem");

Trace.WriteLine(Environment.DownloadCacheDirectory, "FileSystem");
Trace.WriteLine(Environment.ExternalStorageDirectory,
    "FileSystem");
```

The output to these calls identifies the app-specific and public locations:

```
I/mono-stdout(10079): FileSystem: /system
I/mono-stdout(10079): FileSystem: /data
I/mono-stdout(10079): FileSystem: /storage/emulated/0/Android/data/
Xamarin.Master.Android/files/Download
I/mono-stdout(10079): FileSystem: /storage/emulated/0/Android/data/
Xamarin.Master.Android/files/Documents
I/mono-stdout(10079): FileSystem: /storage/emulated/0/Android/data/
Xamarin.Master.Android/files/Movies
I/mono-stdout(10079): FileSystem: /storage/emulated/0/Android/data/
Xamarin.Master.Android/files/Music
I/mono-stdout(10079): FileSystem: /storage/emulated/0/Android/data/
Xamarin.Master.Android/files/Pictures
```

```
I/mono-stdout(10079): FileSystem: /storage/emulated/0/Movies
I/mono-stdout(10079): FileSystem: /storage/emulated/0/Music
I/mono-stdout(10079): FileSystem: /storage/emulated/0/Pictures
I/mono-stdout(10079): FileSystem: /cache
I/mono-stdout(10079): FileSystem: /storage/emulated/0
```

In spite of the fact that Android developers have access to a vast set of options for storage access methods, they are required to implement their own file picker dialogs or use interfaces provided by other installed applications (Android runtime also offers a provider-consumer type of file sharing implementation between applications).

A sample file browser implementation (Xamarin recipes)

If there is an application that, by default, handles the file dialogs (the activity that can handle `ActionGetContent` intent), it can be invoked with an intent and the result can be accessed through the `OnActivityResult` callback method.

SQLite

SQLite database implementations provide a relational persisted data structure in mobile application projects. Unlike the general server/client model that is used by relational databases, SQLite is a local database implementation and the data is stored in application local storage. Both Xamarin.iOS and Xamarin.Android application projects can include a SQLite database and associated implementations.

In order to use SQLite, developers are to choose to between the cross-platform implementation of ADO.Net, where the SQL queries are supposed to be created and included as plain text, or use the linq-2-entities access model of the SQLite.Net portable class library. It is available as a NuGet package and a component.

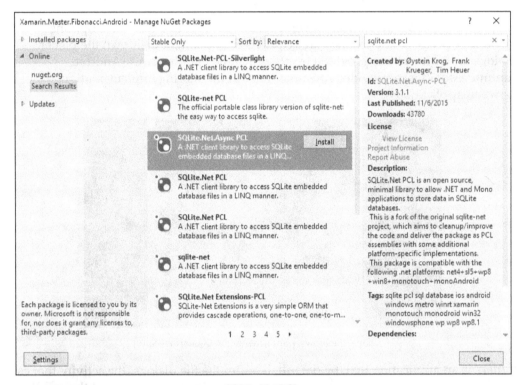

SQLite.Net PCL

For the following demonstration, we will use the asynchronous version of the SQLite.Net library.

Implementation of the SQLite data access layer with SQLite.Net generally follows a code first database programming paradigm. In this pattern, developers first define their data model by creating entity classes and defining the data structure using the provided attributes. The code is as follows:

```
public class LocationInfo
{
    [PrimaryKey, AutoIncrement]
    public int LocationInfoId { get; set; }
```

```
public string Name { get; set; }

public double Latitude { get; set; }

public double Longitude { get; set; }
}
```

Once the data model implementation is finished, we can start creating the SQLite access methods.

In order to create a SQLite connection, first an application storage location has to be defined for the database file. The code is as follows:

```
public TravelContext(string sqlitePath, ISQLitePlatform platform)
{
    var connectionString = new SQLiteConnectionString(sqlitePath,
        false);
    var connectionWithLock =
        new SQLiteConnectionWithLock(platform, connectionString);
    m_SqliteConnection = new SQLiteAsyncConnection(() =>
        connectionWithLock);

    // OR with non-async connection
    //var connection = new SQLiteConnection(platform, sqlitePath);
}
```

In this implementation, ISQLitePlatform provides the much needed abstraction for the platform-specific APIs.

After the SQLite connection is ready for use, we can implement the data tables' access and creation methods. The code is as follows:

```
private void InitTablesAsync()
{
    var tasks = new List<Task<CreateTablesResult>>();

    tasks.Add
        (m_SqliteConnection.CreateTableAsync<LocationInfo>());
    tasks.Add(m_SqliteConnection.CreateTableAsync<City>());
    tasks.Add(m_SqliteConnection.CreateTableAsync<Landmark>());
    tasks.Add(m_SqliteConnection.CreateTableAsync<Comment>());

    // OR
```

```
    //var initTask = m_SqliteConnection.
        CreateTablesAsync<LocationInfo, City, Landmark, Comment>();

    var initTask = Task.WhenAll(tasks);
    initTask.ConfigureAwait(false);
}
```

We can now expose the tables through public properties in our data context, so the upper layers can execute queries against these tables. The code is as follows:

```
var dbPath = Path.Combine(this.FilesDir.Path, "myTravelDb.db3");

// TODO: Use Dependency Injection
var platform = new SQLitePlatformAndroid();

var myDbContext = new TravelContext(dbPath, platform);

var landmarksInCityTask = await myDbContext.Landmarks
    .Where(item => item.CityId == cityId).ToListAsync();
```

It is possible to extend the data model with entity relations and cascade operations. There are also available extensions for the SQLite.Net PCL library for lazy loading and child-related operations.

Patterns and best practices

In this section, we will have a look at two common patterns that are common to mobile applications and how to implement these usage scenarios in a platform agnostic manner.

Application preferences

Application preferences is a common scenario in mobile applications. In order to use the previously described property list on iOS and SharedPreferences on Android, a common dictionary interface is often the most appropriate approach. The interface would then be inherited on platform-specific projects and can be injected into the common library.

For a simple demonstration, we can define a simple interface that will retrieve and save string values. The code is as follows:

```
public interface ISettingsProvider
{
    string this[string key] { get; set; }
}
```

The implementation on the Android side would use a simple dictionary using a shared preference implementation. The code is as follows:

```
public class SettingsProvider : ISettingsProvider
{
    private readonly ISharedPreferences m_SharedPreferences;

    public SettingsProvider(string name = "default")
    {
        // Retrieve and hold the contents of the preference file'
        m_SharedPreferences =
          Application.Context.GetSharedPreferences(name,
            FileCreationMode.Private);
    }

    public string this[string key]
    {
        get
        {
            if (m_SharedPreferences.Contains(key))
                m_SharedPreferences.GetString(key, string.Empty);
            return string.Empty;
        }
        set
        {
            var editor = m_SharedPreferences.Edit();
            editor.PutString(key, value);
            editor.Apply();
        }
    }
}
```

On the iOS side, the implementation would use an NSMutableDictionary class to facilitate the preferences being edited by the user. The code is as follows:

```
public string this[string key]
{
    get
    {
        if (m_MyNSMutableDictionary.ContainsKey(new
          NSString(key)))
        {
```

```
            return MyNSMutableDictionary [key].ToString();
        }

        return string.Empty;
    }
    set
    {
        MyNSMutableDictionary [key] = new NSString(value);
        MyNSMutableDictionary.WriteToFile(GetPropertyListPath(),
            true);
    }
}
```

Now that the persisted dictionary has been implemented on both platforms, we can include the application settings as a singleton to be used with a dependency injection.

This implementation can be extended using the Settings API on the iOS platform and using the preferences views (`PreferencesFragment` and `PreferencesActivity`) on the Android platform to create a more native-looking implementation.

File picker

In a cross-platform application project, if we are following an MVVM pattern, the view-model should reside in a shared project or a PCL so that the business logic can be shared between the apps. However, if we have a requirement to pick a file for processing, the method implementation should reside in the view itself since the platform-specific project that holds the view has access to platform features. Although it would be moving the business logic to the UI components, the work has to be done by the view.

You can, however, delegate the responsibility of the view model to the view without compromising the MVVM implementation. The delegation process can be executed through **Inversion of Control** (**IOC**) into the interface that defines the file picking operation.

To demonstrate this usage, we will use an interface called `IFilePickerService`. In this example, we just want to let the user pick a file and return the resulting file path back to the view-model and maybe the model. The code is as follows:

```
public interface IFilePickerService
{
    Task<string> PickFileAsync();
}
```

We will use this interface in the view-model to call for the view to execute the logic. The code is as follows:

```
return new MvxCommand(() =>
{
    m_FilePickerService.PickFileAsync()
        .ContinueWith(task =>
        {
            Debug.WriteLine("File Picked:" + task.Result);
        });
});
```

For Android implementation, we will be using the default file manager application that supports the respective intent type. We need to convert intent execution and the callback call on the OnActivityResult class into an asynchronous implementation. In order to do this, we will be using a task completion source. The code is as follows:

```
private TaskCompletionSource<string> m_PickFileCompletionSource;
```

The private variable will be initialized every time the intent is called and the result will be set in the callback method. With this pattern in mind, the interface method implementation would look similar to this:

```
public Task<string> PickFileAsync()
{
    m_PickFileCompletionSource = new
      TaskCompletionSource<string>();

    Intent intent = new Intent();
    intent.SetType("*/*");
    intent.SetAction(Intent.ActionGetContent);
    intent.AddCategory(Intent.CategoryOpenable);

    try
    {
        StartActivityForResult(intent, 0);
    }
    catch(ActivityNotFoundException ex)
    {
        throw new InvalidOperationException("Could not find a file
            manager");
    }

    return m_PickFileCompletionSource.Task;
}
```

Finally, the callback method implementation would be just setting the result on the `TaskCompletionSource` class. The code is as follows:

```
protected override void OnActivityResult(int requestCode, Result
    resultCode, Intent data)
{
    base.OnActivityResult(requestCode, resultCode, data);

    if (resultCode == Result.Ok)
    {
        m_PickFileCompletionSource.TrySetResult(data.Data.Path);
    }
    else if(resultCode == Result.Canceled)
    {
        m_PickFileCompletionSource.SetCanceled();
    }
}
```

Now that we have the `IFilePickerService` interface created, at least on the Android side, we have to register the type with the dependency injection provider we are using, and then we can rely on it to resolve the type in the view-model initialization. (We will be using the MVVMCross framework in this example.)

The code is as follows:

```
public MainView()
{
    Mvx.RegisterType<IFilePickerService>(()=>this);
}
```

The resulting application would execute the pick file command and open up the file browser, returning the file path back to the view model. If the user cancels the file selection, the task would throw an exception notifying that the operation has been cancelled.

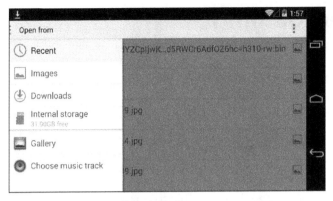

Default file browser

For the iOS side of the story, our job is a little easier:

```
public Task<string> PickFileAsync()
{
    var taskCompletionSource = new TaskCompletionSource<string>();

    var documentTypes = new string[] { UTType.PNG, UTType.Image,
        UTType.BMP };

    var filePicker =
        new UIDocumentPickerViewController(documentTypes,
            UIDocumentPickerMode.Open);

    EventHandler<UIDocumentPickedEventArgs>
        documentPickedHandler = (sender, args) =>
    {
        taskCompletionSource.SetResult(args.Url.Path);
    };

    filePicker.DidPickDocument += documentPickedHandler;

    return taskCompletionSource.Task;
}
```

With this completed, we just need to register the type and we finally have a cross-platform implementation of a command relying on the dependency injected, platform-specific methods.

Backup/Roaming

Xamarin target platforms both offer cloud sync and backup mechanisms. While the Android backup strategy is more of an async background process where backup and restore operations have to be initiated by the calling application, the iOS and iCloud roaming strategy provides seamless integration to the filesystem.

Android and Backup API

Android Backup API and Google-provided backup transport services provide an easily accessible way for application developers to back up and restore application data to remote cloud storage. It is possible to restore data after a factory reset or one device to another using the APIs provided by the BackupManager.

Backup operations are executed by the BackupManager in Android runtime and operations related to the application data are delegated to the BackupAgent registered in the application manifest. It is important to remember the fact that your application has to be registered in the Android Backup Service. It is crucial to include the backup service key that you receive from the registration in the package manifest.

In order to create a BackupAgent, you must implement the OnBackup and OnRestore methods of the BackupAgent abstract class. In these methods, the old and new states of your data are served in the form of ParcelFileDescriptor (file metadata that can be used to access the actual file). In the restore method, you also receive the application version that might be helpful if the data structure has changed between application updates.

Another way to create an agent is to use the existing agent template (BackupAgentHelper) and use the existing helper classes to back up and restore certain subsets of your application data.

For instance, the SharedPreferencesBackupHelper class is a generic implementation of a backup operator on SharedPreferences files that are used by your application. The preferences groups for the application can be passed onto the helper and the helper class can deal with the backup logic implementation.

Another helper class is the FileBackupHelper class that can be used to back up and restore application files.

In order to demonstrate the Backup API and a usual backup scenario, we can create a backup agent that will trace out the backup events and method executions. The implementation class should derive from the `BackupAgentHelper` class:

```
public class PreferencesBackupService : BackupAgentHelper
{
    // TODO: Override the methods we might need
}
```

To include this backup agent in our application, we can either edit the application manifest or use the `ApplicationAttribute` attribute in the assembly info. Both `AssemblyInfo.cs` and `AndroidManifest.xml` can be found under the `Properties` project folder.

Application manifest and AssemblyInfo

Using the `ApplicationManifest.xml` file, let's add the backup agent and backup services key:

```
<application android:label="Xamarin.Master.Android"
             android:icon="@drawable/Icon"
             android:backupAgent="PreferencesBackupService">
   <meta-data android:name="com.google.android.backup.api-key"
             android:value="..." />
</application>
```

The preceding application manifest entry is how it would look if we were dealing with Java class libraries, not Xamarin and the JNI Bridge. In fact, this registration would throw an error as soon as a backup request is received. The code is as follows:

```
09-22 18:28:33.647 E/ActivityThread(32153): Agent threw during creation:
java.lang.ClassNotFoundException: Didn't find class "Xamarin.Master.
Android.PreferencesBackupService" on path: DexPathList[[zip file "/data/
app/Xamarin.Master.Android-1.apk"],nativeLibraryDirectories=[/data/app-
lib/Xamarin.Master.Android-1, /system/lib]]
```

To register the `PreferencesBackupService` class with the Android runtime, we need to add an identifier for the type itself. Since we are not using a namespace qualifier in the manifest declaration, we can register the class in the application default namespace:

```
[Register("Xamarin.Master.Android.PreferencesBackupService")]
public class PreferencesBackupService : BackupAgentHelper
```

If we were to use the `Application` attribute to register our backup agent without the application manifest entries, the attributes would look similar to the following using the `AssemblyInfo.cs` file:

```
[assembly: Application(AllowBackup = true,
   BackupAgent = typeof(PreferencesBackupService))]
[assembly: MetaData("com.google.android.backup.api_key",
   Value = "...")]
```

In this case, the **android callable wrapper (ACW)** is created with the default naming convention for our backup agent and inserted into the application manifest, so we didn't need to register our class additionally. The generated entry for the application manifest contains the MD5 hash of the pair namespace and the containing assembly:

md5d06a1058f86cf8319abb1555c0b54fbf.PreferencesBackupService

If you are developing with Visual Studio and running your application on Emulator, you can see the generated MD5 values for the Android exposed classes in the `<projectdir>\obj\<buildconfig>\android\src` directory.

Android source directory

Once the registration is complete, we can override a couple of methods in the agent class to get the trace information. The code is as follows:

```
public override void OnCreate()
{
    var preferencesHelper =
      new SharedPreferencesBackupHelper(this,
        "ApplicationSettings");
    AddHelper("ApplicationPreferences", preferencesHelper);

    Debug.WriteLine("PreferencesBackupService was created",
      "BackUp");

    base.OnCreate();
}
```

You can now open an Android Adb Console and use the following commands to trigger a backup request:

```
adb shell bmgr enable true
adb shell bmgr run
```

Once your data segments change, you can use the `DataChanged` method of the `BackupManager` class and use it to request restore operations. (Restore operations are, under normal circumstances, scheduled and performed by Android backup services, so the app does not need to explicitly call it.)

The code is as follows:

```
BackupManager backupManager = new BackupManager(this);

// Notifying the backup manager about data changes
backupManager.DataChanged();

// Using an implementations of RestoreObserver class to request
restore
backupManager.RequestRestore(new MyRestoreObserver());
```

iOS and ubiquitous storage

In order to use iCloud features in your iOS applications, they must be configured in the *Apple Provisioning Portal* and the project manifest.

In the provisioning portal, while creating the App ID, iCloud must be selected as one of the enabled services. Then, using the `<TeamID>.<BundeID>` format, the container identifier must be inserted into the `Entitlements.plist` file. The keys that have to be edited are as follows:

```
com.apple.developer.ubiquity-kvstore-identifier
com.apple.developer.ubiquity-container-identifiers
```

On iOS, the simplest synchronization mechanism provided is for primitive data types in the form of key/value pairs. This is used for simple user preferences or application required values that need to be synchronized between separate clients. The total size of a key/value pair cannot exceed 64 kilobytes, while the maximum value size is 64 kB and key size is 64 bytes.

The synchronizing context can be accessed through the
`NSUbiquitousKeyValueStore` class. The code is as follows:

```
/// <summary>
/// Synchronizes local values to the cloud
/// </summary>
private void SyncUpSettings()
{
    var store = NSUbiquitousKeyValueStore.DefaultStore;
    //
    // Can use designated set functions for different value types
    // string, bool, NSData, NSDictionary, NSObject[], long, double
    store.SetString("myStringValue", "New String Value");
    store.SetLong("myLongValue", 1234);
    store.SetBool("myBoolValue", true);
    store.Synchronize();
}
```

Using the same store, you can access the values:

```
/// <summary>
/// Gets the values from synchronized local storage
/// </summary>
/// <returns></returns>
private Dictionary<string,object> GetValues()
{
    var results = new Dictionary<string,object>();
    var store = NSUbiquitousKeyValueStore.DefaultStore;

    //
    // Getting the synchronized LOCAL values
    results.Add("myStringValue",store.GetString("myStringValue"));
    results.Add("myLongValue", store.GetLong("myLongValue"));
    results.Add("myBoolValue", store.GetBool("myBoolValue"));

    return results;
}
```

The synchronization process does not happen right after the synchronize
method is invoked. The process is initiated according to iCloud's own schedule;
up-sync generally happens within 5 seconds, while the only way to exactly
know when the down-sync occurs is by adding an `Observer` delegate to the
`NSUbiquitousKeyValueStore` events.

The code is as follows:

```
NSNotificationCenter.DefaultCenter.AddObserver(
    NSUbiquitousKeyValueStore.DidChangeExternallyNotification,
      (notification) =>
    {
        NSDictionary userInfo = notification.UserInfo;

        // NInt: 0-ServerChange, 1-InitialSyncChange,
        // 2-QuotaViolationChange
        NSNumber reasonNumber = (NSNumber) userInfo.
          ObjectForKey(NSUbiquitousKeyValueStore.ChangeReasonKey);

        // NSString[] You can used the changed items list to sync only
those values
        NSArray changedKeys = (NSArray) userInfo.
          ObjectForKey(NSUbiquitousKeyValueStore.ChangedKeysKey);

        // OR get the latest values from synchronized local storage
        var latestValues = GetValues();
    });
```

For synchronized files, the implementation is a little more complicated. While backup and restore scenarios are automatically handled by the iOS application and iTunes, for keeping a synchronized file storage, developers need to implement the UIDocument class to prepare type of documents that needs to be synced between devices.

The UbiquityContainer directory is managed by the so-called daemons to coordinate the synchronization and modifications of the files on the iCloud context. In order not to cause concurrency problems and interfere with the daemon processing, the files in question need to be accessed and modified with the NSFilePresenter and NSFileCoordinator classes.

The easiest way to use the presenters and coordinators for file operations is to implement the UIDocument base class. There are two virtual methods that need to be implemented to read data and write data to documents.

Let's assume that we want to keep a synchronized context for serialized entity data for our application. First, we need to declare our class as inheriting and implementing the required constructor from the UIDocument class. The code is as follows:

```
public class EntityDocument<T> : UIDocument
{
```

```
public EntityDocument (NSUrl url)
    : base(url)
{
    m_Type = typeof(T);
}
```

We then need to implement the two virtual methods. The following load method defined just deserializes the data from the cloud into the entity defined in the generic class type definition. The code is as follows:

```
/// <summary>
/// Content down-sync'd from the cloud
/// </summary>
public override bool LoadFromContents(NSObject contents,
  string typeName, out NSError outError)
{
    // TODO: Implement a try/catch block to return (if any)
        errors as well as negative result (i.e. return false).
    outError = null;

    if (contents != null)
    {
        var serializedData = NSString.FromData((NSData)contents,
            NSStringEncoding.UTF8);
        m_Entity =
            JsonConvert.DeserializeObject<T>(serializedData);
    }

    // LoadFromContents called when an update occurs
    NSNotificationCenter.DefaultCenter.
        PostNotificationName(string.Format("{0}DocumentModified",
        m_Type.Name), this);

    return true;
}
```

Finally, we can implement the save method that will serialize the object and serve the stream to be saved in the ubiquitous container. The code is as follows:

```
/// <summary>
/// Content to up-sync to the cloud
/// </summary>
public override NSObject ContentsForType(string typeName, out NSError
outError)
```

```
    {
        // TODO: Implement a try/catch block to return (if any)
          errors as well as negative result (i.e. return false).
        outError = null;

        if (m_Entity != null)
        {
            var serializedData =
              JsonConvert.SerializeObject(m_Entity);

            NSData docData = new NSString(serializedData).
              Encode(NSStringEncoding.UTF8);

            return docData;
        }

        return null;
    }
```

In order to be able to use this implementation with an example class, named
LocationInfo, we can first implement a load file procedure (we are using a single
file query for each location loaded, but this can be extended using queries like
ENDSWITH or CONTAINS). The code is as follows:

```
    private void GetLocationsInfo(string locationName)
    {
        var locationDataQuery = new NSMetadataQuery();
        locationDataQuery.SearchScopes = new NSObject[]
          {NSMetadataQuery.UbiquitousDocumentsScope};

        locationDataQuery.Predicate =
          NSPredicate.FromFormat(string.Format("{0} == %@",
            NSMetadataQuery.ItemFSNameKey),
            new NSString(locationName + "Data.txt"));

        NSNotificationCenter.DefaultCenter.AddObserver(this,
          new Selector("locationLoaded:"),
            NSMetadataQuery.DidFinishGatheringNotification,
              locationDataQuery);

        locationDataQuery.StartQuery();
    }
```

Once the query returns, we can expand the object into the data needed. The code is as follows:

```
[Export("locationLoaded:")]
private void DidFinishGatheringHandler(NSNotification notification)
{
    var locationQuery = (NSMetadataQuery) notification.Object;
    locationQuery.DisableUpdates();
    locationQuery.StopQuery();
    NSNotificationCenter.DefaultCenter.RemoveObserver(this,
      NSMetadataQuery.DidFinishGatheringNotification,
      locationQuery);

    LoadLocationInfo(locationQuery);

    // listen for notifications that the document was modified
     via the // server
    NSNotificationCenter.DefaultCenter.AddObserver(this,
      new Selector("itemReloaded:"),
      new NSString("LocationInfoDocumentModified"),
      null);

}
```

The `LoadLocationInfo` function in the example would simply try to open the file and deal with the loaded data. The code is as follows:

```
private void LoadLocationInfo(NSMetadataQuery locationDataQuery)
{
    if (locationDataQuery.ResultCount == 1)
    {
        NSMetadataItem item = (NSMetadataItem)
          locationDataQuery.ResultAtIndex(0);
        var url = (NSUrl)item.
        ValueForAttribute(NSMetadataQuery.ItemURLKey);
        m_LocationData = new EntityDocument<LocationInfo>(url);
        m_LocationData.Open((success) =>
        {
            if (success)
            {
                var info = m_LocationData.Entity;
                // TODO: Do something with the location info
                  loaded
            }
        }
```

```
        else
            Console.WriteLine("failed to open iCloud
                document");
    });
    }
}
```

Notice that we are also subscribing to the data changed event with the notification name we defined in the EntityDocument<T> class (string.Format("{0} DocumentModified", m_Type.Name). The reload implementation is simply gathering the object from the notification itself. The code is as follows:

```
[Export("itemReloaded:")]
private void DataReloadedHandler(NSNotification notification)
{
    var locationData = (EntityDocument<LocationInfo>)
        notification.Object;
    var entityData = locationData.Entity;
    // TODO: Do something with the location info loaded.
}
```

For saving and synchronizing the data, we just need to assign the new data and update the change count on the UIDocument class. The code is as follows:

```
private void SyncLocationDataChanges(LocationInfo info)
{
    m_LocationData.Entity = info;
    m_LocationData.UpdateChangeCount(UIDocumentChangeKind.Done);

}
```

This topic will be discussed further in *Chapter 5, Networking*.

Summary

In this chapter, we discussed some of the local storage containers and access strategies. In both of the Xamarin platforms, with the additional option to back up and synchronize the data to the cloud, developers can create a consistent user interface as well as stateful mobile applications.

In the next chapter, we will discuss the network connectivity options and how to use connected data together with local storage options provided with the target Xamarin platforms.

5
Networking

In this chapter, we will take a detailed look at the networking capabilities of Xamarin applications and various service integration scenarios. The chapter also includes real-world examples on how to use local storage for data caching on connected app scenarios. It is divided into the following sections:

- Connected apps
- Web services
- Push notifications
- SignalR
- Patterns and best practices
- Platform-specific concepts
- Cloud integration

Connected apps

Mobile applications by definition should be as lightweight and resource-efficient as possible. You cannot expect to package media and other content into the application and then distribute the app or create an extravagant size of storage for user data, especially with applications whose main purpose is to provide user access to related content or store and manipulate the data.

For instance, while dealing with cross-platform projects, one of the easiest ways to create unified business logic and storage is to create a web service layer and delegate the responsibility and logic to this layer. In this scenario, the application(s) would be simply responsible for serving the content provided by the service layer or communicating the user input to the service layer.

This approach not only increases the efficiency of the application(s) but also creates an abstraction between the logic implementation and the presentation. This allows the developers to be free from the platform constraints on technology choices for storage and execution.

It is also important to mention that applications' dependency on external resources is not a matter of choice but has rather become a necessity, since applications are more and more dependent on third-party web service APIs and social media networks.

Web services

A web service is generally defined as an interoperable machine-to-machine communication over the wire (network). In the context of cross-platform application, the most important term in this definition would be "interoperable". Web services written in different frameworks or languages and running on different type of runtimes and hardware conform to the same standards, most of which can be consumed by applications running on a variety of platforms, including Xamarin target platforms.

Xamarin target platforms, namely iOS and Android, and Windows Runtime, can access stateless web services using the TCP/IP (short for Transmission Control Protocol / Internet Protocol) stack over a secure or non-secure HTTP (short for Hypertext Transfer Protocol) transport layer. Even though various data representations can be consumed via web services, JSON and XML are the most common text-based notations used.

 While defining or accessing a web service, there are three basic elements that need to be taken into consideration. We can call these the A-B-C of a web service: Address, Binding, and Contract. The address is the remote access location to the service, binding defines the transport and security protocols, and contract defines the data types and the methods used by the service.

While the methods and data types defined in the web service contract are very case-specific, transport and serialization protocols that can be used by Xamarin applications can be generalized.

In web service scenarios, if the consumer is a Xamarin target platform, you should always be persistent about using asynchronous implementation for the client implementation. Asynchronous implementation for the web service clients decreases the chance of blocking the main thread, as discussed previously, and protects the application from network shortage related errors and crashes.

Transport

For Xamarin applications on both iOS and Android platforms, the main communication protocol is HTTP. HTTP transport can be secured on the client and/or message level using a certificate or credentials.

The message-level security is optional in other versions of iOS and Xamarin.Android applications. In iOS 9, the **App Transport Security** (**ATS**) feature enforces secure connections to network resources. Even though it is possible to add certain domains to the exclusion list, or to turn off the ATS altogether for the target applications, it is strongly advised that you use secure transport over HTTP (or HTTPS) for Xamarin. iOS applications.

Even though communication protocols for TCP, UDP, or web sockets over HTTP are fully or partially supported on Xamarin platforms, with the current service infrastructure implementation, these communication channels cannot be used with web services.

Messaging

Messaging specifications of a service define which format should be used while communicating data over the HTTP transport layer.

In Xamarin applications dealing with web services, messages should be constructed either according to the SOAP (Simple Object Access Protocol) or using POX (short for Plain Old XML) or JSON, depending on the service requirements.

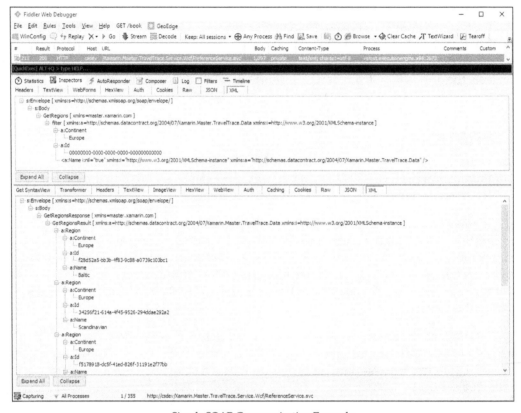

Simple SOAP Communication Example

The messaging structure is mainly important for the serialization and deserialization of request and response pairs between the client and server implementations. Hence, it is possible to employ other types of data communication models, which would require additional custom implementation for the client and the server.

SOAP/XML services

SOAP web services use XML data objects enveloped in SOAP-defined schemas. **Windows Communication Foundation (WCF)** services and ASP.Net Legacy Services (ASMX) are both SOAP services and conform to the SOAP protocol.

SOAP web service contracts are defined in **Web Service Description Language** (**WSDL**) and the WSDL document, together with other XML data schemas (for example, XSD files), are generally accessible through the web service URL. Using this document, web services can be defined in a consistent manner, irrespective of the underlying language, and can be interfaced with and consumed by various clients.

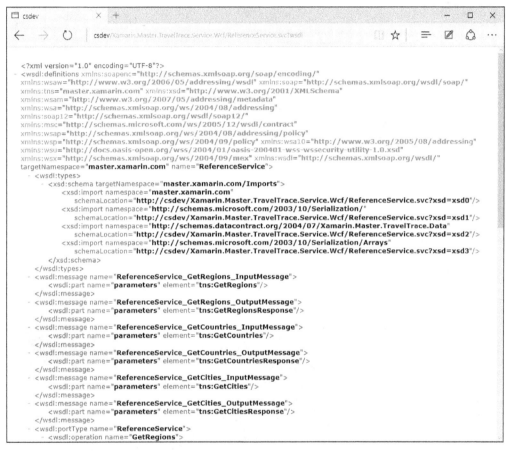

Service WSDL for a SOAP 1.1 Service

In Xamarin applications, one of the possible ways to create a so-called proxy (service consumer) is to use the Silverlight SDK to generate the access code. The main reason for using the Silverlight SDK is the fact that the Windows Communication Foundation client infrastructure is not fully included in the Xamarin core and only a subset of client features, very similar to the Silverlight framework, can be used to access web services.

In order to generate the client, you can simply use the command-line tool to execute the following command:

```
slsvcutil http://localhost/ ReferenceService.svc /d:c:\bin\
```

> SLSvcUtil can be found in various SDKs including Windows Phone 7, Windows Phone 8, Windows Phone 8.1 (Silverlight), as well as the actual Silverlight SDK directories:
>
> - `C:\Program Files (x86)\Microsoft SDKs\Windows Phone\v7.0\Tools\SlSvcUtil.exe`
> - `C:\Program Files (x86)\Microsoft SDKs\Windows Phone\v8.0\Tools\SlSvcUtil.exe`
> - `C:\Program Files (x86)\Microsoft SDKs\Windows Phone\v8.1\Tools\SlSvcUtil.exe`
> - `C:\Program Files (x86)\Microsoft SDKs\ Silverlight\v5.0\Tools\SlSvcUtil.exe`

The preceding command would generate a WCF client that can communicate with any web service that supports the SOAP 1.1 profile. If we were to consume a WCF service, the supported binding configurations would be `BasicHttpBinding` and `WebHttpBinding` (essentially a REST binding). `WSHttpBinding` and similar configurations use other SOAP profiles to envelope the data requests and responses.

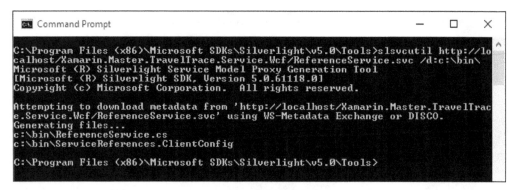

Generating Silverlight Proxy

The generated client would have both the Event-Based and Asynchronous Programming Model (APM) asynchronous methods for accessing the client.

```
[OperationContract (AsyncPattern=true, Action=
  "master.xamarin.com/ReferenceService/GetRegions", ReplyAction=
  "master.xamarin.com/ReferenceService/GetRegionsResponse")]
```

```
IAsyncResult BeginGetRegions(Xamarin.Master.TravelTrace.Data.Region
filter,
  AsyncCallback callback, object asyncState)
List<Xamarin.Master.TravelTrace.Data.Region>
  EndGetRegions(IAsyncResult result)

public void GetRegionsAsync(Xamarin.Master.TravelTrace.Data.Region
filter)
```

Another approach would be to create a web reference in Visual Studio or Xamarin Studio. A web reference can only be used to communicate with services that implement the WS-I Basic Profile 1.1 (in other words, SOAP 1.1). Web reference generated clients use the ASMX communication stack (.NET 2.0 Services Technology) as opposed to the WCF client infrastructure used by service references.

Add Web Reference Dialog (Visual Studio)

If we were to compare the generated clients from the web reference and the Silverlight SDK, we could easily identify the underlying technologies.

```
// Web Service Generated Client.
[System.ComponentModel.DesignerCategoryAttribute("code")]
[System.Web.Services.WebServiceBindingAttribute(Name="BasicHttpBindi
ng_ReferenceService", Namespace="master.xamarin.com")]
[GeneratedCodeAttribute("System.Web.Services", "4.6.79.0")]
```

```
public partial class AsmxReferenceServiceClient : System.Web.Services.
Protocols.SoapHttpClientProtocol

// WCF Generated Client
[GeneratedCodeAttribute("System.ServiceModel", "4.0.0.0")]
public partial class ReferenceServiceClient : System.ServiceModel.
ClientBase<ReferenceService>, ReferenceService
```

Looking at the class diagram for both of the generated proxies, we can get some more insight into the method execution strategies:

Generated Proxy Comparison

The ideal way to integrate the generated proxy in a cross-platform project would be to add the service reference in a portable class library to be used by platform-specific projects. In order to be able to add a service reference in a PCL project in Visual Studio, you must remove Windows Phone 8.1 as one of the targets and/or add a reference to the System.ServiceModel namespace (Visual Studio will automatically remove Windows Phone 8.1 from the targets list). The Windows Phone 8.1 platform does not include the Windows Communication Foundation client assemblies. After this step, the **Add Service Reference** option will appear under the project context menu.

For scenarios involving Windows Phone 8.1, the more appropriate solution would be to use a RESTful service and a client.

RESTful services

RESTful services are one of the most common distributed system implementations involving mobile applications. Compared to SOAP services, they don't have the overhead of SOAP protocols or the enveloping of the request/response pairs. In essence, network traffic caused by a SOAP method call is the same as the request/response pair of a REST call. The simplicity of the **Representational State Transfer (REST)** model increases the performance and maintainability. Stateless and cacheable approaches of RESTful services makes them an optimal solution for Xamarin target platforms.

REST services can essentially be described as static HTTP endpoints. The HTTP verbs (GET, PUT, POST, and DELETE) used to access these endpoints define the type of method to be invoked on the service layer (PUT for update, POST for create, and DELETE for delete actions). The messaging structure can vary from JSON to XML, even to ATOM.

On Xamarin target platforms, there are various out-of-the-box options and additional components available for REST-based web services. Any of these options can be used to execute web requests and request/response pairs can be serialized/deserialized according to the requirements and chosen messaging media-type.

Since we are making ordinary web requests to the REST endpoints, the simplest implementation would involve the `HttpClient`, which is included in the `System.Net.Http` namespace.

For instance, if we were to implement a base class that will handle the CRUD (create, read, update, and delete) methods on the RESTful version of the web service used in the previous section (`TravelTrace.ReferenceDataService`), we could implement a per-call wrapper around the inner HTTP client layer.

```
public BaseClient(string baseAddress, string securityToken)
{
    if (string.IsNullOrEmpty(baseAddress)) throw new ArgumentNullExcep
tion("baseAddress");

    BaseAddress = new Uri(baseAddress);

  // Storing the security token in a class property of type string
    SecurityToken = securityToken.StartsWith("Bearer") ?
securityToken.Substring(7) : securityToken;

    m_HttpClient = CreateHttpClient();
}
```

You will notice that we are using the base address as the server address and, if any, using the security token to initialize our client. In this implementation, the create method will simply create the HTTP client and use the authentication token as a default header. Another important requirement is to set the "Accept" header to announce which type of content the client is expecting from the server (JSON in this example).

```
private HttpClient CreateHttpClient()
{
    var httpClient = new HttpClient();
    httpClient.DefaultRequestHeaders.Accept.Add(new MediaTypeWithQuali
tyHeaderValue("application/json"));

    if (string.IsNullOrEmpty(SecurityToken))
    {
        httpClient.DefaultRequestHeaders.Authorization = new Authentic
ationHeaderValue("Bearer", SecurityToken);
    }

    return httpClient;
}
```

After the HTTP pipeline is ready to execute the requests, we can start implementing the base methods for the REST service.

```
protected async Task<string> GetStringAsync(string path)
{
    // if we are using the BaseClient multiple times
    // we can create a new transport with each method
    //HttpClient httpClient = CreateHttpClient();

    try
    {
        // Get the response from the server url and REST path for the
data
        var response = await m_HttpClient
            .GetAsync(new Uri(BaseAddress, path));

        if (response.StatusCode == HttpStatusCode.Unauthorized)
        {
            throw new UnauthorizedAccessException(
              "Access Denied");
        }
```

```
        if (response.IsSuccessStatusCode)
        {
            return await response.Content.ReadAsStringAsync();
        }

        throw new WebException(response.ReasonPhrase);
    }
    catch (Exception ex)
    {
        // TODO:
        throw ex;
    }
}
```

Now, the `GetRegions` method looks like this:

```
var regions = await GetStringAsync("regions");
```

The result of this request can be visualized in the debug screen:

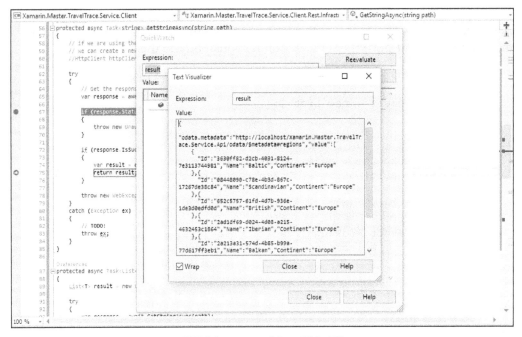

JSON data returned from Web API

However, this is only the string representation of the service data, and we would need to extend our implementation to include a JSON serializer. There are multiple options available for serialization, including the standard libraries available through the *Microsoft BCL* package: `System.Xml` and `System.Json` namespaces. *NewtonSoft Json.NET* is still one of the most popular JSON libraries and available through NuGet.

```
public async Task<List<Region>> GetRegionsAsync(Region filter = null)
{
    var result = new List<Region>();

    var regions = await GetStringAsync("regions");
    var resultingList = JToken.Parse(regions);

    await Task.Run(() =>
    {
        result.AddRange(resultingList["value"]
            .Select(item => item.ToObject<Region>()));
    });

    return result;
}
```

Using this implementation, we can create generic methods in the base class implementation and push the serialization responsibility to this layer.

```
protected async Task<List<T>> GetListAsync<T>(string path)
{
    List<T> result = new List<T>();

    try
    {
        var response = await GetStringAsync(path);
        var resultingList = JToken.Parse(response);

        await Task.Run(() =>
        {
            result.AddRange(resultingList["value"]
                .Select(item => item.ToObject<T>()));
        });
    }
    catch (Exception ex)
    {
        // TODO:
        throw ex;
    }

    return result;
}
```

We can extend this generic implementation for other web methods and create the basis for our RESTful client. The authentication scenario will be discussed further in the following section.

There are many more REST consumer implementations available for the Xamarin developer and these modules can be included in cross-platform projects via components and NuGet packages (RestSharp, Hammock, and so on).

OData and OAuth

OData and OAuth are two widely accepted standards/protocols for RESTful communication scenarios. Xamarin mobile applications that deal with external resources, and especially third-party web service APIs, are generally implementing these protocols.

OData

Unlike SOAP, which is a communication protocol, REST is simply an architectural approach to web service implementations. RESTful services do not need to conform to certain specifications and may vary greatly. In order to identify the requirements for RESTful services and create a uniform structure for data being exchanged between the client applications and the server, OData was initiated by Microsoft in 2007. OData is now an internationally accepted protocol that is maintained by OASIS and supported/used by various applications, platforms, and companies (for example, Microsoft Azure Mobile Services, Microsoft Office 365 Web Access, Salesforce, SAP Netweaver Gateway Solution, IBM WebSphere, and so on).

In OData protocol, each object set is defined by an endpoint in line with REST principles. For GET requests, these entity set endpoints can either accept object identifiers, which results in the details of that specific entity instance, or entities in the list can be queried with OData filter and other query options.

Similar to the WSDL in SOAP/XML services, accessible endpoints (entity sets and functions) and types used in the service contracts are generally served through the metadata endpoint with a CSDL (OData Common Schema Definition Language) file in OData.

To access the whole list of elements, visit `http://localhost/Xamarin.Master.TravelTrace.Service.Api/odata/regions`.

To access a single element in the entity set endpoint, visit `http://localhost/Xamarin.Master.TravelTrace.Service.Api/odata/regions(guid'90222c18-66fa-441a-b069-0115faa1e0f1')`.

To query the list of elements with a filter, visit `http://localhost/Xamarin.Master.TravelTrace.Service.Api/odata/regions?$filter=Continent eq 'Europe'`.

Advanced OData queries involving additional property expansions, lambda operators, and functions are also possible with the OData protocol; however, these topics are beyond the scope of this book.

There are multiple NuGet packages and components available both as open source and/or free to download that help with the client generation for OData services.

OAuth

OAuth is an open standard used generally by service providers for authorization. A general use case for OAuth would be to use third-party identity providers such as Live ID (Microsoft), Google, Facebook, or Twitter for authentication and authorization in a mobile or web application.

A classic OAuth 2.0 implementation scenario is generally a two-step process. The first step involves the user granting access to the client application through the provider web interface. The second step is using the authorization code received from the provider's web interface to get an access token to access the provider's resources.

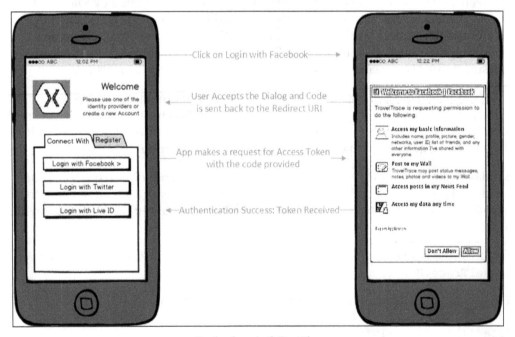

Facebook as Auth Provider

The first step of the authorization process on a web application is generally an `iframe` displaying the provider's authorization page. In a Xamarin application, this step is executed using a web view control or a more specialized implementation (`WebAuthenticationBroker` is an out-of-box control on Windows Phone 8.1). Implementing the two-step authentication process can become quite cumbersome considering the fact that the provider's page makes a callback request to the client application page with the authorization token and the client app is responsible for parsing and extracting this token either from the callback URL or the body of the content.

Xamarin.Auth Components

To provide access to OAuth APIs and simplify the implementation, developers can make use of the available Xamarin OAuth component: Xamarin.Auth (available on Xamarin.iOS and Xamarin.Android platforms). There is also an accompanying component for social media provider APIs: Xamarin.Social.

Using the Xamarin.Auth implementation, authenticating with the Facebook API can become as simple as a few lines of code.

```
var authenticationBroker = new OAuth2Authenticator(
    clientId: "<App ID from https://developers.facebook.com/apps>",
    scope: "",
    authorizeUrl: new Uri("https://m.facebook.com/dialog/oauth/"),
    redirectUrl: new Uri("http://www.facebook.com/connect/login_
success.html"));

authenticationBroker.Completed += (sender, eventArgs) =>
{
    DismissViewController(true, null);

    if (eventArgs.IsAuthenticated)
    {
        // TODO: eventArgs.Account contains the authenticated user
info
    }
    else
    {
```

```
                // TODO: Possibly the user denied access to the account or
                // the user could not authenticate with the provider
        }
    };

    // The GetUI method returns UINavigationControllers on iOS, and
    Intents on Android
    PresentViewController(authenticationBroker.GetUI(), true, null);
```

SignalR

ASP.NET SignalR is a web server-side technology that allows developers to pass real-time updates to their applications. SignalR works in a similar way to WCF duplex channels where the server side is accessible through the main service contract and the server-to-client communication occurs through the callback contract. While WCF duplex channels provide support for the same scenarios as SignalR, duplex channel implementation is currently not supported in any of the Xamarin target platforms. On the other hand, there is a component available for use on all Xamarin target platforms for SignalR.

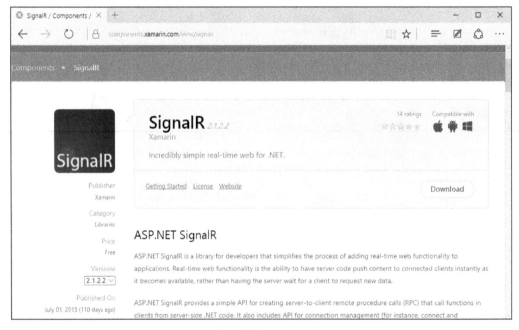

SignalR Component

SignalR takes advantage of `WebSockets`, which enables bidirectional communication over the HTTP transport. In essence, `WebSockets` works almost in the same way as TCP Sockets; however, the connection is established over the HTTP transport layer.

Using SignalR, applications requiring real-time data can be implemented without resorting to polling or listener channel implementations, which is neither scalable nor efficient on mobile platforms.

SignalR is generally implemented with a Hub application on the server-side, which creates different event sinks to be subscribed by different applications. Each client that subscribes to a certain channel gets event notifications and data over these channels in a normal broadcast scenario in a string format or already deserialized as a complex type.

```
// Connect to the server
var hubConnection = new HubConnection("http://xamarin.traveltrace.
com/");

// Create a proxy to the 'MainHub' on the SignalR server
var myHubProxy = hubConnection.CreateHubProxy("MainHub");

// Subscribe to message from the server
myHubProxy.On<string>("ServerStringCall", message =>
{
    // TODO: use the message update from the channel
});

// Subscribe to message with a complex type
myHubProxy.On<Region>("ServerComplexCall", message =>
{
    // TODO: use the message update from the channel
});

// Start the connection
await hubConnection.Start();
```

SignalR server implementations can, generally speaking, replace RESTful service actions. These duplex hubs can provide functions to be called by the consumers as well as update calls from the server to listening clients.

While different message formats can be used to exchange data, most implementations employ the JSON format to serialize and deserialize data, and Json.NET is the default serialization library used by the SignalR component.

```
await myHubProxy.Invoke("MySimpleServerMethod", "myParameter");
await myHubProxy.Invoke<Region>("MyComplexServerMethod", new
Region{Continent = Continent.Europe});
```

On top of the server invoked events, SignalR channels also offer lifetime events:

- **Received**: Raised when any data is received on the connection. Provides the received data.

- **ConnectionSlow**: Raised when the client detects a slow or frequently dropping connection.

- **Reconnecting**: Raised when the underlying transport begins reconnecting.

- **Reconnected**: Raised when the underlying transport has reconnected.

- **StateChanged**: Raised when the connection state changes. Provides the old state and the new state.

- **Closed**: Raised when the connection has disconnected.

SignalR supports SSL transport security as well as having the ability to integrate with the existing authentication and authorization providers already being used by the web server and mobile applications.

Patterns and best practices

In mobile applications, developers often use certain reusable design patterns while using web services and other communication channels in development projects. These patterns aim to increase the efficiency and increase the code sharing not only between platforms but also among various execution domains of cross-platform mobile applications.

Async conversions

The generated proxies for WCF and/or SOAP/XML services generally include either an event-based async implementation or an asynchronous invoke pattern with begin and end methods. Both of these implementations can be converted to a task-based async pattern.

In order to convert the event-based async service method to a task-based one, we can use `TaskCompletionSource<T>` and return the task that is produced (refer to *Chapter 3, Asynchronous Programming*).

```
public Task<List<Region>> GetRegionsAsync(Region filter = null)
{
    var taskAwaiter = new TaskCompletionSource<List<Region>>();

    var client = CreateServiceClient();

    EventHandler<GetRegionsCompletedEventArgs>
      completedDelegate = null;

    completedDelegate = (sender, args) =>
        {
            if (args.Error != null)
            {
                taskAwaiter.SetException(args.Error);
            }

            taskAwaiter.SetResult(args.Result);

            client.GetRegionsCompleted -= completedDelegate;
        };

    client.GetRegionsCompleted += completedDelegate;

    client.GetRegionsAsync(new Region { Continent =
      Continent.Europe });

    return taskAwaiter.Task;
}
```

For the async invoke pattern, we can use the designated methods from the `TaskFactory`. The `FromAsync` method of the `TaskFactory` uses the begin and end methods together with the async state object (which can, for example, be used for cancellation token or progress callback) and creates an awaitable task.

```
public Task<List<Region>> GetRegionsAsync(Region filter = null)
{
    var client = (ReferenceService.ReferenceService)
CreateServiceClient();
```

```
var task = Task<List<Region>>.Factory
    .FromAsync(
    (callback, o) => client.BeginGetRegions(filter, callback, o),
    result => client.EndGetRegions(result),
    null);

    return task;
}
```

Data model abstraction

Following the quality identifiers that were put forward previously, in service-related scenarios, it is important to create a data model abstraction layer which can be used by different branches of a cross-platform application.

Using the travelers' guide application example from previous sections, we can analyze the sharing strategy. In this example, as a development team or a single developer, we are responsible for:

- Implementing the service layer responsible for accessing the database and connecting to external APIs, if necessary
- Implementing the shared common logic which will be used by Xamarin applications
- Implementing the Xamarin.iOS and Xamarin.Android applications
- Implementing the Windows Phone 8.1 application
- Implementing the web interface which will employ a Silverlight component (optional)

For simplicity, we will be implementing only a single data type and a single GET method.

For the contracts and the data objects, we can create a portable library that will be targeting Xamarin platforms together with .NET 4.5. The reason we are including the .NET profile is because we will be using the data model in the service layer implementation as well.

The implementation starts by creating the Data Transfer Model objects. These objects are generally the reflection of the database tables used on the service layer. However, one-to-one mapping between DTOs and DBOs (Entity Framework items) is not absolutely necessary since the DTO abstraction layer's sole purpose is to create an abstraction layer over the actual data repository that we will be dealing with.

```
public class Region
{
```

```
[JsonProperty("id")]
public Guid Id { get; set; }

[JsonProperty("name")]
public string Name { get; set; }

[JsonProperty("continent")]
public Continent Continent { get; set; }
}
```

> Notice that we are including Json.NET attributes to define class
> properties. They are used to format the JSON object attributes during
> serialization/deserialization to camel-case (for example, camelCase),
> which is the JavaScript convention, rather than the .NET convention
> of pascal-case (for example, PascalCase) for property names. These
> property definitions can be used with RESTful clients and web
> service implementations. This will not interfere with other service or
> client layer use cases.

After we create the model, we can define the interface(s) that will be used
by the web service and associated clients. We will define two interfaces
for synchronous implementation on the service layer and asynchronous
consumption on the client side.

```
namespace Xamarin.Master.TravelTrace.Common.Infrastructure
{
    public interface IReferenceService
    {
        List<Region> GetRegions(Region filter = null);

        List<Country> GetCountries(Country filter = null);

        List<City> GetCities(City filter = null);
    }

    public interface IReferenceServiceAsync
    {
        Task<List<Region>> GetRegionsAsync(Region filter = null);

        Task<List<Country>> GetCountriesAsync(Country filter = null);

        Task<List<City>> GetCitiesAsync(City filter = null);
    }
}
```

The service implementation strategy would normally be to use a RESTful layer. For demonstration purposes, let's implement the WCF service in a separate project, reusing the data model defined and the interface previously created.

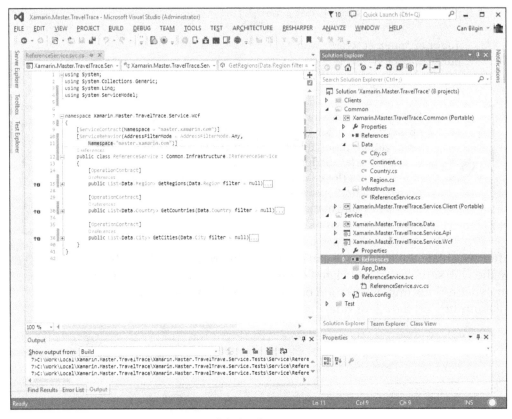

Solution Structure

In this implementation, each service method will be calling a data repository (Entity Framework/MSSQL) and the repository will be returning the DTO objects by converting the database layer entities.

The next section of the project that we need to implement would be the service data consumer layer. We will create a new portable library for this layer and use a generated WCF client. After creating the project and adding the reference to the `System.ServiceModel` namespace and the common portable library that contains the DTO model, an important detail to remember is to make sure that the generated proxy reuses the referenced libraries.

Service Reference Properties

 If you are using the Silverlight SDK to generate the client, it is a little more complicated to include the existing libraries so that the types are reused. In order to do this, you can use the "reference" switch (or simply, / r:) and point the utility to the assemblies that contain the implemented types.

```
slsvcutil http://localhost/ReferenceService.svc
    /d:c:\bin\ /r:C:\Local\Xamarin.Master.TravelTrace.
Common.dll
```

After creating the proxy, we have a structure in which the data model and the contracts are shared by different layers of the application including the service, data access layer, service proxy, and finally, the applications.

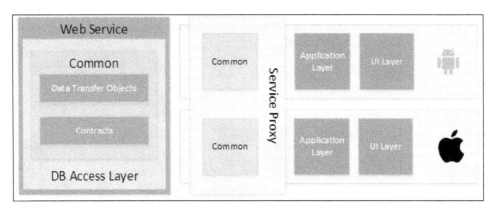

Shared service structure

The implementation, however, should be further extended with conversions to task-based async implementation on the service proxy. Another useful improvement would be to implement local DB caching and offline storage. For this caching layer, the same DTO implementation can be reused.

If we were to include a Windows Phone 8.1 client in this cross-platform project, the only solution to the lack of WCF infrastructure would be to exchange the WCF service with a RESTful implementation.

Service cache

When dealing with network scenarios, it is important to keep in mind that mobile devices do not always have a good network connectivity or network at all. In order to make the Xamarin connected app usable even in offline scenarios, a caching layer can be implemented to store and return data items that do not often change.

For instance, in travel guide applications, users will want to access guides, and possibly maps, even when they are with a roaming connection or, even worse, without any connection at all. To facilitate offline storage, we can implement a SQLite database that uses the existing data transfer objects as storage items and updates the data on certain intervals when there is Internet connectivity.

The first step of the implementation would be to revise our DTO layer classes and add SQLite attributes if needed. This will create a dependency on the service layer for SQLite assemblies; the other option is either to use linked code files between the service layer and the client libraries or to recreate the DTO objects specifically for the SQLite data store.

```
public class Region
{
    public Region()
    {
        Countries = new List<Country>();
    }

    [PrimaryKey]
    [JsonProperty("id")]
    public Guid Id { get; set; }

    [JsonProperty("name")]
    public string Name { get; set; }

    [JsonProperty("continent")]
    public Continent Continent { get; set; }

    [OneToMany(CascadeOperations = CascadeOperation.CascadeInsert |
CascadeOperation.CascadeRead)]
    [JsonProperty("countries")]
    public List<Country> Countries { get; set; }
}
```

In this scenario, in order to create a data context that will use the online storage if available and use the local data storage if Internet connectivity is limited, we can implement the same data interface that we created for the service proxy in the previous examples for the SQLite data source and create one parent handler for the data sync context.

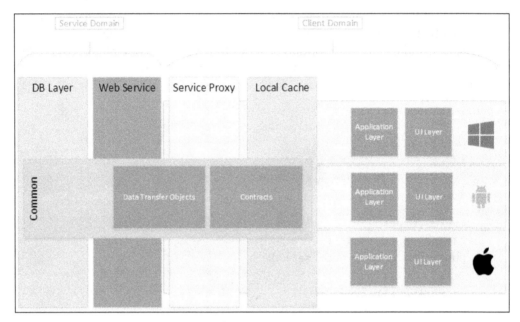

Data Abstraction on App Tiers

In the sync context, for GET methods, the service calls will be used only for updating the local storage and actual results will be returned from the local storage. For PATCH, POST, and PUT calls, depending on the online connectivity, we will be either saving the data locally or pushing the deltas and new object instances to the service and updating the local data with the updates.

```
public class DataSyncContext : IReferenceServiceAsync
{
    public IReferenceServiceAsync LocalDataService { get; set; }

    public IReferenceServiceAsync RemoteDataService { get; set; }

...

    public async Task<List<Region>> GetRegionsAsync(Region filter =
null)
```

```
{
    try
    {
        // Getting the online results
        var results = await RemoteDataService.
GetRegionsAsync(filter);

        // If there were any online changes.
        SyncToLocal(results);
    }
    catch (Exception ex)
    {
        // TODO:
    }

    // Returning the local storage results (with or without
updates)
    return await LocalDataService.GetRegionsAsync(filter);
    }
    ...
}
```

For performance improvement in this implementation, when we are loading data for certain visualizations, we can first call the local data provider and continue with UI updates and then call the web service method and the same continuation delegate.

```
Action<List<Region>> onRegionsLoaded = regions =>
{
    // Update the view-model data or the UI.
};

DataContext.LocalDataService.GetRegionsAsync()
    .ContinueWith((task) =>
    {
        onRegionsLoaded(task.Result);
    });

DataContext.GetRegionsAsync()
    .ContinueWith((task) =>
    {
        onRegionsLoaded(task.Result);
    });
```

Platform-specific concepts

There are other concepts and network communication methods on Xamarin platforms that are provided by the native runtime and supported by Xamarin.

Permissions

In order for an Android or Windows Phone application to access Internet, the application manifest should declare that the application will need to use the network to access resources.

The permission on Android system is declared using the `uses-permission` tag in the manifest node of the XML file:

```
<uses-permission android:name="android.permission.INTERNET" />
```

While this declaration will suffice in most use case scenarios, in order to access the current network status or the Wi-Fi status, you must also declare the network state permissions:

```
<uses-permission android:name="android.permission.ACCESS_NETWORK_
STATE" />
<uses-permission android:name="android.permission.ACCESS_WIFI_STATE"
/>
```

For a Windows phone, the app capability to declare would be `ID_CAP_NETWORKING`.

Application manifests for both platforms can be edited through the application project properties in the designated configuration section.

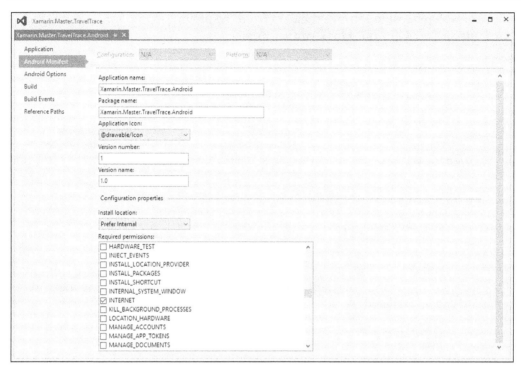

Android Manifest

iOS, other than the App Transport Security (ATS) that was mentioned previously, does not enforce any manifest setup or permissions for applications to use network connection.

NSUrlConnection/NSUrlSession (iOS Only)

Apart from the different client libraries available for use with Xamarin target platforms, some native implementations can also be used to call and receive external web data. One of these available options for Xamarin.iOS platform is NSUrlConnection. With the help of NSUrlConnection, developers can make web requests and use the response.

A simple web request to retrieve the data from the previously demonstrated static data endpoint on iOS would look similar to this:

```
public Task<List<Region>> GetRegionsAsync(Region filter = null)
{
    var nsUrlRequest = new NSUrlRequest(new NSUrl(myServiceEndpoint));

    var taskSource = new TaskCompletionSource<List<Region>>();

    var nsUrlConnection = new NSUrlConnection(nsUrlRequest,
        new ConnectionSerializingHandler<List<Region>>(taskSource));
    nsUrlConnection.Start();

    return taskSource.Task;
}
```

The implementation for the connection delegate would involve the deserialization of the data and assigning the result to the `TaskCompletionSource` so the method execution can be finalized.

```
public class ConnectionSerializingHandler<T> :
        NSUrlConnectionDataDelegate where T:class,new()
{
    private StringBuilder m_ResponseStore;

    private TaskCompletionSource<T> m_TaskCompletion;
    public bool IsFinishedLoading { get; set; }
    public string ResponseContent { get; set; }

    public ConnectionSerializingHandler(TaskCompletionSource<T>
taskCompletionSource)
        : base()
    {
        m_ResponseStore = new StringBuilder();
        m_TaskCompletion = taskCompletionSource;
    }
    public override void ReceivedData(NSUrlConnection connection,
NSData data)
    {
        if (data != null)
        {
            m_ResponseStore.Append(data);
        }
```

```
    }

    public override void FinishedLoading(NSUrlConnection connection)
    {
        IsFinishedLoading = true;
        ResponseContent = m_ResponseStore.ToString();

        // TODO: implement deserialization and
        m_TaskCompletion.SetResult(result);
    }
}
```

Even though this implementation is possible on the iOS platform, considering the cost of passing the mono to iOS bridge (likewise on Android and JNC Bridge), this type of implementation should be avoided, and either only native or mono runtime code should be used to communicate over the network.

In a similar manner, we can implement the usage scenario for the new NSUrlSession class in iOS. However, NSUrlSession can also be used in background download scenarios. Therefore, we will discuss it in the next section.

Background downloads

When the application requires larger network resources than the client UI can wait for, in Xamarin mobile applications we can resort to background downloads. Both iOS and Android platforms offer implementations for background downloads and these strategies can be executed on Xamarin runtime.

For Xamarin.Android application developers, the easiest way to execute a background download is to use the Download Manager API service/application provided since API level 9. The download manager can be initialized with a request and the application can subscribe to event notification(s) regarding the download status.

First, we need to create a request to pass onto the DownloadManager:

```
global::Android.Net.Uri downloadUri = global::Android.Net.Uri.
Parse("<URL to Download>");
DownloadManager.Request request = new DownloadManager.
Request(downloadUri);

// Types of networks on which this download will be executed.
```

```
request.SetAllowedNetworkTypes(DownloadNetwork.Wifi);

// Allowed on Roaming connection?
request.SetAllowedOverRoaming(false);

// Allowed on Metered Connection?
request.SetAllowedOverMetered(false);

//Set the title of this downloaded
request.SetTitle("My Background Download");

//Set the description of this downloaded
request.SetDescription("Xamarin.Android download using
DownloadManager");

//Set the local destination for the downloaded file
request.SetDestinationInExternalFilesDir(this, global::Android.
OS.Environment.DirectoryDownloads, "MyDownloadedData.xml");
// or use the request.SetDestinationUri()
```

Once the request is ready to be executed, we can get the `DownloadManager` instance and queue the download request:

```
m_DownloadManager = (DownloadManager)GetSystemService(DownloadService
);

// Enqueue the request
// The download reference will be used to retrieve the status
m_CurrentDownloadReference = m_DownloadManager.Enqueue(request);
```

The download reference can be used to get the current status information about the queued download or cancel the ongoing background download.

To get the current status of the download or cancel it, we can use the respective methods on the `DownloadManager` instance.

```
// Removing the queued request from the DownloadManager queue.
m_DownloadManager.Remove(m_CurrentDownloadReference);

//
// Retrieving the current status of the download queue
// Create a query to retrieve the download status(s)
```

```
DownloadManager.Query myDownloadQuery = new DownloadManager.Query();
myDownloadQuery.SetFilterById(m_CurrentDownloadReference);
// Request the queued download items as a data table.
var cursor = m_DownloadManager.InvokeQuery(myDownloadQuery);
var statusColumn =
  cursor.GetColumnIndex(DownloadManager.ColumnStatus);
var status = (DownloadStatus)cursor.GetInt(statusColumn);
```

This implementation can be extended with the notification(s) that are received from the DownloadManager application using a BroadcastReceiver class.

```
public class DownloadBroadcastReceiver : BroadcastReceiver
{
    public override void OnReceive(Context context, Intent intent)
    {
        // Get the download reference from the intent broadcast
        long referenceId =
          intent.GetLongExtra(DownloadManager.ExtraDownloadId, -1);

        // TODO: Implement the delegated execution
    }
}
```

We can now register the broadcast receiver with the DownloadManager instance and update the UI with a possible delegated implementation for updating it.

```
//set filter to only when download is complete and register broadcast
receiver
IntentFilter filter = new IntentFilter(DownloadManager.
ActionDownloadComplete);
// TODO: We can extend the DownloadBroadcastReceiver with delegates
RegisterReceiver(new DownloadBroadcastReceiver(), filter);
```

On top of the broadcasts mechanism, the Download Manager App UI can also be invoked within the Xamarin applications to give a uniform UI about on-going or completed transfers.

On the iOS platform (at least post iOS 7), background transfers (both download and upload operations) are made possible with NSUrlSession. NSUrlSession provides an easy to implement interface that lets developers create an efficient and reliable transfer processes.

The implementation strategy for NSUrlSession initially involves the implementation of an NSUrlSessionDelegate, which will be the responsible "handler" for the transfer process. Basic methods related to the health and status of the transfer are exposed through this delegate and can be implemented to provide required information for the transfer or give real-time updates to the application user.

- DidFinishEventsForBackgroundSession is called when the background session is complete
- DidReceiveChallenge is invoked when the server requests credentials
- DidBecomeInvalid is invoked when there is a problem with the session

NSUrlSessionDelegate provides the base implementation for more specialized transfer delegates: NSUrlSessionDownloadDelegate for download operations and NSUrlSessionTaskDelegate for upload operations. These delegate classes expose additional status methods related to the transfer tasks (for example, download delegate provides methods to retrieve notifications about the download progress).

For instance, if we were to use the same example as on Xamarin.Android with the BroadcastReceiver implementation, the NSUrlSessionDownloadDelegate implementation would require three basic methods for completion, error, and progress.

```
public class DownloadTaskDelegate : NSUrlSessionDownloadDelegate
{
    public override void DidFinishDownloading(
      NSUrlSession session, NSUrlSessionDownloadTask downloadTask,
        NSUrl location)
    {
        // TODO: Implement the delegate for download finished
    }
    public override void DidBecomeInvalid(NSUrlSession session,
      NSError error)
    {
        //base.DidBecomeInvalid(session, error);

        // TODO: Implement the delegate for error
    }
    public override void DidWriteData(NSUrlSession session,
      NSUrlSessionDownloadTask downloadTask, long bytesWritten,
      long totalBytesWritten,
        long totalBytesExpectedToWrite)
    {
```

```
        //base.DidWriteData(session, downloadTask, bytesWritten,
        //  totalBytesWritten, totalBytesExpectedToWrite);

        // TODO: Implement the delegate for download progress
    }
}
```

After the delegate implementation is complete, we can create the session and start the download operation using the NSUrlSession.

```
NSUrlSessionConfiguration downloadSessionConfiguration =
NSUrlSessionConfiguration.BackgroundSessionConfiguration ("com.
TravelTravel.BackgroundTransfer");
m_DownloadSession = NSUrlSession
    .FromConfiguration(downloadSessionConfiguration,
    new DownloadTaskDelegate(),
    new NSOperationQueue());
NSUrl url = NSUrl.FromString("<URL to Download>");
NSUrlRequest request = NSUrlRequest.FromUrl(url);
m_DownloadTask = m_DownloadSession.CreateDownloadTask(request);
```

On top of the handler implementation, the iOS app can be woken to execute certain code, such as a local mobile notification to inform the user about the completed sessions. For the task complete event, one needs to use the iOS application delegate (refer to *Chapter 2, Memory Management*) for DidFinishEventsForBackgroundSession.

Mobile notifications (also called pushed notifications for remote scenarios) are user notifications that are executed on the OS level to inform the user about application-related updates. They can be triggered both locally or by using a remote server.

Push notifications

Push notifications are subtle UI messages that can help an application to provide the user information about an asynchronous task being executed by the service layer or about an external event that is related to the application instance itself (for example, messages from social networks, approval for a travel reservation, and so on).

It is possible to create and receive push notifications on both Xamarin platforms and Windows Phone. These notifications are triggered by a secondary server/application (for example, service layer), brokered by the corresponding messaging infrastructure provider for the platform and displayed by the application on the target client. For the Android platform, the messaging provider is **Google Cloud Messaging (GCM)** and it is the **Apple Notification Push Service (APNS)** for iOS. Both of these service providers require your application to be registered to receive push notifications and the server application to have the credentials to be able to authenticate with the notification services. Similarly, **Windows Notification Services (WNS)** adopts a federated authentication mechanism.

Both GCM and APNS use a subscription model in which the client app on a specific device subscribes/registers for the push notifications and an addressing token is created. The addressing token is used, later on, by the server to send push notifications to the message broker service (for example, GCM) and the queued messages are delivered to the specific client.

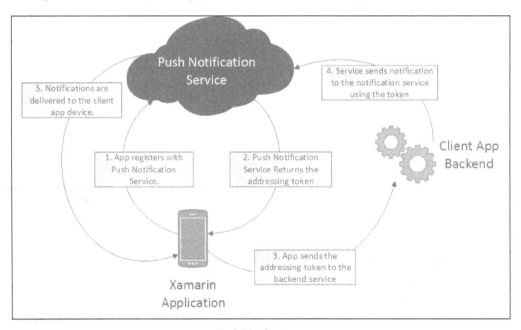

Push Notifications

On top of the classic messaging model, GCM also supports topic-based and group-based messages where the receivers are not limited to a single device/application pair. It is also possible with GCM to create a duplex channel where the client is able to send messages back to the server layer.

Push notifications on these platforms can be used to trigger various tasks, the most common of which is to navigate to a certain view and continue the business process flow initialized by the notification.

Although it is relatively elementary on the client side to subscribe to push notifications, cross-platform scenarios require complex implementation to introduce a single server environment to provide messages to both GCM and APNS. However, there are platform-agnostic implementations available for both of these platforms. The Microsoft Azure platform and the notification hub is one of these solutions, where communication with GCM and APNS are both supported through usage of the same business logic implementation.

Cloud integration

Even though there are multiple cloud service providers as development platforms for creating the backend for mobile applications, Microsoft Azure stands out among the competitors with its inherent natural bond to the .NET platform and subsequently Xamarin, considering its evolution. Most of the features supported by Azure have a specific implementation for Xamarin target platforms.

Azure Mobile Services

Azure Mobile Services is a scalable cloud development platform that helps developers add functionality to their mobile applications with ease. The patterns and features described in this chapter related to network services such as OData services, offline data storage, push notifications, and OAuth authentication providers are already included in the mobile services SDK and can be configured through the Azure management console.

In order to demonstrate aforementioned features, we can incorporate them into our demo application.

The initial step would be to create a mobile service on the Azure management console. For this purpose, we will select a compute service and create the mobile service.

Create Compute Service

Then, we will set up the mobile service endpoint and create the SQL database to store the online data.

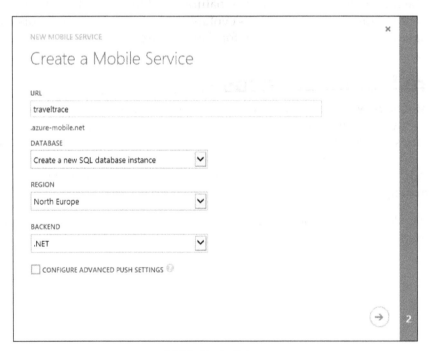

Mobile Service Setup

Once the setup is complete, the "personalized" service layer project can be downloaded in order to integrate the mobile services into the application project.

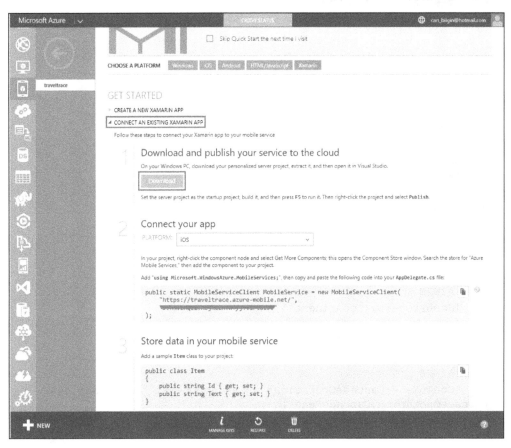

Connect Mobile Services to an existing Xamarin app

In the service layer project, you will notice that there is only a single controller created for your convenience. We will be extending the project with additional controllers and adding a reference to our own DTO data model. In order to reuse the types created in the previous sections, instead of referencing the common data model project directly, we add the data type files as a reference to the new service project that we downloaded from the Azure portal. The reason for the referenced files is that the data objects in the service project have to derive from `EntityData` class. Another change we need to make is to convert the class definitions to partial and remove the SQLite references, for example, you can comment out the SQLite property descriptors or use conditional compilation.

In this example, we are using AZURE as the build constant for the Azure web service.

```csharp
public partial class Region
{
    public Region()
    {
        Countries = new List<Country>();
    }

#if !AZURE
    [PrimaryKey]
    [JsonProperty("id")]
    public Guid Id { get; set; }
#endif

#if !AZURE
    [JsonProperty("name")]
#endif
    public string Name { get; set; }

#if !AZURE
    [JsonProperty("continent")]
#endif
    public Continent Continent { get; set; }

#if !AZURE
    [OneToMany(CascadeOperations = CascadeOperation.CascadeInsert |
CascadeOperation.CascadeRead)]
    [JsonProperty("countries")]
#endif

    public List<Country> Countries { get; set; }
}
```

Finally, create a data object definition using a `partial` declaration for the
`Region` class:

```csharp
public partial class Region : EntityData
{
}
```

After this step, you can simply use the existing project item template for the controller to add the specialized data endpoint (Microsoft Azure Mobile Services Table Controller).

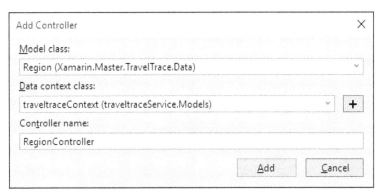

Microsoft Azure Mobile Services Table Controller

This will create a controller for the data object and insert the type into the data context.

Once the project is published and the mobile services are running, SQL database tables are going to be migrated automatically. This migration also applies to data table column changes or future additions to the DTO model.

Now we can add the NuGet package or the component to our client application and add the necessary initialization code, as described in the start page of mobile services section on the Azure management console.

In the main activity, we create the following mobile service instance:

```
public static MobileServiceClient MobileService =
  new MobileServiceClient(
    "https://traveltrace.azure-mobile.net/",
    "<Removed for security reasons>"
    );
```

Add the following to an event handler or the OnCreate function:

```
// Intialization the mobile services on the mobile platform
CurrentPlatform.Init();

// Adding a region item to the database
var item = new Region {Continent = Continent.Europe,
  Name = "Balkan"};
```

```
MobileService.GetTable<Region>().InsertAsync(item)
  .ContinueWith((result) =>
{
    System.Diagnostics.Debug.Write(result.Status);
});
```

After the code is successfully executed, the data on the Azure database can be observed using SQL Management Studio or the Visual Studio SQL Server tools.

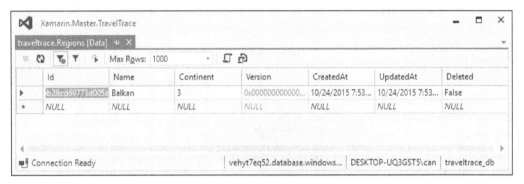

Azure Data Sample

Now that we have a working service layer and a client that can communicate with it, we can have a look at the local synchronization.

Azure offline data

For local data caching and offline scenarios, Azure Mobile Services SDK already implements a synchronization framework where the local data is stored in SQLite database and the synchronization is handled by pull and push commands (push requests upload local changes to the cloud store whereas pull requests download the latest changes from the server) using a default conflict handler. Each pull request automatically issues a push request where the local data is pushed to the cloud storage. Conflicts are resolved according to the created and updated fields, which are members of each object type defined using the `EntityData` base class.

Before starting the implementation, we need to download and install the Azure Mobile Services SQLiteStore NuGet package.

In order to initialize the default local data store, we will use the
`MobileServicesSQLiteStore` implementation. Custom local store implementation
can be incorporated using the `IMobileServiceLocalStore` interface.

```
private async Task InitLocalStoreAsync()
{
    // new code to initialize the SQLite store
    string path = Path.Combine(
        Environment.GetFolderPath(
        Environment.SpecialFolder.Personal), "traveltrace.db");

    if (!File.Exists(path))
    {
        File.Create(path).Dispose();
    }

    var store = new MobileServiceSQLiteStore(path);
    store.DefineTable<Region>();

    // Uses the default conflict handler, which fails on conflict
    await MobileService.SyncContext.InitializeAsync(store);
}
```

After the local store is initialized and the synchronization context is created,
we can implement the synchronization method that can be called every time
the application starts.

```
private async Task SyncAsync()
{
    // IMobileServiceSyncTable<Region> RegionsTable = MobileService.
GetSyncTable<Region>();
    await MobileService.SyncContext.PushAsync();
    await RegionsTable.PullAsync("AllRegions", RegionsTable.
CreateQuery());
}
```

Both the `PushAsync` and `PullAsync` methods additionally accept filter expressions so
one can limit the synchronization to certain entities.

In this implementation, once the synchronization context is in place, if the
service connection is not available, the `IMobileServiceSyncTable<T>` interface
implementations handle the offline data and the data is kept in the local store until
the next push operation.

Azure authentication

The Azure platform provides various authentication mechanisms for Xamarin mobile applications. Each authentication mechanism can be integrated into existing mobile applications with a service backend through NuGet packages and/or components.

Being a multi-tenant, cloud-based directory and identity management service, Azure Active Directory (Azure AD) provides application developers an easy way to create single sign-on experience on a large number of cloud SaaS applications. It is also possible to incorporate an existing Windows Server Active Directory into applications and leverage the existing on-premise identity stores. These features make the Azure AD an ideal candidate for LOB applications.

Another authentication strategy for Azure Mobile Services is to configure an existing authentication provider such as Facebook, Google, Twitter, or Microsoft and secure the service requests using the Azure Mobile SDK. In order to register an authentication provider, the first step would be to create a consumer app on the target platform.

For instance, if we were to use Live ID for our authentication scenarios, we would need to use the Live Connect App management site (`https://account.live.com/developers/applications/index`). Similarly, for Twitter, we would need to create a Twitter consumer application on the Twitter application management console (`https://apps.twitter.com/`).

Live Connect app management site

Once the application setup is in place, the Azure management console can be used to update the mobile services configuration.

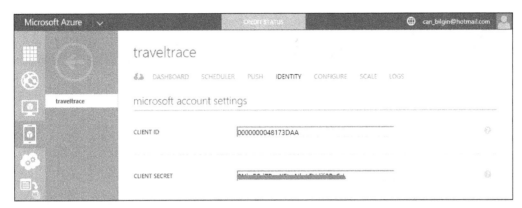

Mobile Services Identity Configuration

After the identity provider for the mobile services has been set up, the web service project can be easily protected simply by adding the Authorize attribute.

```
[AuthorizeLevel(AuthorizationLevel.User)]
public class RegionController : TableController<Region>
```

On the client apps, the authentication is handled by simply using the LoginAsync method on the Azure Mobile Services SDK client with the correct authentication provider.

```
MobileService.LoginAsync(this, MobileServiceAuthenticationProvider.
MicrosoftAccount).ContinueWith((task) =>
{
    System.Diagnostics.Debug.WriteLine("Currently authenticated user's
ID is {0}", task.Result.UserId);
});
```

The result is the same authentication screen received using the Xamarin.
Auth component.

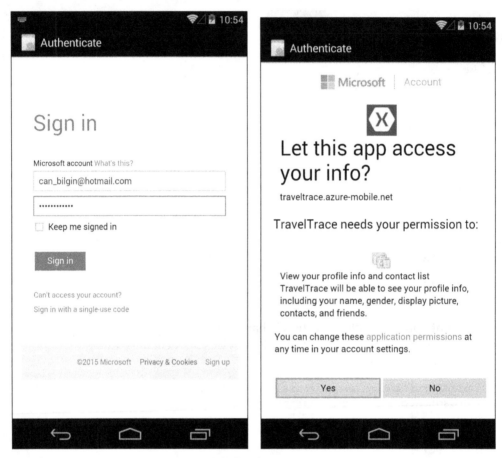

Brokered Authentication

Azure Cloud integration scenarios extend far beyond the ones described here.
The features that are included in this cloud-based development platform can
help developers enhance their Xamarin apps with ease and scalability.

Summary

This chapter provided an overview of various network channels that can be used in Xamarin applications to create connected applications.

Web services are definitely on the essentials list for modern mobile applications because of the interoperability of the protocols in place for web services (both SOAP/ XML and REST/JSON). Unfortunately, XML services are a little harder to integrate with Windows Phone 8.1 runtime (even though they are still supported by Windows Phone Silverlight runtime) because the Windows Communication Foundation client infrastructure is not included in Windows Phone runtime. However, the same RESTful service proxies can be used by applications on each Xamarin target platform and Windows Phone.

Cloud integration options such as mobile services and Azure Active Directory were discussed with demonstration samples. Each of these technologies provides additional connectivity and integration opportunities for Xamarin mobile apps. SignalR is another web technology that grants additional communication capabilities to mobile applications by means of bidirectional communication between the client apps and the server.

Several common service and web implementation patterns were demonstrated using the TravelTrace application scope that we will be using for various scenarios in the remainder of this book. Each pattern described targets different quality identifiers initially mentioned.

Finally, we discussed some of the platform-specific network options.

6
Platform Extras

This chapter concentrates on platform-specific APIs and features. It explains some of the peripherals that can be employed in Xamarin applications. We will also discuss native libraries and how to include them in cross platform Xamarin applications. The following topics will be discussed:

- Content sharing
- Peripherals
- Location data
- Native libraries

Content sharing

Each Xamarin target platform implements a certain strategy to share formatted content between the applications. Sharing implementations increases the visibility of your applications by allowing users to open files from your application in any other app. In addition, these types of implementations provide added value to the quality of your cross platform projects from the nativity perspective.

The inter-application sharing occurs with the underlying runtime acting as a broker between the sharing source and target applications. On iOS and Windows Store applications, the sharing is facilitated in the form of abstract file elements. Android applications, however, can take it one step further by sharing formatted data that can be manipulated by the receiving application, which essentially allows the source application to almost act as a data repository.

On Windows Store, applications can actively share content such as media elements, URIs, text content, and other types of data. However, in this implementation strategy, that is, sharing contact implementation, the source application has to initiate the sharing process. The content sharing scenarios described in this book are about target applications accessing the content via the source application.

On Windows Runtime, applications interact with each other or with the operating system through the usage of so-called application contracts. With the help of contracts, applications can immerse into the runtime and get one step closer to become part of the runtime.

The same functionality is achieved by the implementation of the base ContentProviders on Android and the implementation of document provider extensions on the iOS platform.

File pickers and contracts (Windows Store apps)

One of the most commonly used contracts is the File Open Picker contract on Windows Runtime. In this contract implementation, the source application has to implement the activation strategy for when it is called to provide file content for the target application. When the target application requires a certain type of file, the runtime lists all possible source applications that declares this type in their app manifest (for example, on a Windows Phone, when you want to attach a document on the mail client together along with a picture, the OneDrive application is displayed as one of the possible sources).

The user then selects the file that they want to use in the current application and the provider app is responsible for either creating or providing the file to the target application.

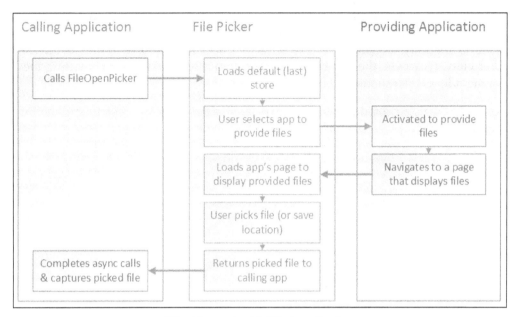

File picker contract in Windows Runtime

In this methodology, the file does not necessarily need to be an actual document item, but it can be a conceptual one. For instance, if we were to implement the File Open Picker in the TravelTrace app, we would not need to use actual documents in the File Open Picker to provide content. The shared content items could be the previous trips that the user kept track of and the selected trip could provide a generated scrap book or a collage of images in an image format or as a PDF document according to the type of document that is being requested by the consumer app.

Document Provider extensions (iOS)

The Document Provider extensions (introduced in iOS 8) allow applications, that is, consuming applications) to access documents outside their application sandbox. Document Provider extensions are twofold. The Document Picker View Controller extension provides a UI implementation for the operating system to display whenever the source application is selected as a document source in the document picker view. However, the File Provider extension is responsible for providing the document level operations.

In order to create a provider extension, we can use the existing project template in Xamarin Studio.

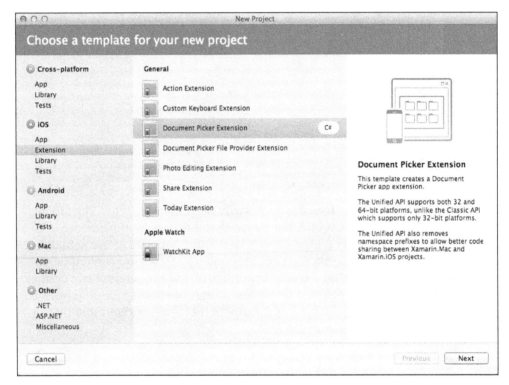

The Document Picker extension project template

Once the project is created, we are responsible for creating the view on the storyboard and implementing DocumentPickerViewController so that the available files are listed on the UI when our application is selected to provide files. DocumentPickerViewController initially has two methods that require our attention. The PrepareForPresentation method receives the picker mode (Import, Open, ExportToService, or MoveToService) so the user interface can be prepared according to the requested operation. The OpenDocument method is implemented just for our convenience to demonstrate the fact that once the user selects a document, we should prepare the corresponding file URL and pass it onto the runtime using the DismissGrantingAccess method.

It is important to keep in mind that the URL provided from our Document Picker extension should already point to an actual file, or we should go on to implement the Document File Provider extension that will provide the files when either the consuming app displays the document picker and the user selects the file or the consuming app opens the file directly using the cached URL.

In the Document File Provider extension project, the crucial implementation is located in the StartProvidingItemAtUrl method. This method uses the FileCoordinator class provided to create the file at the target URL (for example, generates the file or downloads it from a remote location).

```
public override void StartProvidingItemAtUrl (NSUrl url,
Action<NSError> completionHandler)
{
  NSError error, fileError = null;
  NSData fileData;

  // TODO: get the file data for file at <url> from model
  fileData = new NSData ();

  FileCoordinator.CoordinateWrite (url, 0, out error, (newUrl) =>
    fileData.Save (newUrl, 0, out fileError));

  if (error != null)
    completionHandler (error);
  else
    completionHandler (fileError);
}
```

After the implementation of the extensions is complete, we have to prepare the project metadata entries. Each project (both extensions and the container application) needs to make use of the **App Groups** capability. This capability needs to be set up in the **Entitlements** option list. Other settings involve the base document storage URL, type of operations supported for the document picker, and so on. However, these configuration values are inserted in the `Info.plist` option list.

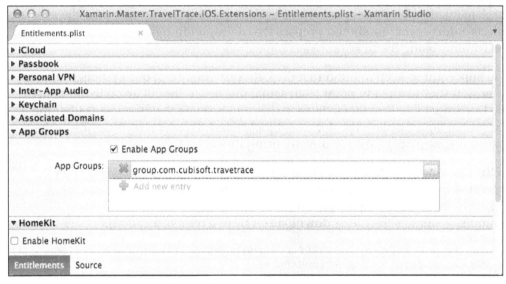

Entitlements for Document Provider extensions

In order to add the extensions to the containing application, the only thing we need to do is to add them as references to the main project. If you look at the project file of the main project, you will notice that the references are added with the `IsExtension` flag set to true.

ContentProvider and ContentResolver (Android)

Content providers on Android platform act as data repositories. These repositories are exposed to consuming applications through structured endpoint descriptions (similar to REST endpoints on web services). Using the metadata provided, providers' content is resolved by the consuming app through the implementation of `ContentResolvers`. Using content providers, applications can expose well-known data types such as contact list photos or calendar events, as well as custom data types and formatted data.

On the consumer side of this infrastructure, there are many content providers already implemented by default on Android runtime, such as `Contacts`, `MediaStore`, `UserDictionary`, and so on. These providers can be accessed by implementing base classes such as `ContentResolver` and `CursorAdapter`. `CursorAdapter` is used to feed the data that is retrieved by `ContentResolver` to a UI list view control. The `ContentProvider` API operations can involve list queries and CRUD operations on individual records.

Provider applications are responsible for registering an authority that is unique to the application. The authority entry can be described as the base content URI for a specific application. Either it can be added to the manifest file, or an attribute entry could be used on the class that is implementing `ContentProvider`.

```
[ContentProvider(new string[] {
"com.xamarin.master.traveltrace.TripProvider" })]
public class TripDataProvider : ContentProvider
```

Another important piece of metadata that the content provider needs to provide is the Mime-Type information. In order to facilitate the use of `CursorAdapter` on consumer applications, the content provider needs to provide a Mime-Type for a list of items (starting with `vnd.android.cursor.dir`) as well as for a single item (starting with `vnd.android.cursor.item`).

Finally, the content provider needs to expose the data columns for the data that is being made available to other applications. This is achieved by hiding the `InterfaceConstants` nested class from the base abstract class.

```
public new static class InterfaceConsts
{
    public const string Id = "Id";
    public const string Name = "Name";
    public const string Description = "Description";
    public const string Date = "Date";
    public const string Location = "Location";
    public const string ContentPath = "ContentPath";
}
```

Another optional implementation would be to create a `UriMatcher` class that could ease the implementation process for the query methods.

```
private UriMatcher GetUriMatcher()
{
    var matcher = new UriMatcher(UriMatcher.NoMatch);
```

```
        // to get data...
        matcher.AddURI(Authority, _basePath, (int) QueryType.List);
        matcher.AddURI(Authority, _basePath + "/#", (int)
          QueryType.Single);

        return matcher;
    }
```

The final implementation is related to the query, update, insert, and delete methods. Each of these methods needs to return the ICursor implementations according to the abstract class defined.

```
    public override global::Android.Database.ICursor
    Query(global::Android.Net.Uri uri, string[] projection, string
    selection, string[] selectionArgs, string sortOrder)
    {
        switch ((QueryType) m_UriMatcher.Match(uri))
        {
            case QueryType.List:
                // TODO:
            case QueryType.Single:
                // TODO:
            default:
                throw new Java.Lang.IllegalArgumentException("Unknown
                    Uri: " + uri);
        }
    }
```

Overall, while providing more flexibility for content sharing, Android makes it a little more difficult for other applications to consume the data provided by the source application. The data provided by a content provider implementation on a Xamarin.Android application cannot be consumed by another without a specialized implementation.

Peripherals

In this section, we will discuss several communication protocols that enable applications to communicate with other platforms and other devices.

Bluetooth

The Bluetooth communication protocol has become an invaluable feature on mobile devices. Especially with the emerging technologies related to **IoT** (**Internet of Things**), and various accessories we use in daily life, our dependency on the Bluetooth stack on mobile platforms has increased.

While Xamarin.Android applications and Windows Runtime applications can make use of both GATT (Bluetooth Low Energy) and RFCOMM (Bluetooth Serial), iOS applications can only communicate through the Bluetooth LE protocol. The main reason for this discrepancy is the fact that Android and Windows Runtime implement the serial communication port according to shared specifications. However, Apple implements a propriety communication stack using an encryption system. This, unfortunately, limits the serial communication to between only Apple produced/compliant accessories or devices.

For Xamarin.Android, Bluetooth APIs reside in the `Android.Bluetooth` namespace. Using the provided classes, developers can enhance their applications with features like:

- Scanning for discoverable Bluetooth devices (including LE protocol)
- Getting information on the local BT adapter and paired devices
- Creating Serial Communication Sockets using the RFCOMM protocol
- Acting both as a GATT client or a GATT server

Bluetooth protocols can be accessed only with the user permission manifest entry for Bluetooth.

```
<manifest ... >
  <uses-permission android:name="android.permission.BLUETOOTH"
    />
  ...
</manifest>
```

On Windows Runtime, Bluetooth-related features are implemented in the `Windows.Devices.Bluetooth` namespace. Similar to the feature-set in Android, Windows Runtime Bluetooth stack requires the applications to declare the adapter access requirement and the protocol to be used in the application manifest (for some specific devices and protocols, the Bluetooth capability declaration has to be inserted manually into the manifest). An important feature on this platform is that the Bluetooth connectivity can be facilitated and kept alive by background tasks, enabling the devices to continue their operations in the backgrounded or suspended states.

For Xamarin.iOS, Bluetooth LE related implementations would need to use the `CoreBluetooth` framework.

An important component that is currently in the Xamarin store for cross-platform peripherals integration is the Monkey.Robotics project. While implementing the basic APIs for Bluetooth LE and Wi-Fi, some other vendor-specific peripherals, such as health monitoring devices and smart watches, can be used with this component.

Wi-Fi Direct

Wi-Fi Direct is another communication protocol that allows Wi-Fi enabled devices to create **peer-to-peer** (**P2P**) networks and exchange information using the Wi-Fi adapter without using a common provider network connection.

Out of the Xamarin target platforms that are described in this book, only the Android platform supports this protocol. The Windows 10 platform will support Wi-Fi Direct; however, this implementation will be targeting only Windows based devices.

On Android devices, with the introduction of Wi-Fi P2P, developers can create applications that can communicate with higher speeds and through much longer distances than with Bluetooth adapters. Wi-Fi P2P features were introduced in Android 4.0 (API level 14) and they comply with the Wi-Fi Alliance's Wi-Fi Direct standards.

In order to be able to use this feature, the application manifest should contain permissions for `ACCESS_WIFI_STATE`, `CHANGE_WIFI_STATE`, and `INTERNET`.

Access to these services is provided with the WifiP2pManager, which is located in the Android.Net.Wifi.P2P namespace. Using this manager, applications can broadcast, create groups, request peers, and developers can create applications that can communicate over P2P sockets via Wi-Fi Direct.

Near Field Communication

The **Near Field Communication** (**NFC**) protocol provides an easy alternative to Bluetooth for pairing and advertising scenarios (for example, NFC tags). With NFC, it is possible to create sockets and transfer data between mobile devices that are in proximity to each other.

Unfortunately, the NFC protocol is another unsupported communication protocol on iOS devices. (Reports suggest that iPhone 6 technically has the ability to use this protocol; however, this API is not made available to developers.)

The NFC stacks on Windows Phone and Android devices, however, implement most of the same profiles. In essence, it is technically possible to communicate over NFC across Windows and Android devices in proximity (by default, the tap and send feature works as a cross-platform feature). In spite of the fact that Windows devices use a propriety messaging scheme (`Windows:`), there are third-party frameworks for NDEF. NDEF is a cross-platform messaging scheme that is currently the default for Android.

Location data

Nowadays, geo-context (location awareness) is becoming more and more crucial for applications, especially the ones running on mobile platforms. For instance, search engines optimize results according to the location information they gather from the client platform, social media and photo applications add geo-tags to posts and media items, and there are many more use cases for the data about *not how or on which platform the application is running, but where.*

On Xamarin platforms, the location information is provided making use of several different sources. The most accurate of these sources is **GPS** (**Global Position System**). This option consumes the most power and, generally, is only available for foreground applications. Other options that can provide somewhat less accurate data are network providers such as Wi-Fi or Cellular data. iBeacon is another technology introduced by Apple and applicable to iOS 7+ devices. iBeacon-compatible devices transmit location information using the Bluetooth LE protocol, and this transmission is then used by the Bluetooth adapter on mobile phones and tablets.

On Xamarin target platforms, location information can be accessed both proactively and through system events and triggers. In each platform, access to a location is limited by the privacy settings and it is always up to the user whether a certain (or every) application can access the location services.

Android location and Google Play services

In early versions of Android runtime, the `android.location` API was the framework-designated module for adding location awareness to applications. However, after the release of Google Play Services SDK (compatible with Android v2.2, API level 8, or higher), location APIs provided by Google became the preferred way to access location data on Android platform.

LocationManager, a LocationServices implementation, is a system-wide service and can be accessed through the application context in Xamarin.Android applications. In order to get location information, the application has to subscribe to the location updates with an implementation of ILocationListener.

```
m_LocationService = GetSystemService(LocationService) as
  LocationManager;

if (m_LocationService != null)
{
    if (m_LocationService.
      IsProviderEnabled(LocationManager.GpsProvider))
    {
        // Get updates in min every 5 seconds for every minimum 2m
        change
        m_LocationService.
          RequestLocationUpdates(LocationManager.
          GpsProvider, 5000, 2, m_LocationListener);
    }
    else if (m_LocationService.
      IsProviderEnabled(LocationManager.NetworkProvider))
    {
        // Get updates in min every 10 seconds for every minimum
        // 10m change
        m_LocationService.RequestLocationUpdates
          (LocationManager.NetworkProvider,
          10000, 10, m_LocationListener);
    }
}
```

In the location listener interface, there are several events that can be utilized. Other than the location change information, developers are provided with the updates related to different location provider status changes.

A simple location listener implementation used in the previous example would resemble this:

```
public class LocationListener : Java.Lang.Object,
  ILocationListener
{
    public void OnLocationChanged(Location location)
```

```
    {
        Trace.WriteLine(string.Format("Lat:{0}, Long {1}",
            location.Latitude, location.Longitude),
            "OnLocationChanged");
    }

    public void OnProviderDisabled(string provider)
    {
        Trace.WriteLine(string.Format("Location Provider '{0}' is
            disabled", provider), "OnProviderDisabled");
    }

    public void OnProviderEnabled(string provider)
    {
        Trace.WriteLine(string.Format("Location Provider '{0}' is
            enabled", provider), "OnProviderEnabled");
    }

    public void OnStatusChanged(string provider, Availability
        status, Bundle extras)
    {
        Trace.WriteLine(string.Format("Location Provider '{0}'
            status changed to {1}", provider, status),
            "OnStatusChanged");
    }
}
```

The listener interface can be implemented on the current `Activity` itself or any other `JavaObject` class implementation. Using the backgrounding techniques defined in *Chapter 3, Asynchronous Programming,* the listener interface can also be implemented on a custom started service and the application can receive background updates on the location changes through the service data directly (bound scenario) or through information persisted by the service.

Testing location information can be difficult on mobile applications. In order to facilitate GPS data testing and diagnostics, Android Emulator in Android SDK and Visual Studio Android Emulator are equipped with location emulation functionality.

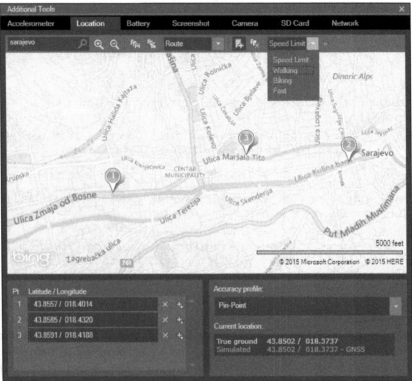

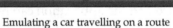

Emulating a car travelling on a route

Visual Studio Android Emulator also provides features to emulate the usage of an automobile, or other means of transport, on a route or GPS location changing according to the defined pins with defined intervals.

On top of the location information, using the location provider status information, location info can be gathered in a more efficient and reliable way (for example, switching between GPS and network provided information according to connectivity and requirement for accuracy). In order to get the optimal provider that is currently available for the application scope, you can use the `GetBestProvider` method with the desired criteria for accuracy (Coarse or Fine Location Info) and for power consumption (high, medium, and low).

This intelligent switch between location data providers is the main advantage of using the Fused Location Provider (Google Play Services SDK) and Google Location Services over the default location API.

Google Play services Xamarin components

Xamarin binding libraries to Google Play Services SDK, which are available as components for Xamarin.Android v4.8+ developers, provide an easy way to integrate various services, including location APIs, into Xamarin.Android applications. These components implement the Java Binding projects and take care of the cumbersome implementation and compilation of the Google provided Android libraries.

After installing the Google Play services' location component, while trying to build the Xamarin.Android application, you might receive a compilation error similar to this:

"No resource found that matches the given name (at 'value' with value '@integer/ google_play_services_version')."

The reason for this error is the fact that the Xamarin component is dependent on the Google Play Services SDK and the SDK modules are supposed to be installed manually using the Android SDK Manager.

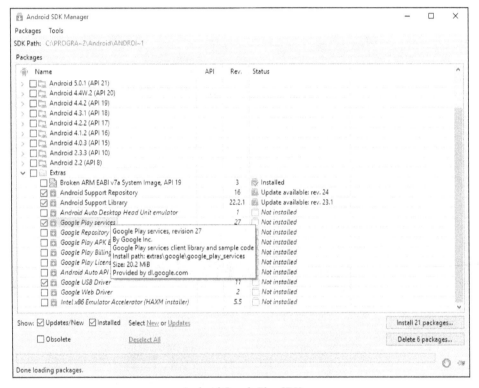

Android Google Play SDK

After installing the SDK module, the Xamarin.Android application can be built without errors.

Once the setup and configuration is complete, the `GoogleApiClient` class can be initialized and used in Xamarin applications. `GoogleApiClient` requires the implementation of two interfaces to gather information about the client connection status: `GoogleApiClient.IConnectionCallbacks` and `GoogleApiClient. IOnConnectionFailedListener`.

If the application you are implementing does not depend on continuous updates of location data, but rather just the current location, you can use the `GetLastLocation` method provided on the `GoogleApiClient`. This method provides a one-time reading option.

```
m_GoogleClient = new GoogleApiClient.Builder(this)
        .AddApi(Gms.Location.LocationServices.API)
        .AddConnectionCallbacks(this)
        .AddOnConnectionFailedListener(this)
        .Build();


m_GoogleClient.Connect();
```

In order to receive real-time updates with the fused location provider, you must implement the `ILocationListener` interface for the Google Location Services API. This listener is different from the default one; it only contains a single event handler implementation for location changes. The events related to the data providers do not need to be implemented since the fused location provider itself is responsible for smart switching between the location data providers.

Although the type of provider and provider status changes are not relevant for us using the fused location provider, it is still possible to let the fused provider know which type of accuracy and priority our application scope demands. For this purpose, we can use the `SetPriority` method with the appropriate flag on `LocationRequest` while subscribing to the location updates.

- **High accuracy (100)**: Requests the finest location available
- **Balanced power/accuracy (102) (default)**: Requests the `block` level accuracy (~100m accuracy)
- **Low power (104)**: Requests the `city` level accuracy (~10km accuracy)
- **No power (105)**: Sets the location updates to use passive mode; waits for location updates delivered to other client applications (also known as **piggybacking**)

As well as the priority, a fused location provider lets developers set other important delineations of location updates, such as minimum interval, smallest displacement, and expiration time.

```
private async Task RequestLocationUpdates(GoogleApiClient
  apiClient)
{
    // Describe our location request
```

```
    var locationRequest = new Gms.Location.LocationRequest()
        .SetInterval(5000) // Setting the interval to 5 seconds
        .SetSmallestDisplacement(5) // Setting the smallest update
            delta to 5 meters
        .SetPriority(Gms.Location.LocationRequest.
            PriorityHighAccuracy)
        // Setting the priority to Fine and High Power
        .SetExpirationDuration(20000); // Stopping the location
            updates after 20 seconds.

    // Request updates
    await Gms.Location.LocationServices.FusedLocationApi
        .RequestLocationUpdates(apiClient, locationRequest,
            m_LocationListener);
}
```

Unfortunately, Google Play services are only preinstalled on Android SDK emulator and for the other emulators, the Google applications package has to be downloaded and installed on the emulator image.

Location services on iOS

On the iOS platform, the location data is accessed through the CoreLocation library, and similar to the android location API, location changes are sent to the subscribing application with the help of event delegates. The CLLocationManager class makes it a trivial task to get location data updates from the mobile device.

The Xamarin.iOS location data access implementation starts with creating the required Info.plist entries, which will explain why the application requires access to the user's location. In order to do this, we have to edit the Info.plist file, adding one or both of the following entries:

Info.plist entries for location info

In addition to the Info.plist entry, you should also keep in mind that starting with iOS 8, applications have to explicitly ask for permission to use the location data. In order to get consent from the user, the location manager exposes two methods: one for authorizing the app for continuous local data updates and the other one just to be used when the application is in the foreground.

```
_LocationManager = new CLLocationManager();

_LocationManager.RequestWhenInUseAuthorization();

_LocationManager.RequestAlwaysAuthorization();
```

Finally, we can subscribe to the `LocationsUpdated` event to receive the latest location update information.

```
if (CLLocationManager.LocationServicesEnabled)
{
    _LocationManager.LocationsUpdated += (sender, eventArgs) =>
    {
        Debug.WriteLine(
            string.Format("Lat:{0}, Long {1}",
```

```
                eventArgs.Locations[0].Coordinate.Latitude,
                eventArgs.Locations[0].Coordinate.Longitude),
                "OnLocationChanged");
    };

    // Every ~500m an update
    _LocationManager.StartMonitoringSignificantLocationChanges();

    // Every 10m send an update event
    _LocationManager.DistanceFilter = 10;
    _LocationManager.StartUpdatingLocation();
}
```

The location information can be further optimized for the application scope using the exposed criteria properties and methods. It is also possible to retrieve other types of information such as heading direction. However, it is important to first check if the service is available and request updates according to the system status information.

```
if (CLLocationManager.HeadingAvailable)
{
    // update the heading
    _LocationManager.StartUpdatingHeading();
    _LocationManager.UpdatedHeading += (sender, eventArgs) =>
    {
        Debug.WriteLine("New Heading: X: {0} Y: {1} Z: {2}",
            eventArgs.NewHeading.X,
            eventArgs.NewHeading.Y,
            eventArgs.NewHeading.Z);
    };
}
```

Location data on Windows Runtime

On Windows Runtime (Windows Store apps), the `Windows.Device.Geolocation` namespace is dedicated for tracking the device's location over time. The `Geolocator` class replaces the main access points in the previous platforms and can give on-demand data and information updates through events.

Similar to iOS access request, the application can request consent from the application user with the `RequestAccessAsync` method and according to the response, methods or events can be accessed through the `Geolocator` class.

```
var accessStatus = await Geolocator.RequestAccessAsync();
if(accessStatus == GeolocationAccessStatus.Allowed)
```

```
{
    // Give update in every 5 meters
    Geolocator geolocator = new Geolocator {
      DesiredAccuracyInMeters = 5 };

    // Use StatusChanged event for Geolocator status change
    geolocator.StatusChanged += OnStatusChanged;

    // Use PositionChanged event for Geolocator status change
    geolocator.PositionChanged += (sender, eventArgs) =>
    {
        UpdateLocationData(eventArgs.Position);
    }

    // Get the current position
    Geoposition pos = await geolocator.GetGeopositionAsync();

    UpdateLocationData(pos);
}
```

Geofencing

A geofence is an abstract boundary that can be defined with location services so that the application which created the geofence receives an update from the mobile device whenever the user is entering or exiting this boundary. This eliminates the need for polling for the location info and opens up different implementation opportunities for mobile applications.

The use cases for geofences vary from simple reminders on certain locations to virtual tours created by showing certain images or information according to the current region.

All the Xamarin target platforms support the creation and usage of geofences. For instance, in order to create a geofence on an iOS platform, we would need to use `CLCircularRegion` and the location monitoring feature of the `CoreLocation` library. There are two events of interest that are fired when the mobile device enters and exists in the region.

```
var region = new CLCircularRegion(
new CLLocationCoordinate2D(43.8592, 018.4315), 600,
"Old Town");
```

```
if (CLLocationManager.IsMonitoringAvailable(typeof
  (CLCircularRegion)))
{
    _LocationManager.DidStartMonitoringForRegion += (sender,
      eventArgs) =>
    {
        Debug.WriteLine(string.Format("Starting region monitoring
          for {0}",
        eventArgs.Region.Identifier));
    };

    _LocationManager.RegionEntered += (sender, eventArgs) =>
    {
        CreateLocalNotification("Welcome to Old Town",
            "Don't forget to take stroll down the Bascarsija and
             visit the historic national library!");
    };

    _LocationManager.RegionLeft += (sender, eventArgs) =>
    {
        Debug.WriteLine(string.Format("User left {0}",
        eventArgs.Region.Identifier));
    };

    _LocationManager.StartMonitoring(region);
}
```

This implementation creates a geofence around the described region (with a center defined by the coordinates and a radius of 600 m) and sends out a notification when the specified fence is entered, giving information about the location.

Old town geofence

The same implementation on Android platform would use LocationServices in conjunction with the GeofenceBuilder class to create IGeofence type boundaries and add them to the watch list. One important difference on the Android platform is that the events are handled through delegates and are generally implemented by an intent service.

The implementation starts with creating GoogleApiClient like in the previous examples, and once the API client is connected, we can go ahead and create the geofence(s) and the intent service that is going to handle the callbacks.

```
public void OnConnected(Bundle connectionHint)
{
    var intent = new Intent(this,
    typeof(GeofenceListenerService));
    var pendingIntent = PendingIntent.GetService(this, 0, intent,
    PendingIntentFlags.UpdateCurrent);


    var geoFence =
        new GeofenceBuilder().SetRequestId("OldTown")
            .SetTransitionTypes(Geofence.GeofenceTransitionEnter |
            Geofence.GeofenceTransitionExit)
            .SetCircularRegion(43.8592, 018.4315, 600)
            .SetExpirationDuration(200000) // Expiration Duration
            is obligatory
            .Build();

    var geofenceRequest = (new
    GeofencingRequest.Builder()).AddGeofence(geoFence).Build();

    //
    // The async version can be used instead
    // await LocationServices.GeofencingApi.
    AddGeofencesAsync(m_GoogleClient,
    geofenceRequest, pendingIntent);
    LocationServices.GeofencingApi.AddGeofences(m_GoogleClient,
    geofenceRequest, pendingIntent);
}
```

The intent service implementation for sending out a local toast notification on location updates would look similar to this:

```
[Service(Exported = false)]
public class GeofenceListenerService : IntentService
{
    public GeofenceListenerService() :
    base("GeoFenceListenerService")
    {
    }

    protected override void OnHandleIntent(Intent intent)
    {
        var geofencingEvent = GeofencingEvent.FromIntent(intent);

        if (geofencingEvent.HasError)
        {
            int errorCode = geofencingEvent.ErrorCode;
            // TODO: Log Error
        }
        else
        {
            var requestId =
            geofencingEvent.TriggeringGeofences[0].RequestId;

            switch (geofencingEvent.GeofenceTransition)
            {
                case Geofence.GeofenceTransitionEnter:
                    if (requestId == "OldTown")
                    {
                        Toast.MakeText(Application.Context,
                            "Don't forget to take stroll down the
                            Bascarsija and visit the historic
                            national library!",
                            ToastLength.Short);
                    }
                    break;
                case Geofence.GeofenceTransitionExit:
                    Debug.WriteLine(string.Format("User left {0}",
                    requestId));
                    break;
            }
        }
    }
}
```

The classes used by Windows Store apps for geofences are the `GeofenceMonitor` and `Geofence/GeoCircle` descriptive classes. A simple `Geofence` class would consist of a `Geocircle` class and the associated ID.

```
string fenceId = "OldTown";

// Define fence properties
BasicGeoposition position;
position.Latitude = 43.8592;
position.Longitude = 018.4315;
position.Altitude = 0.0;
double radius = 600; // in meters

Geocircle geocircle = new Geocircle(position, radius);

// Create the geofence
Geofence geofence = new Geofence(fenceId, geocircle);
```

Once the geofence is initialized, we can use the `GeofenceMonitor` class to add the geofence and subscribe to the events.

```
GeofenceMonitor.Current.GeofenceStateChanged +=
    OnGeofenceStateChanged;
GeofenceMonitor.Current.StatusChanged += OnGeofenceStatusChanged;
```

It is also possible to use the geofence status change events as triggers for a background task so that the registering application does not need to be in the foreground or even in the running state.

Native libraries

In spite of the fact that the Xamarin framework and .NET core implementations on Xamarin.Android and Xamarin.iOS platforms provide a vast amount of features, in some cases it is unavoidable to include native code in cross-platform implementations. Fortunately, it is possible to bind or link native libraries on both of these platforms.

Managed callable wrappers (Android)

As mentioned in previous chapters, managed callable wrappers are generated managed code libraries which provide a way to interact with the Java Runtime over the JNI bridge to execute code from certain Java libraries.

Java libraries are often packaged in Java archive files (JAR files) and it is possible, using the compiled Java library project, to create a binding library which can be included in Xamarin.Android applications.

In order to demonstrate this usage, we will be creating a MCW for a simple JSON parsing library. The first step of creating our binding library would be to use the built-in project template to create our binding project.

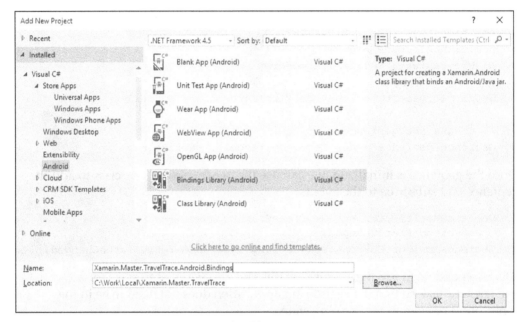

Binding library project

Once the binding project is created, we can copy the JAR into the created Jars folder in the binding project. After the copying is completed, an important step would be to check the **Build Action** configuration for the JAR resource. The copied JAVA library files can be used in two ways:

- **InputJar**: This is a Java library archive that is going to be used to generate the managed wrapper.

- **ReferenceJar**: This is a Java library archive that is only going to be used as a reference and not to generate a wrapper.

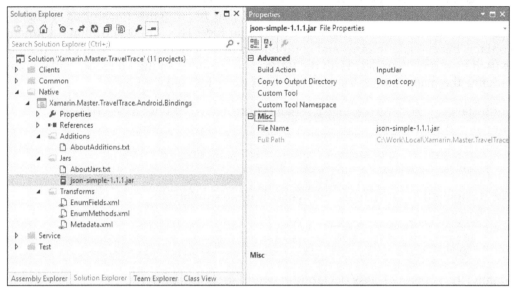

Binding library structure and build action

After setting the **Build Action** field to `InputJar` (this simple library does not have any dependencies), we can build the library project. Once the build is successful, you can see the generated managed files in the `<Project Directory>\obj\Debug\ generated\src` directory.

```
namespace Org.Json.Simple.Parser {

    // Metadata.xml XPath class reference:
      path="/api/package[@name='org.json.
      simple.parser']/class[@name='JSONParser']"
      [global::Android.Runtime.Register (
                "org/json/simple/parser/JSONParser",
                DoNotGenerateAcw=true)]
    public partial class JSONParser : global::Java.Lang.Object {
        ...
```

Looking at the main parser file, you will notice that the definition for a class consists of an Android runtime registration and a class deriving from a Java object. Metadata about the class or class members also has a metadata comment, which defines the path of the item in the Java library package.

If we wanted to change the name of a namespace (by default, they are generated from the package names defined in the api.xml file), or the name of any members of a class or the class itself, we could make use of the Metadata.xml file that is located in the bindings project. The Metadata.xml file contains transforms on the api.xml document that is generated from the jar files. This API description document contains the class definitions and components in a format similar to that of GAPI that is used by mono compiler. With the transforms included in the Metadata.xml, we can redefine the managed names designated for the generated C# items.

For instance, in order to change the namespace, we would use a description similar to this:

```
<attr path="/api/package[@name='org.json.simple']"
name="managedName">Json.Simple</attr>
```

For changing the class names, the syntax is quite similar:

```
<attr path="/api/package
  [@name='org.json.simple']/class
  [@name='JSONParser']" name="managedName">JsonParser</attr>
```

Finally, the generated class declaration would look similar to this:

```
namespace Json.Simple.Parser {

  // Metadata.xml XPath class reference:
  path="/api/package[@name='org.json.simple.
  parser']/class[@name='JSONParser']"
  [global::Android.Runtime.Register
  ("org/json/simple/parser/JSONParser", DoNotGenerateAcw=true)]
  public partial class JsonParser : global::Java.Lang.Object {
```

Linking versus binding (iOS)

While dealing with native code on the Xamarin.iOS platform, there are several options developers can use.

If we were dealing with simple static utility libraries on C or Objective-C, it is possible to create so-called **fat binaries** and then link them at the compile time. Later in Xamarin runtime (remember there is no Xamarin runtime in iOS, everything is compiled into static code), methods from the native library can be invoked using the P/Invoke functionality in the Xamarin framework.

The other option, which enables users to create a stronger "bridge" (at the cost of performance) with native libraries, is to create bindings to Objective-C classes and methods. Using this approach, similar to managed callable wrappers in Android runtime, we would need to create a C# wrapper over the Objective-C framework library and use the managed wrapper to access the native implementation. Even though this approach creates a more intuitive and manageable access point to native code, since the managed wrapper is, in essence, a high-level implementation and the mono compiler actually generates the P/Invoke and Imports for accessing native functionality, it is inherently a little more costly than native linking.

Both implementations require the creation of the fat binary as a starting point. A fat binary is the colloquial term used to describe binary packages that contain native binary compilations for all possible CPU architectures (i386 for the Simulator and ARMv7/ARM64 for the devices). In order to create the universal binary that is suitable for use in all iOS development targets, one needs to make use of the command-line utility in Mac OS X.

```
lipo -create -output libFatBinary.a libThinBinary-i386.a libThinBinary-arm64.a libThinBinary-armv7.a
```

After the universal binary is created, you can now copy the universal package into a project folder in the Xamarin.iOS application, set the build action to **None**, and instruct the mtouch compiler to link the binary in compile time. For build instructions, you would need to use the build arguments section in project properties and gcc flags.

```
-gcc_flags "-L${ProjectDir} -lFatBinary -force_load ${ProjectDir}/libFatBinary.a
```

Additional parameters might need to be included according to the frameworks being used or if the binary includes C++ code (for example, the –cxx flag for C++ code).

The other option is to create a `LinkWith` declaration (in most cases, this is created automatically) in an Objective-C binding project. The code is as follows:

```
[assembly: LinkWith ("libFatBinary.a",
LinkTarget.ArmV7|LinkTarget.ArmV7s|LinkTarget.Simulator|LinkTarget.
Simulator64|LinkTarget.Arm64,
ForceLoad = true,
Frameworks = "CoreFoundation CoreData CoreLocation",
LinkerFlags = "-lz -lsqlite3",
IsCxx = true)]
```

In an Objective-C binding project, you must first familiarize yourself with the types, methods, and other constructs in the native library to be able to start implementing the responding managed types in the binding library.

 Objective Sharpie is a useful tool for creating managed wrappers for Objective-C libraries. Initially, an internal tool used by the Xamarin team, it soon was released to public. Even though the implementation is not complete and it is not fully supported as an official product, it can help accelerate the implementation against native libraries.

Summary

In this chapter, we talked about some platform-specific features related to inter-app communications, peripherals, and location data.

Using platform-specific features can make your applications more attractive to platform users by providing scenarios that they are familiar with and increase the native look and feel of your applications.

Platform-specific features related to different communication protocols, such as Bluetooth, NFC, and Wi-Direct, can be employed for various scenarios. However, most of the protocols and profiles described here target Android and Windows Phone. Xamarin.iOS applications can only benefit from the Bluetooth LE profile.

Location awareness is another platform-specific implementation that all mobile applications can benefit from. By adding a location context to the business logic of applications, developers can create a more personalized experience for users.

Finally, if needed, Xamarin provides important features for binding and linking native libraries for Android and iOS platforms, which transform a complex porting task into merely imports.

In the next chapter, we will discuss the user interface components on different platforms and how they correlate with each other.

7
View Elements

In this chapter, you will find introductory information about **User Experience** (UX) design concepts and explanations on the differences and similarities of design principles on Xamarin platforms. Correlation between the UI elements will be illustrated and useful design patterns will be demonstrated with real-life examples to create a consistent user experience across platforms without compromising the native look-and-feel. This chapter is divided into the following sections:

- Design philosophy
- Design elements
- User interaction

Design philosophy

One of the biggest pitfalls while designing an application for cross-platform use is to impose the design patterns from one OS to the other one. In the mobile world, each platform and users of those platforms have certain expectations from an application. These expectations can be as insignificant as an icon on a common feature access button (for example, the share button on iOS and Android), or as important as the layout of a view (for example, tab buttons on the bottom and top of a view on iOS and Windows Phone, respectively). In this paradigm, the designer's responsibility becomes much more complex, since the design, while creating a brand for the application, would need to be inviting and appealing for the users of the platform.

User expectations

Mobile platform users are creatures of habit. One of the key deciding factors of the adoption rate of a mobile application is how easy it is to use and how discoverable the features are for the platform users. It is important to remember that when users become acquainted with a specific platform, they will expect certain patterns and behaviors while interacting with that device. Trying to change these habits and forcing the users into usage patterns that they are not accustomed to might be costly.

Platform imperatives

Both iOS and Windows Runtime have well-defined design guidelines that were refined over the years with the help of Microsoft's and Apple's experience on various software platforms. Android, being an open source development platform, has been searching for an identity since the early versions and it was a general implementation principle to design first on iOS and port the design to Android. However, with the release of Material Design guidelines by Google, the Android platform and app developers finally seem to have found a scheme to adhere to and create a unified experience on the Android platform across different applications.

With the emergence of minimalism and flat design patterns in software design, Microsoft was the pioneer to release the Microsoft design language (the Modern UI, codenamed Metro). Modern UI design heavily depended on typograph and geometry. The motto of this design pattern is "content over chrome", and application developers were encouraged to use the content itself to provide the interactivity and remove any unnecessary ornaments that are not crucial to the content or the functionality.

Panorama View from Windows Phone 7

With the release of iOS 7, Apple joined the minimalist movement with an overhaul of their user interface, which is described by Jonathan Ive (Senior VP of Design) as bringing order to complexity. Translucency, typography, and layering were the highlighted features of this new design. It was a major change of Apple's design direction which, at the time, was famous for its skeuomorphic designs on various applications and platforms.

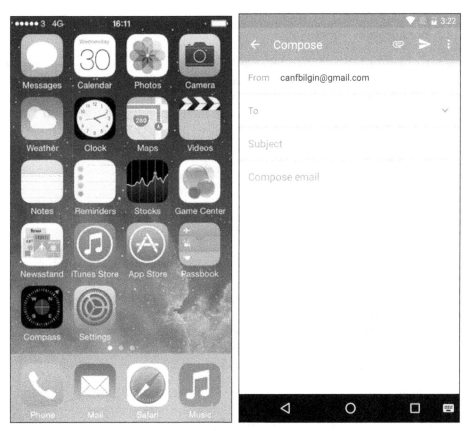

iOS 7 Home Page and an Android dialog

Google's take on flat design principles, Material Design (codenamed Quantum Paper), tries to address the same type of design concerns by reducing the design elements to their very basics and recreating interactive surfaces with strong typography resembling paper and ink in essence.

Hardware dependency

Similar to web applications, on Xamarin target platforms, especially on Windows and Android, the hardware that the Xamarin application is going to be running or displayed on varies greatly. An application designed for a specific platform can be used on a low-end touchscreen device with a mediocre resolution or on a high-end phablet with an HD display on landscape or portrait rotations. This hardware dependency should be one of the main concerns while designing the UI for mobile applications.

For instance, pre-Android 3.0 phones used to have hardware buttons that helped with the navigation throughout the application and the OS itself. These buttons consisted of a back, menu, search, and home buttons. Even though the hardware buttons were replaced with the bottom system navigation bar (software buttons) on later devices, this trait is followed by Windows Phone devices that still have the back, Windows, and search hardware buttons. On iOS, the navigation hierarchy implementation is completely up to the application and generally handled by the back button placed on the top navigation bar.

Design metrics on Android

For varying resolutions, in order to create an adaptive user interface, each platform uses different methodologies. However, in each platform, the important metric unit is the pixel density. Pixel density can be defined as the number of pixels that can fit into an inch in length. According to the pixel density (PPI or pixels per inch), independent from the total physical width and height of the screen, developers can create consistent views across various mobile devices. In other words, total screen resolution (pixel density multiplied by screen dimensions) is a declining trait that is taken into consideration while designing cross device/platform applications.

On the Android platform, to create a uniform experience on different pixel densities, developers and designers are encouraged to use density-independent pixels (dp) unit for expressing various dimensions and measurements of UI controls. Density-independent pixels are calculated by considering the 160 pixel density as a norm and calculating the display size in normalized pixel values.

Check out the following table for more information on Android density-independent pixels:

Screen Density	Density Bucket	Screen Resolution (pixels)	Screen Resolution (dp)
120	LDPI	360 x 480	480 x 640
160	MDPI	480 x 640	480 x 640
240	HDPI	720 x 960	480 x 640
320	XHDPI	960 x 1280	480 x 640

Android Density-Independent pixels (dp)

In order to demonstrate the scaling and density independent pixels, we can compare the following views on different devices. Using the pixels to design the content would be visualized differently on different devices:

Using pixels to design the UI

However, if we were to use the same design elements with dp as the measurement unit, the UI would be much more uniform.

Using dp to design the UI

Similar to dp, another density-independent measure unit on Android is "sp", or scalable pixels. The main difference between dp and sp is that sp is scaled according to the user's font settings and generally associated with text content, while dp is managed by the operating system and the user generally does not have any control over it.

For media resources (for example, images) and layouts, the Android solution structure supports creating specialized design elements. Icons and other graphics can be provided in alternative sizes and resolutions using the correct density bucket identifier as a suffix to the `drawable` folder (for example, `drawable-xhdpi` for extra high density). Similarly, if needed, multiple alternative layouts can be provided according to the screen size groups in the layouts folder (for example, `layout-xlarge` or `layout-xlarge-land` for portrait and landscape displays on an extra-large screen).

Design metrics on iOS

In the iOS ecosystem, there are only a handful of devices and screen resolutions. On this platform, the identifier on display scaling is the point (pt) notation. A point is displayed as one physical pixel on a non-retina display. On retina display and higher configurations (iPhone 6 Plus), the scaling factor is calculated as 2x and 3x, respectively, while the point measurements are kept as they are.

 iPhone 6 Plus has the scale factor of 3 and screen resolution of 414 x 736 points. This would translate to 1242 x 2208 pixel resolution. However, the physical supported resolution on this device is 1080 x 1920. For this reason, images rendered (or rasterized) with the 3x scale factor are then down-sampled with a ratio of 1:1.15 on this device.

Design metrics on Windows Runtime

On Windows Runtime, the scaling of the application view is taken care of by the scaling algorithms that normalize the size of controls, fonts, and other UI elements. This normalization process occurs on the runtime and developers generally do not need to deal with it. When designing Windows Runtime applications, the measurement unit is pixels. However, the pixels are referred to as effective pixels. Effective pixels are the normalized size unit of the operating system.

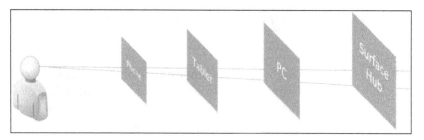

Effective Pixels on Windows Runtime

A common example for the effective pixels is to consider a font of size 24px. Text visualized with this font is displayed the same way on a phone 5-10 cm away from the user and on a surface hub couple of meters away.

Design elements

In order to create a consistent layout across platforms, while conforming to the platform requirements, developers and designers need to familiarize themselves with each platform and draw parallels between the layouts and UI controls on these platforms. We will discuss this in the next chapter within the scope of Xamarin. Forms. The existence of parallels between these platforms makes the foundation of the Xamarin.Forms framework.

The basic layout

The main layout elements in all three platforms are very similar to each other. However, the placement of these elements differs greatly according to the platform.

The User Interface Layout

On each platform, the status bar displaying the system information is located at the top of the screen (marked as "1" in the preceding screenshot). This section is one of the constant elements that should be kept in mind when designing applications for Xamarin target platforms.

 On Windows 10 operating system, the system bar can be expanded on user's initiative to give detailed information about the system. This expansion causes the elements to be hidden on the application canvas. However, this does not cause elements to offset, and the expansion occurs on a different layer of the screen.

On all three platforms, the second element is generally the navigation bar (marked as "2" on the screenshot). This element is only used to display information about the current view on Windows Phone. However, on iOS and especially on Android, the navigation bar has additional functions. The navigation bar on iOS applications can be used for hierarchical navigational items. However, on the Android platform, the so-called app-bar contains the context-related commands and navigation items. The context menu presenting the additional context-related commands that do not fit on the main app-bar (navigation panel on the right-hand side) and the Navigation Drawer that reveals the left navigation panel are the functional and structural elements of the main app-bar on Android applications. Having application and content-related buttons or links on the title area on Windows Phone applications has been discouraged. However, on Windows 10, similar to the Navigation Drawer on the Android platform, developers can implement an application-level switch.

On Windows platform, context-related application commands and the additional items that are displayed inside a context menu are generally located at the bottom of the screen on the application bar (marked as "5"). Even though the application bar can be created on the top of the screen, this is generally a use case for applications that use the peer-to-peer/horizontal navigation patterns (refer to the next section, *Navigation*).

The system navigation bar (marked as "4") is located at the bottom of the screen on the Android platform. This bar contains three buttons, namely Back, Home, and History. These buttons used to be hardware buttons prior to Android 4.0.

Instead of the bottom app-bar on Windows Phone and the system navigation bar on Android, on iOS this area is generally occupied by the tab bar (marked as "3"). The tab bar provides the main navigation functionality in iOS applications and should be available on each screen of the application (similar to the peer-to-peer navigation app-bar on Windows Phone).

Navigation

In application design, the navigation strategy should be one of the first decision items. According to the requirements of the application or the elements to focus on, developers can adopt different navigations strategies.

While building the navigation tree and preparing the flowchart for the application, you can make use of two types of traverses: hierarchical (vertical) and peer-to-peer (horizontal). Horizontal navigation occurs when the user wants to navigate between pages that are on the same level of the navigation tree. Hierarchical navigation can be on either direction on the vertical path. As a rule of thumb, as the user navigates deeper, the number of similarly typed objects on the screen decreases and the details about a single object increases. In other words, it is rare to see list views in the lower nodes of a sub-tree in an app navigation hierarchy.

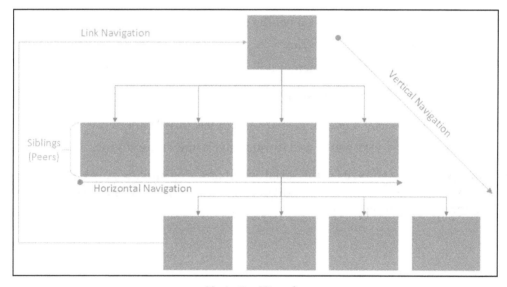

Navigation Hierarchy

On top of the traditional navigation methods, jump links among the pages on various levels and sub-trees can also be used to provide easy access to these nodes (for example, a Home link navigating from the bottom of the hierarchy back to the main page).

In order to demonstrate the navigation design, we will be creating an interface for the TravelTrace application that was used as an example for functional implementations in the previous chapters.

Horizontal navigation

Navigation between peers or siblings can provide an easy way to switch context between the items on the *top level*. In this case, peers would be representing the main features of an application that should generally be accessible to the user at all times. On this level, the navigation can be implemented with tabbed controls or application-level navigation providers such as the Navigation Drawer on the Android platform. The homepage should have clear design and focus; it should make a statement about what your app is tailored to do.

For instance, if we were to use our travel application to demonstrate the top-level peers, we would first need to decide on the main features that the application has to offer.

Possible features of this travel companion application could be:

- Get detailed information on nearby attractions
- Allow users to plan their trips
- Create and share travel memorabilia (photos, notes, tips, and so on)

Identifying features of the application could be:

- Creating a social medium to share and re-use travel experience
- Assisting the user before and during travels and cultural visits

Overall, we want to emphasize the social aspect and also provide personal assistance for users during their visits. In the light of this "decision", we can start designing the initial concept for our application.

Home Screen Sample

On the Windows Phone platform, the home screen can be either implemented as a hub or a pivot view. Although each view has similar navigational properties, pivot control is generally used to display segregated groups of content that carry similar traits.

Hence, it is generally preferable to use a hub view as a homepage to make different top level sections of the application available and sub-nodes easily discoverable.

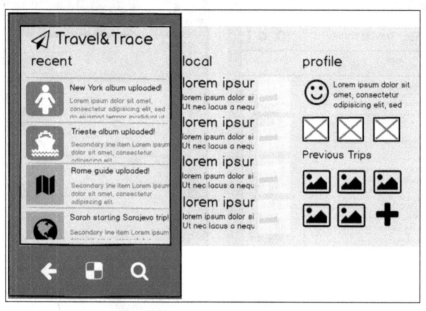

Hub View (Windows Phone)

When considering Windows Phone and HubView, the only possible way of navigating between the top-level items in the hierarchy is a swipe gesture, while it is possible to tap on the tab bar buttons on the other platforms.

Another type of horizontal navigation can occur when navigating through different categories or filtered views of content items. On the Android platform, the main app-bar can host a filter dropdown to select the proper category to display content items. On iOS, the navigation bar, or a secondary bottom tool bar, can be used to create a button to display a picker (aka spinner) to select the proper sibling on the navigation tree. Another possible horizontal navigation provider control on iOS would be the SegmentedView control, which can be used to display different perspectives of the same type of content (for example, previous trips as opposed to future plans or recent guides and recent albums).

SegmentedView control on iOS

On the Windows platform, it is generally a better idea to choose a master/detail type of implementation for use-cases with more than "several" categories where the possible categories are always visible and displayed side-by-side with the content area. It is also possible to use a drop-down menu on a fly-out attached to one of the command bar buttons. If the number of categories is limited, the `PivotView` control can be employed in the view implementation.

Command bar flyout on Windows Phone

It is also possible, on all platforms, to include in-content selection controls that help the user navigate between the categories (dropdowns, pickers, spinners, hyperlinks, buttons, and so on).

For instance, a catalog view for our travel application that allows users to browse the uploaded content freely would need to categorize the country items on different continents.

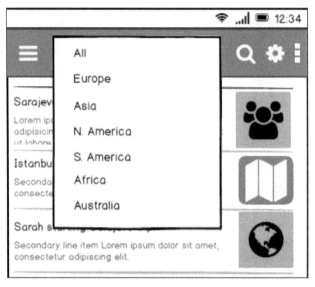

Main App Bar Filter on Android

Finally, the Next/Previous buttons used on the top navigation bar and the main app-bar on iOS and Android, respectively, together with the swipe left/right gestures on Windows Phone, can create a pleasant experience when navigating between the siblings and/or collection items. This type of navigation is generally used at the bottom of the hierarchical navigation tree or at the bottom of a sub-tree.

Vertical navigation

Elements that have a parent-child relationship (for example, the parent page can be the country view and the child views can be the city details) can use the vertical traversal of the navigation tree. The simplest and most common way of vertical traversal is navigating to the details view of a content element when the user clicks on the item.

A common mistake related to the details concept is to make it a two-step process where the user first needs to select the item and then click on a details command button. In modern applications, it is crucial to make the UI intuitive by means of using the content elements themselves as interaction elements.

Once the user is in the details view, backward navigation to ascend in the navigation tree is implemented either with a back button on the main app-bar (on Android) and the navigation bar (on iOS), or by using the hardware back button (on Windows Phone) and the soft back button on the system bar (on Android). It is not recommended to use an additional back button on the Windows Phone platform since the design real estate is already limited and the same functionality can be implemented with the hardware button, as opposed to its desktop counterpart where there is no hardware button and the design canvas is relatively generous.

Semantic Zoom on Windows Phone

On the Windows Phone platform, another way of creating a different perspective on the content elements without having to implement a secondary view is to use the SemanticZoom control. The SemanticZoom control provides two views of the same list of content elements where the first one is generally a categorized view with a smaller number of elements and the second one is the full list view with additional details on content items. The navigation between the two views is generally implemented with pinch-in and pinch-out gestures (see the *Gestures* section for details).

Jump navigation

Jump or cross navigation occurs when the application navigates between different nodes without conforming to the navigation hierarchy (for example, it is possible to navigate to the details view of an item that is on the third-level from the hub page that is on the top level of a Windows Phone application).

This type of navigation is generally used with very particular features that do not relate to the general outline of the application. The navigation commands can be included on the navigation bar or as hyperlinks embedded into the content. It is also common to use the command bars to create item related navigation links.

Navigation Drawer on Android

Another possible way to create navigation access points for switching the context in an easy way is to use the Navigation Drawer type functionality on Android. A similar experience can be achieved with the persistent tab bar on iOS. As mentioned before, comparable functionality was added to the Windows Phone platform with the release of Windows 10.

Content elements

Each Xamarin target platform puts forward certain strategies and guidelines to visualize the content. Although developers are given the freedom to create appealing and innovative design blocks, especially on the Android and Windows Phone platforms, there are strict guidelines to adhere to. We can group these content blocks and controls in several categories.

Collection views

Collection views provide an efficient way to display collection-based content elements. In most implementation use cases, collection elements are interactive and display attributes of the content items with text and image controls. It is also common to add item-related commands or flags on the content items themselves in the shape of tokens (for example, the command to add an item to favorites, display a status icon, and so on).

UITableView (iOS)

On the iOS platform, `UITableView` provides a flexible way to display collection data on a customizable layout. On a table view, each cell can be customized to display a batch of attributes from the content items and developers are free to make use of the inbuilt events and commands to implement additional command logic (for example, row actions).

Grouped table view & table view with details

Another out-of-the-box feature of the UITableView and the associated controller (UITableViewSource) is the so-called indexing of the content elements. Indexing works in a similar way as the jump lists on the Windows platform and provides an easy way to catalog the content items and enables the user to easily jump into the correct section or the group.

A search display controller can also be associated with a UITableView, creating a standard iOS search experience on a collection of items.

Some of the possible artefacts that can be included in a table view cell by default are as follows:

✓	Checkmark	Signifies that the row is selected
>	Disclosure indicator	Signifies that another table is associated with the row
(i)	Detail disclosure indicator	Identifies that the user can click to see details about the current row (for example, Popover)
≡	Row reorder	Identifies that the row can be dragged to re-order
+	Row insert	Adds a new row to the table
–	Delete view/hide	Reveals or hides the delete button for the current row
Delete	Delete button	Deletes the row

Table view artifacts

UICollectionView (iOS)

UICollectionView is used to create a grid-like layout on the iOS platform. Collection views are also customizable using the in-built properties and base-classes. Collection views are more flexible in nature compared to the table views which are inherently bound by the table structure and contained cells.

Collection views are also made up of cells that can be displayed in numerous layouts. The default layout can be customized using a `UICollectionViewFlowLayout`. The flow layout can define parameters such as the minimum line spacing between the rows, the minimum interim spacing between the items, item sizes, and section insets (margins assigned to the sections in the collection).

The following code sample creates a simple flow layout structure:

```
UICollectionViewFlowLayout flowLayout =
                        new UICollectionViewFlowLayout();
flowLayout.MinimumLineSpacing = 20f;
flowLayout.MinimumInteritemSpacing = 4f;
flowLayout.SectionInset = new UIEdgeInset(4f, 4f, 4f, 4f);
flowLayout.ItemSize = new SizeF(20f, 20f);
myCollectionView.CollectionViewLayout = flowLayout;
```

Another option for customizing the layout of a collection view is to inherit the `UICollectionViewLayout` class and implement a custom layout. In the custom layout implementation, the class is responsible for providing the layout attributes such as the size and the location of the cells according to the collection size and available layout area.

`UICollectionViewController` is used to normalize the data that is to be presented and act as a delegate for the collection and item level events such as cell selection and context menus.

Additionally, the `SupplementaryView` and `DecorationView` classes provide additional customizations by giving section related details and UI customizations on the collection view layer.

ListView (Android)

`Listview` is one of the most overused components on the Android Platform. While it can be used to display a relatively small list of menu items, with adapters it can also be used to visualize data from other applications and services. It is possible to compare the `ListView` control to the `UITableView` control on the iOS platform and the data provider interfaces. Adapters on Android can be compared to `UITableViewSource` on iOS.

By default, `ListView` has 12 built-in views that can be accessed through the `Android.Resource.Layout` class. These layouts vary from simple single line of text to expandable grouped category views. Each layout uses several control references such as Text1, Text2, and Icon, which should be populated by the adapter assigning the values to the content fields. Implementing a custom layout is also possible by creating an AXML markup file and later referencing the markup in the adapter.

A sample custom layout implementation could look like the following:

```xml
<RelativeLayout xmlns:android="http://schemas.android.com/apk/res/
android"
    android:layout_width="fill_parent"
    android:layout_height="wrap_content"
    android:background="@drawable/CustomSelector"
    android:padding="8dp">
    <LinearLayout
        android:id="@+id/Text"
        android:orientation="vertical"
        android:layout_width="wrap_content"
        android:layout_height="wrap_content"
        android:paddingLeft="10dip">
        <TextView
            android:id="@+id/Title"
            android:layout_width="wrap_content"
            android:layout_height="wrap_content"
            android:textSize="20dip" />
        <TextView
            android:id="@+id/Description"
            android:layout_width="wrap_content"
            android:layout_height="wrap_content"
            android:textSize="14dip" />
    </LinearLayout>
    <ImageView
        android:id="@+id/Image"
        android:layout_width="48dp"
        android:layout_height="48dp"
        android:padding="5dp"
        android:src="@drawable/icon"
        android:layout_alignParentRight="true" />
</RelativeLayout>
```

We can also extend the style by adding visual state selectors (see the background color assignment in the previous sample).

The custom visual state selector implementation could be defined as the following:

```xml
<?xml version="1.0" encoding="utf-8"?>
<selector xmlns:android="http://schemas.android.com/apk/res/android">
  <item android:state_pressed="false"
        android:state_selected="false"
```

```
                android:drawable="@color/blue" />
    <item android:state_pressed="true"
          android:state_selected="false"
          android:drawable="@color/red" />
</selector>
```

Finally, the list adapter implementation would look like:

```
    public class CountriesDataAdapter : BaseAdapter<Country>
    {
        private List<Country> m_Items;

        private Activity m_Context;

        public CountriesDataAdapter(Activity context, List<Country>
items)
        {
            m_Context = context;
            m_Items = items;
        }

        public override long GetItemId(int position)
        {
            return position;
        }

        public override View GetView(int position, View convertView,
ViewGroup parent)
        {
            var item = m_Items[position];

            View view = convertView ??
m_Context.LayoutInflater
.Inflate(Resource.Layout.CustomRowView, null);

            view.FindViewById<TextView>(Resource.Id.Title).Text =
item.Name;
            view.FindViewById<TextView>(Resource.Id.Description).Text
= string.Format("In {0} region of {1}", item.Region.Name, item.Region.
Continent);
            view.FindViewById<ImageView>(Resource.Id.Image).
SetImageResource(Resource.Drawable.Icon);
```

```
            return view;
        }

        public override int Count
        {
            get { return m_Items.Count; }
        }

        public override Country this[int position]
        {
            get { return m_Items[position]; }
        }
    }
```

The preceding code should generate a view similar to the following screenshot:

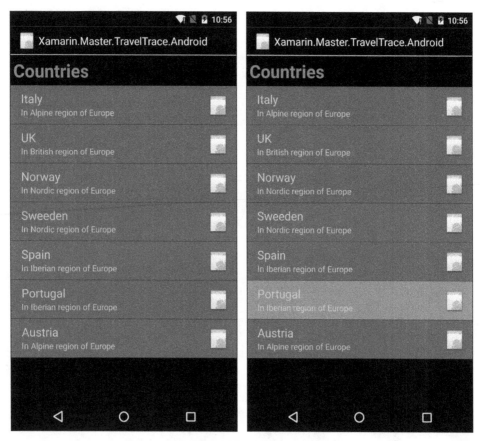

List View with custom layout

GridView (Android)

Other than the `ListView` control, on the Android platform, collections can be visualized in `ViewGroup`. View groups are used to bundle different visual trees and display the items in a scrollable view element. The most common implementation of the `ViewGroup` is the `GridView` widget. `GridView` is a scrollable grid control where content items are again provided with a `ListAdapter` implementation.

`GridView` is generally used with a homogenous set of content items. These content items consist of a set of text content and a related image item. Content items are generally referred to as tiles and they can also include several content related commands.

Tiles are conceptually similar to the live tile blocks of Modern UI design of Windows applications. They are made up of primary and secondary content. The primary content fills the entire cell (for example, album cover in a photo gallery application), while the secondary is represented by icons or text. The primary action is, in most cases, a vertical descending navigation command (navigating to the details view). Context actions related to the content item are generally considered to be the secondary content on a tile.

If the amount of actions on a content item or the content is not homogenous, it is advised to consider using cards rather than tiles in a grid view.

CardView (Android)

The `CardView` control was introduced in Android 5.0, and it can be described as a self contained content unit. The term self-contained here would refer to the fact that cards generally include multiple actions and various content-related items. Users generally do not need to resort to secondary actions (select and then use the context menu) to interact with these content items.

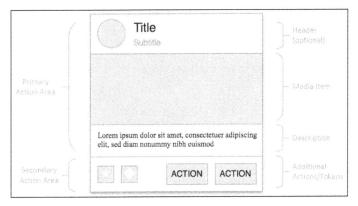

A standard card layout

Cards are generally used when there is neither the need nor the possibility for direct comparison between the collection elements and the content consists of various types of data. Cards can be interactive through the use of action buttons or, in some cases, in-content input controls. They can be expandable and generally have a fixed width.

CardView is implemented as a FrameLayout widget and can be used in association with a ListView or GridView to represent content elements.

ListView and ListBox (Windows Phone)

ListView and ListBox are the main collection visualization controls on the Windows Phone platform. ListView is a more specialized implementation of ListBox, and it is primarily used for displaying text-based content. Its counterpart ListBox is highly customizable and can be adopted to display content composed of multiple data types.

Both of these containers can be used for item-level context actions. However, ListBox, similar to CardViews on the Android platform, is used to create interactive content elements that might include actions and input controls.

Two-way data binding is available for both of these controls and items can be styled and customized using behaviors, item templates, and/or control styles. Orientation is vertical by default for both controls, but this can be set to horizontal if the content items are desired to be displayed on a horizontal line.

In case there is the need for more customization on the template level and how the items are laid out, developers can also use the ItemsControl, which is the base implementation for most of the collection views on the Windows Phone platform.

In order to customize how the items are displayed on a ListView, we would first need to create the DataTemplate that will be the template used for ListViewItems.

A sample DataTemplate declaration could look like the following:

```
<DataTemplate x:Key="SampleItemTemplate">
  <Grid>
    <Grid.ColumnDefinitions>
      <ColumnDefinition Width="Auto" />
      <ColumnDefinition />
    </Grid.ColumnDefinitions>
    <Border Margin="0,10,0,0">
      <Image Source="{Binding ImageUrl}" Height="80" Width="80" />
    </Border>
    <StackPanel Grid.Column="1" Margin="15,0,0,0">
      <TextBlock Text="{Binding Title}"
```

```
      Style="{ThemeResource ListViewItemTextBlockStyle}" />
    <TextBlock Text="{Binding Subtitle}"
      Style="{ThemeResource ListViewItemSubheaderTextBlockStyle}" />
  </StackPanel>
  </Grid>
</DataTemplate>
```

Once our template is ready, we can assign the template to our `ListView` together with the collection data source, which is a list of simple `SampleItem` objects with the properties described in the `DataTemplate`.

The code is as follows:

```
<Grid>
  <ListView
    ItemTemplate="{StaticResource SampleItemTemplate}"
    ItemsSource="{Binding MyItems}" />
</Grid>
```

Now, the content items are displayed in the `ListView` in a two-column style with an image, title, and description text.

GridView (Windows Phone)

`GridView` is another implementation of the `ItemsControl` on the Windows Phone platform, which allows the developers to create collection views in a flow layout. `GridView` should generally be preferred over `ListBox` or `ListView` when dealing with media elements.

ListView versus GridView

Similar to the previously defined elements, `GridView` supports two-way data binding and can be customized using standard methodologies.

Virtualizing panels (Windows Phone)

It is important to realize the fact that mobile platforms are not as performant as desktop or tablet devices. Especially when dealing with big sets of data, even though applications can perform well visually on a desktop workstation, memory resources might cause the UI to flicker, lag, or even block on a mobile device. In order to decrease the memory usage and improve performance by means of loading only the needed data, Windows Runtime provides the virtualizing panel controls (for example, `VirtualizingStackPanel`). `ItemsControl`, which is the base for most of the collection view controls described here, supports both data and UI virtualizations.

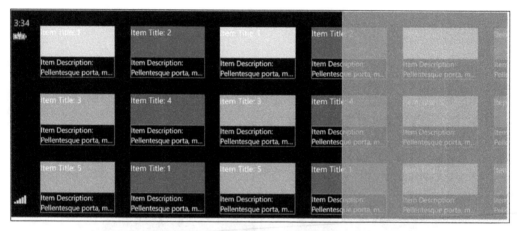

UI Virtualization on Windows Runtime

UI virtualization deals with the controls being rendered on the application viewport. The application list view bound to a large number of items, in this case, does not need to render and keep the controls in the runtime memory but only deal with the ones that are in the viewport. In this paradigm, controls that are removed from the screen with a scrolling action need to be destroyed and redrawn if the user scrolls back.

Data virtualization deals with paged data sources. For instance, with a "virtualizable" data source (a collection that implements `ISupportIncrementalLoading`), only the data needed for the current viewport is loaded into the application and additional batches are requested from the data source when the UI control needs to display additional items. Random access virtualization lets developers retrieve a subset of data on any random ordinal. For this type of data virtualization, the data source needs to implement `INotifyCollectionChanged` and `IObservableVector`.

Modal views

Modal views are temporary view components that can provide an interactive interface to get the user's input on a certain task or decide on the execution path of a workflow. It is also common to use alert dialogs to inform the user about critical information that is crucial for the execution of the application.

Popover and alerts (iOS)

The iOS platform provides various modal dialogs to display, edit, and manipulate data in different scenarios. Each of these dialog types look different but the common denominator is the fact that they always get the focus and are displayed on the highest layer on the screen, while the content under the dialog is hidden with a translucent overlay layer.

Action sheets are one of the most-frequently used modal dialogs. This dialog type is generally used to give the user an option before starting a task or cancelling the task. It is generally displayed as a list of buttons; the last of which is generally the "cancel" button, at the bottom of the screen.

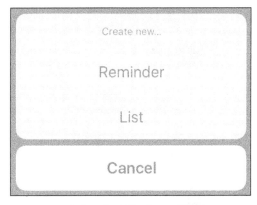

Action sheet display on iOS

Action sheets can be initialized using a UIAlertController and specifying the UIAlertControllerStyleActionSheet. If the screen size permits (on a horizontally regular environment), action sheets are displayed as a popover.

Alert dialogs are another type of modal dialogs on iOS. Alerts are generally used to inform or ask consent from the user about an issue that affects the execution of the application. Unlike action sheets, alert dialogs can contain descriptive text, a title, and even a text input field.

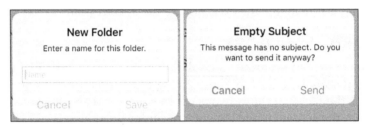

Alert dialog with input field and with only description and title

Alert dialogs can be invoked with `UIAlertController`, using the `UIAlertControllerStyleAlert`. Alert dialogs should avoid any kind of redundant, informal, and negative content. If the title provides enough information for the user to continue with the execution, description text could be omitted.

Popovers are another type of temporary context views on the iOS platform. However, popovers only are displayed on a horizontally regular environment (in both portrait and landscape in iPad, and only in landscape rotation in iPhone 6 Plus). In horizontally compact environments, they are displayed as full screen modal dialogs.

In order to initialize a popover, `UIPopoverPresentationController` can be used.

Modal dialogs are another type of temporary view display used on iOS. Modal dialogs can be used in scenarios where a self-contained and compact view is needed to execute a very particular task or workflow.

Modal dialog with page sheet style

Modal dialogs can be created using the UIPresentationController with various modal presentation styles (full screen, page sheet, form sheet, and current context). However, the presentation styles associated with modal dialogs behave almost the same on horizontally compact environments (all iPhone models except iPhone 6 Plus in landscape orientation).

Flyout, popups, and menus (Windows Phone)

Flyouts are the main modal dialogs on the Windows Phone platform. They can be used in various scenarios, including showing a context menu, showing additional details of an item, or getting consent from the user. The common behavior of different types of flyouts is that they are always displayed with the highest z-index on screen and the elements underneath are disabled with a translucent overlay. Flyouts have, by default, a light-dismiss mechanism. In other words, they can be dismissed if the user taps anywhere outside the flyout control's borders.

Flyouts are generally associated with another control on the current view either by using the attached properties or using the ShowAt function of the Flyout class. The Content property of the Flyout class is used to assign a UIElement to display on screen.

```
var flyout = new Flyout();
var stackPanel = new StackPanel { Orientation = Orientation.
Vertical, Margin = new Thickness(5)};
var textBlock = new TextBlock { Text = "Flyout Text Content",
FontSize = 20 };
var textInput = new TextBox { PlaceholderText = "Input Value",
FontSize = 18 };
var button = new Button { Content = "Apply", FontSize = 18 };
stackPanel.Children.Add(textBlock);
stackPanel.Children.Add(textInput);
stackPanel.Children.Add(button);
flyout.Content = stackPanel;
flyout.ShowAt(TextBlock);
```

The preceding sample code would create a flyout which has text content, an input field, and a button as its content:

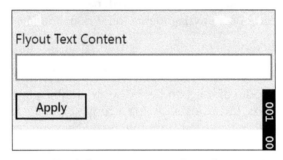

Simple flyout menu on Windows Phone

 In spite of the fact that flyouts are always attached to a UIElement (either using XAML or through code) and the dialog should be displayed in the vicinity of the associated element, on Windows Phone, flyouts behave like message dialogs displaying on the top of the screen.

In Windows Runtime, it is possible to use the derived types of flyouts for specific scenarios. MenuFlyout, TimePickerFlyout, and DateTimePickerFlyout are examples for these implementations.

Menu Flyout Usage

Other than flyouts, popup control can also be used to display a temporary view or details of a content item. Popups are generally stand-alone controls and can directly be included in the view XAML. They can optionally use light-dismiss and can be shown or hidden using the IsOpen property.

For alert dialogs or critical input requirements, the MessageDialog class provides developers a familiar implementation tool. MessageDialog is a simple dialog used to display text content and numerous UI commands. The UICommand class represents a button and the associated action (if any) and is used to display actions on the dialog and provide a result to the dialog once selected by the user. The following implementation creates a message dialog with a text field and two commands:

```
MessageDialog dialog = new MessageDialog("You are about to delete an
important item", "Important Deletion");
dialog.Commands.Add(new UICommand("Sure"));
dialog.Commands.Add(new UICommand("Not Really"));
dialog.ShowAsync();
```

This would be shown on the UI similar to how flyouts are visualized:

MessageDialog example on Windows Phone

Dialogs (Android)

Dialogs on Android can be implemented as simple as an alert dialog or a full screen dialog that retrieves the required form data to continue the current task. Dialogs behave the same way as modal dialog implementations on other platforms; they interrupt the current task and are displayed on top of the underlying layer. The content underneath is hidden with a translucent grey overlay layer.

Simple alert dialogs, like their parallel implementations on other platforms, consist of a title, a descriptive content, and confirmation actions. They are invoked on critical scenarios where the user's input is crucial to continue with the execution.

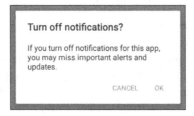

Android Alert Dialog

It is important to be careful to avoid any ambiguity in the descriptive content and the action button contents.

Another popular dialog used in Android applications are the context menu dialogs. This type of dialog does not require any confirmation once the item from the list is selected. They also have the light dismiss behavior. If the dialogs have additional information about the selection item and maybe additional actions, they are referred to as simple dialogs. The selection on these dialogs do not require confirmation either.

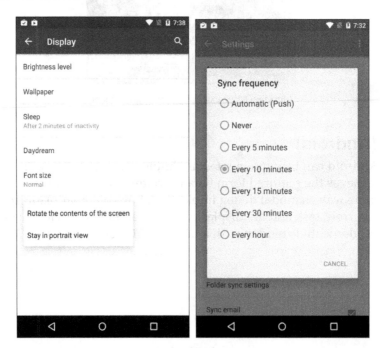

Android Dialogs

If the dialog implementation requires the user to explicitly confirm the choice made, these dialogs are generally referred to as confirmation dialogs. It is common to have a "cancel" button at the bottom of the dialog screen so the previous selected option can be kept.

Text views

On all three platforms, with the emergence of the minimalist design inclinations, typography and text content items became the focus of UX design. Each platform has well-defined guidelines on font sizes and typefaces for different scenarios. More importantly, each of these platforms has specialized ways to display and edit rich text formats.

- **Windows**: On the Windows Phone platform, Run elements are used to define specific sections of text that have a certain formatting applied to. Run elements can then be included in `TextBlock` elements or `RichTextBlock` controls. In addition to the Runs, `RichTextBlocks` can be used in conjunction with HTML-like styling elements (for example, bold, span, italics, and so on). Using the `RichTextBlocks` and `RichTextBlockOverflow` as a container, any shape and style text displays can be supported in Windows Phone applications.

- **Android**: On the Android platform, text formatting is achieved using the so-called spans. There are numerous pre-styled span implementations such as `RelativeSizeSpan`, `ForegroundColorSpan`, and `ClickableSpan`. These span implementations are used to set certain sections of a `SpannableString` with the described styles. There is a `SpannableStringBuilder` class that can be used to create the styled paragraphs/text content. Once the `SpannableString` is complete, it can be used as content for the `TextView` control.

- **iOS**: On the iOS platform, text-related features and controls are introduced by the Core Text library. The `UITextView` control is the visualization element in this library. Text formatting is achieved by using the `NSMutableAttributedText` class. For attributed text content, different text ranges can be set to use certain attributes such as `NSUnderlineStyleAttribute`, `NSBackgroundColorAttribute`, and so on. When displaying attributed text blocks a `NSTextContainer` can be used to describe a shape as line fragments in which the text should be displayed.

Web views

Web view controls are used to display rich HTML content on Xamarin target platforms. These web view controls build their own navigation stack independent from the application runtime. On Android and Windows phone, it is also possible to inject JavaScript into the HTML content that is being displayed on the control.

On all the platforms, it is possible to load not only remote, but also local web applications from the application resources.

Feedback

One of the pillars of modern application design is keeping the user informed at all times about the actions being executed by the application and the progress of these tasks. Even if the application is dealing with a blocking call (the execution cannot continue before finishing the task), displaying a progress ring creates the illusion that the application is still responsive.

Progress indicators can be categorized into two groups: indeterminate and determinate.

Indeterminate progress

Indeterminate tasks and the associated progress indicators are related to the operations where the application cannot provide neither an estimated completion time nor progress information. These operations might depend on completion of multiple sub-procedures and might be related to the whole application or only a single UI element.

With indeterminate processes, we first need to decide on how crucial the process is for the application. If the application cannot continue without completing the current process, this would be an application-level blocking call. In cases of blocking calls (involving single step or multiple steps), it is a good idea to use a progress ring on the main content area. A good example for this scenario would be a main client trying to retrieve e-mail messages from the server without knowing how many items there are on the server. If there are multiple steps involved in this process, you can additionally show an information text near or over the progress ring.

This implementation on Android can be achieved with the `ProgressDialog` class. Instantiating this control provides a modal dialog with the possibility to include a descriptive text. It is important to set the indeterminate flag to true before displaying it on the UI.

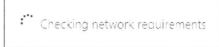

Progress rings on Android, iOS and Windows Phone

On iOS, the same visualization is achieved with the `UIActivityIndicatorView`. You can modify the behavior to animate and change the color.

On Windows Phone, the `ProgressRing` class provides the same type of functionality.

In indeterminate scenarios where the process being executed does not stop the user from continuing with application interaction, it is better to give a more subtle indication about the process and the controls involved in the execution. This can be achieved by using a progress ring or a bar in the vicinity of or over the control where the process started. On iOS, the only distinction between the progress bar and the ring is the process being determinate or indeterminate. However, on Android and Windows Phone, a progress bar can also act as an indeterminate task indicator. On the Windows Phone platform, it is also general practice to display an indeterminate progress bar on top of the screen if the process is an application level task, but the interaction with the application can continue without waiting for the result of this process.

Determinate progress

Determinate tasks and associated indicators are related to processes where the application can provide a current state information to the user. A determinate progress indicator of choice on Xamarin target platforms is the progress bar. Progress bars, while providing a visual indication of the current completion state of the process, can also include a label giving a text description of the current state of the task.

It is important to also provide a cancellation method (for example, a cancel button near the progress bar) if the process is relatively long.

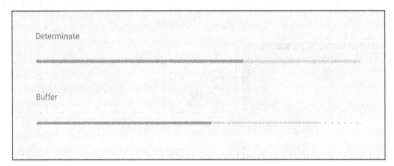

Android determinate progress bar displays

On the Android platform, in addition to the progress indication, a buffering percentage can also be displayed on the progress bar.

User interaction

Another important element in cross-platform development projects is the set of user interaction patterns for the application. Users already using the application on other platforms would want to find the same interaction patterns on clients running on another platform. This decision process gets even more complicated with platform specific interaction patterns, since the application should provide a familiar interface for platform users. It is important to achieve a balanced compromise between platform nativity and application identity in such scenarios and find the optimum solution.

A good example for branding by means of using an interaction pattern, would be the "pull-to-refresh" interactive pattern used in iOS applications. Most application providers dealing with information feeds (for example, Facebook, Twitter, and so on) used this implementation in their iOS applications. Even though this is not a native interaction pattern on Android and Windows Phone, a similar approach quickly became popular on these platforms; hence, most developers and users are now adopting this use-case on various platforms.

Interactive controls

In most cases, applications built for Xamarin target platforms would require input and other interactive controls to collect necessary information from the user. By interactive, we are referring to almost all the UI controls that can be used in a Xamarin application. In this case, even a simple filter dropdown control to select a different view perspective would be an interaction control, requesting information from the user display appropriate data or perspective.

Text input

Text input fields are one of the most used type of input fields. Text fields can be implemented as a single line of text or as a multiline. An important aspect of text fields is the fact that as soon as a text input field gets selected on a touch-enabled device, the virtual keyboard appears on the screen. It is generally a good idea to keep this in mind while designing the user interface and implementing it later on.

On iOS, while the `UITextField` provides an input mechanism for single line of text requirements, `UITextView` can be used to create editable rich text content. Both of these controls provide options such as capitalization and correction.

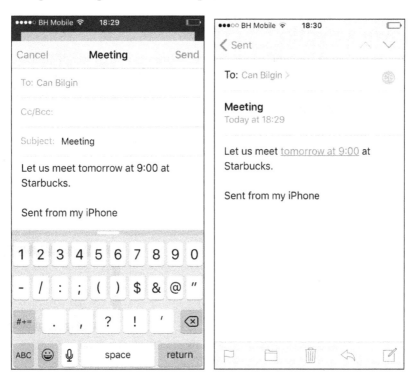

UITextView Edit and Read-only Views

Additionally, UITextView provides detectors that can transform Internet addresses to links, addresses to map links, phone numbers into deep-links to make a phone call, and date/time values to calendar event items.

Android text input fields are similar to the ones on iOS platform. The key difference is that on Android, instead of two different controls, only the EditText control exists for multiline and single line text inputs. This is achieved by settings the InputType property of the control (or inputType attribute in AXML). Other input scopes, besides the text format, can be set such as postal address, capitalized words, autocorrect, and capitalized sentence beginnings. Note that these scope parameters are bit-wise combinations. Another specialized control that provides auto suggestions is the AutoCompleteTextView, to which developers can assign an ArrayAdapter as a source for suggestions.

On Windows Phone, TextBox is the most commonly used text input control. It can be highly customized to meet the previously mentioned requirements. Moreover, the input scope field lets developers control the virtual keyboard displayed for entering the value. For instance, setting the scope to be a telephone number would display a keyboard with only digits. AutoSuggestBox, PasswordBox, and RichEditBox are other controls that can be used for more specialized scenarios.

Dropdown selection

Dropdown elements can be used, on each platform, utilizing the specialized controls. While the UIPickerView is used on iOS, the same implementation is achieved on Android by so-called spinners. Spinners, very much like other content-driven controls, are populated with a SpinnerAdapter.

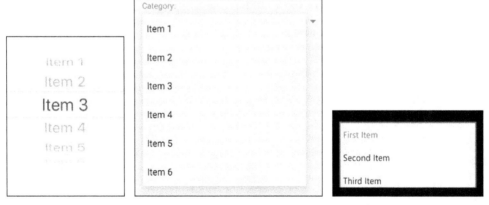

Dropdown controls on iOS, Android and Windows Phone

In addition to the spinner control, simple menu dialogs can also be used for users' input. Windows Runtime provides additional specialized controls, the ComboBox and ListView, for different selection use cases.

Option selection

Similar to the radio or check boxes on HTML forms, each platform provides options related UI elements. On Android, specialized controls for this scenario are Checkbox, RadioButton, and ToggleButton. Starting with Android 4.0 (API 14), Switch control can also be used. Other than the visual difference between these controls, the behavior is the same. On iOS, the main toggle control for Boolean data types is the Switch. Similar to Android, Windows Phone offers checkbox, radio button, and toggle switch control with option selections and Boolean types.

> There are many other controls on each platform, and each provides a specific use case for different UI interaction scenarios. UX guides for Windows Runtime and Material Design are great resources for the respective platforms. Even though the Apple human interface design documents do not provide extensive UX guidelines as the other platforms, they are great resources to learn about user control use cases.

Gestures

When developing for Xamarin target platforms, you should always keep in mind that the devices that are going to run the application will most probably have a touchscreen.

Touchscreen devices, apart from the classic pointer-like gestures (for example, tap, double tap, scroll, and so on), also provide various interaction gestures that help developers create an interface that can interact with the user in a more natural way.

	Tap	In most scenarios, the tap gesture is analogous to a single click with a pointer device. It is primarily used to select a control.
	Long Press	Long press or tap and hold is used to access a context menu on Windows Phone. It is used for item selection on Android.
	Double-Tap	Double tap is generally used for scaling up / zooming-in on a control.
	Swipe Down	Swipe down or pan down is used on vertical scroll scenarios. Also, list controls support swipe down for selection on Windows. It is also common to be used with "Pull to Refresh" implementations.
	Swipe Right	Similar to swipe down, swipe right is used on vertical scroll scenarios and sibling navigation scenarios. It is called "flick" if the gesture is fast.
	Swipe Left	This is same as other pan gestures. It can also be used to delete a list item on iOS and Windows Phone 10.
	Swipe Up	This is another panning gesture. It can additionally be used to reveal a bottom sheet on Android applications.
	Tap & Drag	This is generally used as an active gesture to interact with draggable components.
	Pinch Out	This is used in active canvas application patterns. It is used to zoom in on a view. On Windows, semantic zoom control makes use of this.
	Pinch In	This is similar to the Pinch-Out gesture and is used to zoom out of an active content area of application screen (for example, zoom in on a photo).
	Rotate	This is another gesture used on active canvas applications (for example, a map client). It is used to rotate the current view-port.

Common Gestures

While some of these gestures are already implemented by out-of-box controls on Xamarin platforms, there might be scenarios where you need to use them to create a new interaction use case in your application. For these type of requirements, specialized implementations can be found on respective frameworks.

On the iOS platform, the starting point for gesture recognizer implementation is the abstract class UIGestureRecognizer. There are numerous implementations of gesture recognizer in the UIKit and they can be combined and used with delegate implementations.

On Android, the GestureDetector class and the IOnGestureListener interface can be used to provide implementations for various gesture events and user actions. Classic interaction events such as pan gestures and tap actions can already be accessed through the OnTouchEvent method of any Activity implementation.

On the Windows Phone platform, most of the default controls provide interaction with pointer or touch events for classic manipulation scenarios. However, for more complicated gestures, the GestureRecognizer class available in the Windows. UI.Input namespace can be used.

Summary

This chapter presented an overview of the design philosophy of, and patterns on, Xamarin target platforms. The design elements section outlined the main controls and layouts that are at the disposal of designers and developers while providing various content display strategies. There were additional sections about interactive and modern user interface design.

Even though each platform provides its own UI design patterns and guidelines, the main focus of the design effort in a cross-platform application is to find an optimal compromise between native look-and-feel and application brand design.

In the next chapter, we will discuss the Xamarin.Forms framework and make use of the correlation between the design elements that are outlined here.

8
Xamarin.Forms

Xamarin.Forms is an extension module to Xamarin compiler technologies; an abstraction layer on top of the native UI components on target platforms. This chapter will focus on the various features and extensibility options of Xamarin.Forms that help developers create cross-platform application user interfaces that can then be compiled into Xamarin projects, increasing the code-sharing quality markers, and making cross-platform application development projects more manageable and unified. This chapter is divided into the following sections:

- Under the hood
- Components
- Extending forms
- Patterns and best practices

Under the hood

As previously mentioned, Xamarin, being a cross-platform development framework, provides developers the toolset to create applications that depend on and use the same code base. The shared amount of code is directly proportional to the manageability in these types of implementation.

Xamarin.Forms adds an abstraction layer on top of the mono runtime on Android and the pre-compiler .NET stack on iOS platforms. This abstraction layer's sole responsibility is to provide the Xamarin compilers with the necessary instructions to normalize the code or markup for GUI elements to render native controls in Xamarin apps. Since the platform language for Xamarin is C#, **Extensible Application Markup Language (XAML)** is the design markup language of choice. Xamarin.Forms provides the same abstraction as a runtime library for Windows Store applications.

The abstraction layer provided by Xamarin.Forms makes use of the similar UI elements and layout patterns which were illustrated in the previous chapter (see *Chapter 7, View Elements*). In this context, Xamarin.Forms only provides controls and views that are common to all three platforms and omits platform-specific UI elements. It is important to understand that Xamarin.Forms is not a replacement for a native user interface implementation, but more of a foundation to build upon while creating cross-platform applications.

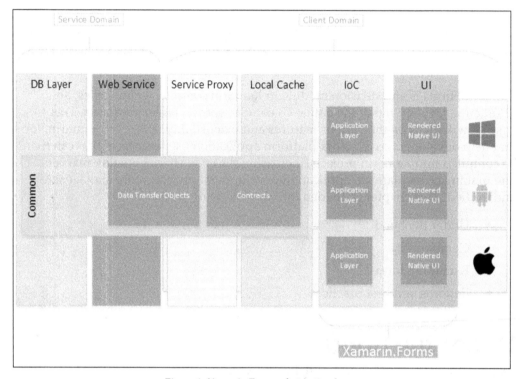

Figure 1: Xamarin.Forms abstraction layer

Xamarin.Forms not only provides a uniform native UI development framework, but also additional features that are generally associated with loosely-coupled UI development, such as data binding, dependency injection, and messenger infrastructure. To a certain extent, these features render third-party MVVM libraries used in various mobile application projects obsolete.

Anatomy of Xamarin.Forms

Xamarin.Forms libraries are distributed through NuGet packages and can be freely included in cross-platform development projects.

Whilst the NuGet package for iOS does not present any dependencies, the Android and Windows Phone versions depend on several support libraries (that is, WPToolKit for Windows Phone; and several design and compatibility packages for Android).

The Xamarin.Forms.Core library contains the UI elements and the necessary XAML declarations together with additional features related to data binding and similar operations. This assembly can be included in portable class library projects that provide the view implementation to platform-specific projects. Native client projects, in return, should reference Xamarin.Forms.Core and the platform-specific assemblies of Xamarin.Forms (for example, Xamarin.Forms.Platform.iOS). Xamarin. Forms platform libraries contain the so-called renderer implementations that are responsible for rendering Xamarin.Form elements using native controls. In other words, these platform assemblies provide the mapping between native elements and their Xamarin. Forms counterparts.

Project structure

In order to create a Xamarin.Forms application project targeting iOS, Android, and/ or Windows Phone 8, it is sufficient to use one of the project templates located in the **Cross-Platform** section. While the portable library project template makes use of a PCL to create the Xamarin.Forms application boilerplate, the shared project template creates a shared project with file references linked to the native client app projects.

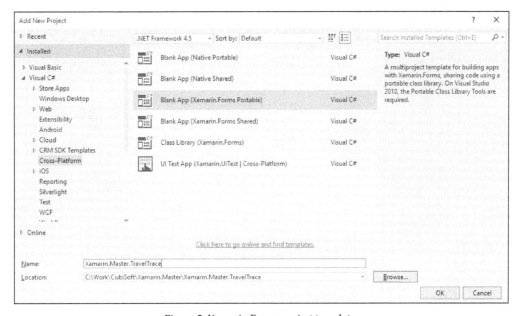

Figure 2: Xamarin.Forms project templates

Project templates can be found in the **Mobile Apps** section in older versions of Xamarin.

Once the project is initialized, by selecting the **Blank App (Xamarin.Forms Portable)** project template, the created solution will include four projects, one project carrying the same name as the entered project name and three platform-specific projects with the platform suffixes.

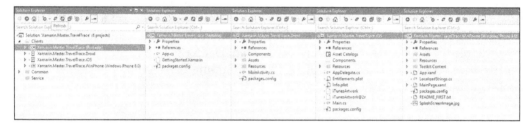

Figure 3: Xamarin.Forms solution main view and project scopes

One caveat of using this project template for Xamarin.Forms is the fact that other platforms that are actually supported by this framework (for example, Windows Phone 8.1 and Windows 10) are not included in this multi-project template. These projects can be created manually, and the NuGet package for Xamarin.Forms can be added using the NuGet package manager. It is also important to mention that the NuGet package referenced in the project template might not be the latest version of Xamarin.Forms and therefore can be updated using the NuGet package manager.

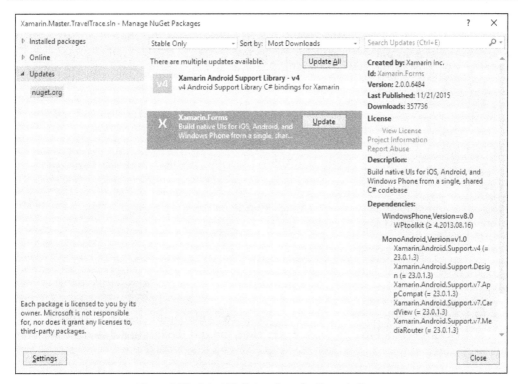

Figure 4: The latest NuGet package for Xamarin.Forms

If you take a look at the generated code in the portable library, `App.cs`, and the platform-specific projects, the implementation pattern immediately becomes apparent.

The Xamarin.Forms implementation contains the application class implementation as the root node. This application is initialized and invoked by the generated code in the app delegates in platform-specific projects (similar to the following code excerpt from the Xamarin.Forms iOS application sample):

```
[Register("AppDelegate")]
public partial class AppDelegate : global::Xamarin.Forms.Platform.iOS.
FormsApplicationDelegate
{
    public override bool FinishedLaunching(UIApplication app,
NSDictionary options)
    {
        global::Xamarin.Forms.Forms.Init();
        LoadApplication(new App());

        return base.FinishedLaunching(app, options);
    }
}
```

The initialization code for the app in the template boilerplate creates a content page with a single label in a StackLayout element and designates this view as the main page:

```
public App()
{
    // The root page of your application
    MainPage = new ContentPage
    {
        Content = new StackLayout
        {
            VerticalOptions = LayoutOptions.Center,
            Children = {
                new Label {
                    XAlign = TextAlignment.Center,
                    Text = "Welcome to Xamarin Forms!"
                }
            }
        }
    };
}
```

As you can see, the Xamarin.Forms application structure is made up of controls wrapped in different layout configurations that are presented through various page types.

Components

Xamarin.Forms components can be categorized into three main groups according to their position in the view hierarchy and their usage.

Pages

Conceptually, pages are navigational elements. They provide a general hierarchical organization of the view elements whilst also acting as a container for the layouts. There are various page types that can be inherited and implemented or designed using XAML markups.

Tabbed page

When discussing the top-level navigation pages in the previous chapter, we mentioned several controls that can provide horizontal navigation throughout top-level pages. Using Xamarin.Forms, `TabbedPage` allows developers to create these horizontal navigational view elements. `TabbedPage` generates a tabbed action bar and associated activities on Android. On Windows Phone, the generated view contains a pivot control. Finally on iOS, generated view contains a tab bar and associated views.

`TabbedPage` contains the navigation pages as its children (that is, the `Children` property accepts different page implementations), and the page titles of the child elements are used as navigation links.

Implementing the tabbed view example from the previous chapter for our TravelTrace application would look similar to the following snippet:

```
var tabbedPage = new TabbedPage();

tabbedPage.Children.Add(new ContentPage
{
    Title = "Recent",
    Content = new StackLayout
    {
        VerticalOptions = LayoutOptions.Center,
        Children = {
            new Label {
                HorizontalTextAlignment = TextAlignment.Center,
```

```
                    Text = "Recent uploads page"
                }
            }
        }
});

// ...
// TODO: Add the other tab nav items

MainPage = tabbedPage;
```

The same implementation can be done using XAML and creating a
`TabbedPage` implementation:

```xml
<TabbedPage xmlns="http://xamarin.com/schemas/2014/forms"
  xmlns:x="http://schemas.microsoft.com/winfx/2009/xaml"
  x:Class="Xamarin.Master.TravelTrace.Views.MainTabView">
  <ContentPage Title="Recent" Icon="social.png">
    <StackLayout VerticalOptions="Center">
      <Label Text="Recent uploads page"
        HorizontalTextAlignment="Center"></Label>
    </StackLayout>
  </ContentPage>
  <ContentPage Title="Local" Icon="map.png">
    <StackLayout VerticalOptions="Center">
      <Label Text="Local landmarks page"
        HorizontalTextAlignment="Center"></Label>
    </StackLayout>
  </ContentPage>
  <ContentPage Title="Friends" Icon="people.png">
    <StackLayout VerticalOptions="Center">
      <Label Text="Friends related page"
        HorizontalTextAlignment="Center"></Label>
    </StackLayout>
  </ContentPage>
</TabbedPage>
```

Assigning the newly created `MainTabView` class instance to `MainPage` in `App.cs` would result in the same view as the code implementation:

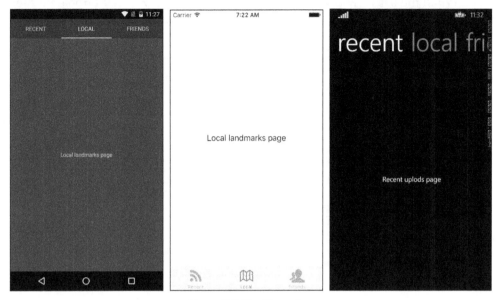

Figure 5: TabbedPage view

It is important here to mention that the `Icon` property provided for individual peers in a `TabbedPage` implementation only applies to the iOS platform. Icons in tab and pivot views are not supported by Xamarin and it is not an accepted design approach for Android and Windows Phone.

The MasterDetail page

The example with the tabbed view satisfies the horizontal navigation requirements of our design, but we also need a navigation drawer and associated main menu navigation items for our Android applications.

`MasterDetailPage` provides a structure in which the master page selection menu can initiate a navigation request on the detail page. Moreover, if the content of the `Detail` page is encapsulated in a `NavigationPage`, the generated view is added to the navigation stack so that the previously displayed pages can easily be pulled into the master view using the event methods. In order to include an additional layer of navigation and a global menu, we can now use the `MasterDetailPage` class to create the desired navigation structure.

The first step of the implementation is to create our master view. The master view in this case will include a simple list view with menu and a profile display as the list header. When the list view content items are selected, we can either bubble up the event to the `MasterDetailPage` or pass the parent page as a parameter to the menu page we are implementing.

```
public NavigationMenuView(Page root)
{
    Icon = "toggle.png";

    InitializeComponent();

    ListViewMenu.ItemsSource = m_MenuItems =
        new List<Tuple<string, string, string>
        {
            new Tuple<string, string, string>("Profile",
                "profile", "profileicon.png"),
            new Tuple<string, string, string>("Map", "map",
                "mapicon.png"),
            new Tuple<string, string, string>("Settings",
                "settings", "settingsicon.png")
        };

    ListViewMenu.SelectedItem = m_MenuItems[0];

    ListViewMenu.ItemSelected += async (sender, e) =>
    {
        if(ListViewMenu.SelectedItem == null)
            return;

        // TODO: Implement the navigation strategy
        Debug.WriteLine("Item selected {0}",
            ((Tuple<string, string, string>)e.SelectedItem).Item2);
    };
}
```

In this implementation, we are using a `Tuple` with three parameters for the label, tag, and icon of the menu item. It would, of course, be better to implement a class to contain these data values.

Now we can construct our `MasterDetailPage` by setting the `Master` and `Detail` properties:

```
var masterDetailPage = new MasterDetailPage();

// Can select any of the behaviors:
// Default, Popover, Split, SplitOnLandscape, SplitOnPortrait
```

```
masterDetailPage.MasterBehavior = MasterBehavior.Popover;
masterDetailPage.Master = new NavigationMenuView(masterDetailPage);
masterDetailPage.Detail = new NavigationPage(new ContentPage
{
    Title = "Detail Page",
    Content = new StackLayout
    {
        VerticalOptions = LayoutOptions.Center,
        Children = {
            new Label {
                HorizontalTextAlignment = TextAlignment.Center,
                Text = "Here is the Detail"
            }
        }
    }
});

MainPage = masterDetailPage;
```

`MasterBehavior` can be adjusted according to the platform. In this example, we will be using the popover behavior, which displays a flyout and a toggle button in the main app bar on Android and creates a navigation command icon to open the flyout on other platforms.

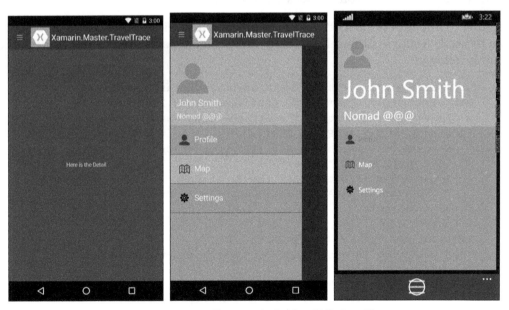

Figure 6: Navigation flyout on Android and Windows Phone

When using `MasterDetailPage`, it is important to anticipate the outcome of the design decisions made in Xamarin.Forms markups so that final applications for the target platforms still follow the design guidelines.

NavigationPage

`NavigationPage` is the most abstract implementation of the `Page` class. The main purpose of using NavigationPage is to create a navigational stack in the application context. This navigational context is supported natively on Windows Phone. However, other platforms do not create a stack for previously viewed pages. Using `NavigationPage`, one can utilize the items in the navigational history and manipulate the stack using push and pop methods.

CarouselPage

`CarouselPage` is another horizontal navigation implementation that the user can use to navigate through the peer pages using swipe or flick gestures. `CarouselPage` is very similar to the panorama view and pivot controls from the Windows Phone 7 platform, except for the fact that `CarouselPage` has strict snap points (that is, when the free scrolling view snaps to the borders of a control or a page) and it does not have an endless loop of items, in contrast with pivot control, but instead has more linear navigation. Behaviorally, it resembles and uses a similar navigation strategy as the `FlipView` control from Windows Runtime.

In order to initiate a carousel-type navigation structure, either XAML or code-behind can be used. A simple carousel view with three content page implementations would look as follows:

```
<CarouselPage xmlns="http://xamarin.com/schemas/2014/forms"
  xmlns:x="http://schemas.microsoft.com/winfx/2009/xaml"
  x:Class="Xamarin.Master.TravelTrace.Views.GuidesView">
  <ContentPage Title="First Peer">
    <StackLayout  HeightRequest="50" VerticalOptions="Center"
      BackgroundColor="Silver">
      <Label Text="Content for the First Peer"
        HorizontalTextAlignment="Center"></Label>
    </StackLayout>
  </ContentPage>
  <ContentPage Title="Second Per">
    <StackLayout HeightRequest="50" VerticalOptions="Center"
      BackgroundColor="Gray">
      <Label Text="Content for the Second Peer"
        HorizontalTextAlignment="Center"></Label>
    </StackLayout>
  </ContentPage>
```

```
    <ContentPage Title="Third Peer">
      <StackLayout HeightRequest="50" VerticalOptions="Center"
        BackgroundColor="Silver">
        <Label Text="Content for the Third Peer"
          HorizontalTextAlignment="Center"></Label>
      </StackLayout>
    </ContentPage>
  </CarouselPage>
```

The resulting view would be a container for touch-initiated horizontal navigation between peers.

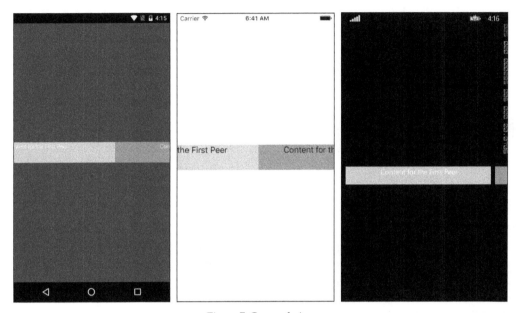

Figure 7: Carousel view

ContentPage

ContentPage is a simple page implementation used generally in cooperation with previously described page structures. It can be described as the actual content presenter. Child views in other navigation implementations are generally made up of ContentPage implementations.

In order to set the content to be visualized on the user interface, you can use the Content property, which accepts a list of view objects. Layout elements are generally used as the direct children of ContentPage and other user controls are appended to this visual tree.

Layouts

Layouts are structural design elements that allow developers to organize the UI controls using various strategies. We can classify layouts into two groups according to their class inheritance hierarchy: single view and multiple view.

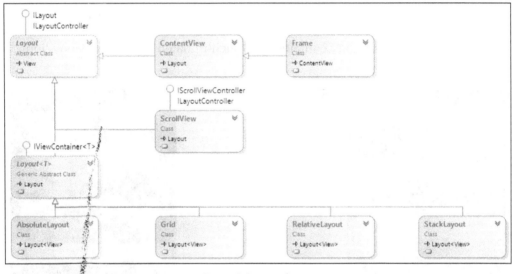

Figure 8: Layout classes

Single view layouts are direct descendants of the base layout implementation and they are capable of displaying only a single view item (they can also be a branch of a visual tree). Examples of this category are ContentView, Frame, and ScrollView. ContentView and Frame elements are rarely used and can be helpful while dealing with fewer content elements and/or an application with an active screen pattern (for example, a drawing application would use a single canvas implementation with absolute positioning; drawn geometry items would be the children of the canvas).

ScrollView, on the other hand, is one of the most popular controls and can be used together with another layout element, such as StackLayout. When used with StackLayout, if the calculated height of StackLayout is greater than the client area, the parent control, ScrollView, makes it possible to change the viewport of the child control. Even though it is not very common, ScrollView can still be used with simple controls such as Label or Image.

For instance, if we were to implement the primary content of the `TabbedPage` created in the previous section, we can use a `ScrollView` to display the `StackLayout` that is displaying the recently uploaded items from the TravelTrace server. The markup for this implementation would look similar to the following snippet:

```
<ScrollView>
  <StackLayout x:Name="StackLayout">
    <Grid Padding="10" ColumnSpacing="4">…</Grid>
    <Grid Padding="10" ColumnSpacing="4">…</Grid>
    <!-- Omitted for clarity -->
  </StackLayout>
</ScrollView>
```

It would be displayed almost like a scrolling `ListView:`.

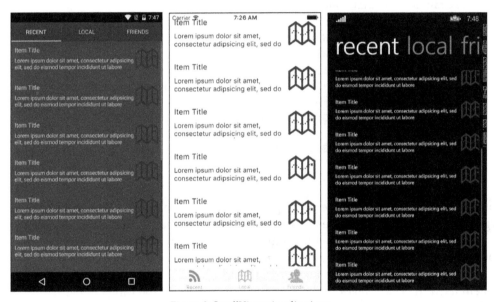

Figure 9: ScrollView visualizations

 Under normal circumstances, when dealing with a long list of data items, `ListView` should be the main control to be used. This implementation is only for demonstration purposes.

The multi-page layouts category consists of `AbsoluteLayout`, `Grid`, `RelativeLayout`, and, as seen in the previous example, `StackLayout`. Each layout is used for a specific scenario for various design-related requirements.

`Grid`, similar to the `Grid` in Windows Presentation Foundation, is used to organize child elements in a grid structure. The initial step of creating a grid is to define `ColumnDefinitions` and `RowDefinitions`, which describe the cells that are going to be used to render the elements. After this step, view elements can be added to the grid using the attached properties of `Grid`, such as `Grid.Row`, `Grid.Column`, `Grid.RowSpan`, and `Grid.ColumnSpan`.

Using the example cells from the previous implementation, we could have a classic cell view with two lines of text and an image on the right-most section of the cell:

```
<Grid Padding="10" ColumnSpacing="4">
  <Grid.RowDefinitions>
    <RowDefinition Height="Auto" />
    <RowDefinition Height="40" />
  </Grid.RowDefinitions>
  <Grid.ColumnDefinitions>
    <ColumnDefinition Width="*" />
    <ColumnDefinition Width="60" />
  </Grid.ColumnDefinitions>
  <Image Grid.RowSpan="2" Grid.Column="1" Source="mapicon.png"
    HeightRequest="40" WidthRequest="40"/>
  <Label Grid.Row="0" Grid.Column="0" Text="Item Title"
  FontSize="16"/>
  <Label Grid.Row="1" Grid.Column="0" Text="{Binding
  LongTextPlaceholder}" FontSize="14" />
</Grid>
```

`AbsoluteLayout` provides a rendering mechanism in which the child elements are organized in floating rectangles. Placement geometry (that is, the `LayoutBounds` property) defines the X and Y coordinates of the element and the size of the bounding rectangle. The `LayoutBounds` property can accept device units or proportional units. The notion used for proportional units is similar to the "%" system used in HTML layouts. These values have to be in the range of 0-1 to designate an element on the screen area. The `AbsoluteLayoutFlags` enumeration can be used to define the bounding rectangle values that follow the proportional unit system or otherwise (for example, `PositionProportional`, `HeightProportional`, `SizeProportional`, or `All`).

`RelativeLayout` is conceptually similar to relative layouts on the Android and Windows 10 platforms. It also uses a similar constraint mechanism as iOS auto-layout implementation. In a relative layout, elements can be positioned in a bounding rectangle similar to an absolute layout. However, values for this bounding rectangle are defined in reference to the parent element (`RelativeToParent`) or another control in the visual tree (`RelativeToView`). Developers are also allowed to use constant values without referencing another control.

In relative layouts, if the arrangement is being created in code-behind, constraints are defined using a lambda expression or anonymous functions. For instance, in order to add an image element to the center of the page of size (100,100), we would use the `RelativeToParent` constraint:

```
relativeLayout.Children.Add(image,
    Constraint.RelativeToParent(parent => parent.Width/2 - 50),
    Constraint.RelativeToParent(parent => parent.Height/2 - 50),
    Constraint.Constant(100), Constraint.Constant(100));
```

If we were to insert a label 10 units underneath the image in the center, it would look as follows:

```
relativeLayout.Children.Add(label,
    Constraint.RelativeToParent(parent => parent.Width/2 - 100),
    Constraint.RelativeToView(image, (parent, view) =>
    {
        // Here view is referring to the other relative control
        return view.Y + view.Height + 10;
    }),
    Constraint.Constant(200),
    Constraint.Constant(100));
```

The outcome would be as follows:

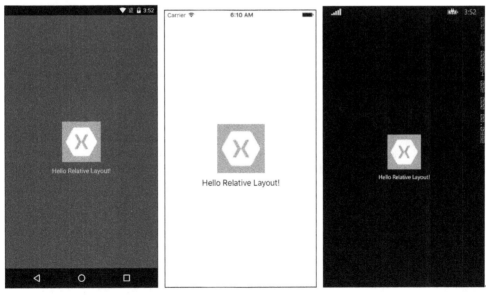

Figure 10: Relative layouts

A similar implementation using the markup extensions in XAML can be employed. Even though the constraint expression options are limited by factor and constant values (that is, using relative layout, factor multiplies the value of the selected property and constant is used for offset values), it can prove useful in data-bound scenarios.

```xaml
<RelativeLayout x:Name="relativeLayout">
    <Image x:Name="Image" Source="icon.png" HeightRequest="100"
        WidthRequest="100"
            RelativeLayout.XConstraint=
            "{ConstraintExpression Type=RelativeToParent,
                                    Property=Width,
                                    Factor=0.5,
                                    Constant=-50}"
            RelativeLayout.YConstraint=
            "{ConstraintExpression Type=RelativeToParent,
                                    Property=Height,
                                    Factor=0.5,
                                    Constant=-50}" />
    <Label Text="Hello Relative Layout!" HeightRequest="100"
        WidthRequest="200" HorizontalTextAlignment="Center"
            RelativeLayout.XConstraint=
            "{ConstraintExpression Type=RelativeToParent,
                                    Property=Width,
                                    Factor=0.5,
                                    Constant=-100}"
            RelativeLayout.YConstraint=
            "{ConstraintExpression Type=RelativeToView,
                                    ElementName=Image,
                                    Property=Y,
                                    Constant=110}"/>
</RelativeLayout>
```

Finally, `StackLayout`, similar to `StackPanel` on the Windows platform and `LinearLayout` on the Android platform, provides a flow layout where child views (that is, controls) are arranged automatically according to the orientation set and the calculated or requested dimensions of elements.

Views

User interface controls in Xamarin.Forms are referred to as views. Views are abstractions of controls or widgets in Xamarin target platforms, and each of them is rendered with a native control on the respective platform.

For text-related scenarios, there are three controls: `Editor`, `Entry`, and `Label`. The `Editor` and `Entry` views provide multi-line and single-line editing capabilities to the user interface respectively. On the other hand, the label view can be used in either scenario as a read-only control.

For dropdown-related scenarios, the `Picker` view can be used. More specialized implementations of pickers are `TimePicker` and `DatePicker`. `Stepper` and `Slider` are other views that can provide a constraint value, such as an integer within a certain range. For option scenarios, the only available control is the `Switch` view. The `Switch` view renders a `Switch` control on Android and iOS and a `ToggleButton` on Windows.

For process feedback implementation, there are two views available, namely `ProgressBar` and `ActivityIndicator`. `ProgressBar` provides a determinate progress indicator, and `ActivityIndicator` is rendered as an indeterminate progress ring on target platforms.

For web resource-related scenarios, `WebView` can be utilized. In a similar fashion to embedded web view native controls on target platforms, `WebView` can be used to display either a local (that is, a web element constructed from application resources or a text value) or a remote web page. It provides access to the navigation stack and navigation events of the displayed web document.

For collection views, there are two main controls in Xamarin.Forms: `ListView` and `TableView`. `ListView`, undoubtedly, is the most specialized control to display a collection of content items. It supports data binding scenarios together with more specialized actions such as pull-to-refresh, context-related commands, and selections. `TableView`, on the other hand, is used for scenarios where the content items are more heterogeneous and instead of a data-bound source, fixed UI element declarations are required. It can be used for a menu display of selections, configuration values, or as an input form.

Both `ListView` and `TableView` consist of cells. Cells are visual templates used to render content elements in these collection views. While `TableView` is generally associated with default templates such as `SwitchCell` and `EntryCell`, which are used to create form elements in a table, `ListView` generally uses a templated implementation of `ViewCell`. For simpler implementation scenarios, built-in cell implementations, such as `TextCell` and `ImageCell`, can also be used with the `ListView` control.

For `TableView` collection control, the iOS platform currently does not support the `HasUnevenRows` property and automatic layout of the cells. This is a known platform limitation that was recently fixed for the `ListView` control. Developers are expected to either define a fixed `RowHeight` for `TableView` or define a `Height` value for each cell.

In order to demonstrate the `ListView` utilization, we can make use of the previous implementation in which we used `StackLayout` together with `ScrollView`. In the previous scenario, we created hard-coded UI elements that were defined as `Grid` items. In this implementation, let us assume that we have a data source that can be set as the data provider for the `ListView`:

```
RecentUploadsList.ItemsSource = new List<Tuple<string, string,
string>>
{
    new Tuple<string, string, string>("Sarajevo trip on 04.10",
        longText, "profileicon.png"),
    new Tuple<string, string, string>("Istanbul trip on 23.09",
        longText, "mapicon.png"),
    new Tuple<string, string, string>("Rome trip on 12.09",
        longText, "settingsicon.png"),
    new Tuple<string, string, string>("Sarajevo trip on 04.10",
        longText, "profileicon.png"),
    new Tuple<string, string, string>("Istanbul trip on 23.09",
        longText, "mapicon.png"),
    new Tuple<string, string, string>("Rome trip on 12.09",
        longText, "settingsicon.png"),
    new Tuple<string, string, string>("Sarajevo trip on 04.10",
        longText, "profileicon.png"),
    new Tuple<string, string, string>("Istanbul trip on 23.09",
        longText, "mapicon.png"),
    new Tuple<string, string, string>("Rome trip on 12.09",
        longText, "settingsicon.png")
};
```

In this provider, we are using a three value `Tuple` that provides the display name, description, and image values for the content entries.

`Tuple` values are accessed using Item1, Item2... properties.

`ListView` can contain three visual templates defining the respective sections of the collection view: `HeaderTemplate`, `FooterTemplate`, and `ItemTemplate`. A header and footer can also be set directly using a view element:

```
<ListView BackgroundColor="Gray" SeparatorColor="Black"
  HasUnevenRows="true" x:Name="RecentUploadsList" >
  <ListView.Header>
    <Label TranslationX="10" Text="Recent Uploads"></Label>
  </ListView.Header>
  <!--<ListView.ItemTemplate> TODO: Insert DataTemplate </ListView.
ItemTemplate>-->
</ListView>
```

`ItemTemplate` defines how the content elements are to be rendered in the collection view. If `ItemTemplate` is not defined, the list renderer will try to convert the content elements to a string and display them as `TextCells`. Re-using the grid implementation from the previous example(s), we can define `DataTemplate` for the `ItemTemplate` property of `ListView`:

```
<ListView.ItemTemplate>
  <DataTemplate>
    <ViewCell>
        <Grid Padding="10" ColumnSpacing="4">
          <Grid.RowDefinitions>
            <RowDefinition Height="Auto" />
            <RowDefinition Height="40" />
          </Grid.RowDefinitions>
          <Grid.ColumnDefinitions>
            <ColumnDefinition Width="*" />
            <ColumnDefinition Width="60" />
          </Grid.ColumnDefinitions>
          <Image Grid.RowSpan="2" Grid.Column="1"
            Source="{Binding Item3}"
                    HeightRequest="40" WidthRequest="60"/>
          <Label Grid.Row="0" Grid.Column="0"
                    Text="{Binding Item1}" FontSize="16" />
          <Label Grid.Row="1" Grid.Column="0"
                    Text="{Binding Item2}" FontSize="14" />
        </Grid>
    </ViewCell>
  </DataTemplate>
</ListView.ItemTemplate>
```

This implementation will be displayed in a scroll-enabled list container similar to the following screenshots:

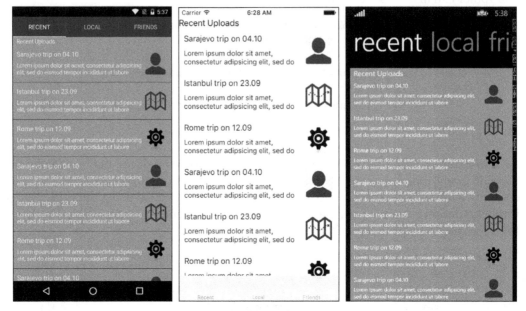

Figure 11: ListView with item source

In order to implement context-related functions, the item data template, view cell, can be edited to include context menu elements. It is also possible to modify view cell in the code-behind file.

The following XAML snippet can be used to create two context menu actions: Favourite and Remove:

```
<ViewCell.ContextActions>
  <MenuItem Text="Favourite" Clicked="OnFavouriteClicked"
    CommandParameter="{Binding .}">
  </MenuItem>
  <MenuItem Text="Remove" IsDestructive="True"
    Clicked="OnRemoveClicked" CommandParameter="{Binding .}">
  </MenuItem>
</ViewCell.ContextActions>
```

Notice that the `Remove` command is marked as destructive. The `IsDestructive` flag is used to create the slide-to-delete behavior on iOS. On other platforms, destructive actions are rendered similar to other commands.

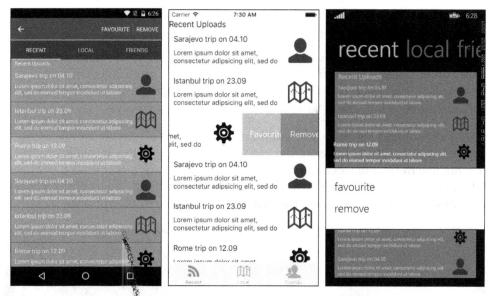

Figure 12: Context menu actions

`ListView` also has a flag called `IsPullToRefreshEnabled`. This property can be used to support the pull-to-refresh behavior. `RefreshCommand` can be used to bind the action required to refresh the list.

Extending forms

Even though the Xamarin.Forms framework provides an extensive set of customizable UI elements, in certain scenarios you might want to change how a certain control looks or behaves. Moreover, at times, providing an application-wide customization scheme can provide consistency and decrease redundancy. XAML markup infrastructure used in Xamarin.Forms provides various custom implementation scenarios.

Styles

When implementing certain UI patterns, view elements have to be declared independent of each other, and yet they have to carry the same design attributes, such as typography, layout properties, colors, and so on. Styles can be used in this situation to organize and re-use the element attributes.

Using `ListView`, the only view container defined would be the item data template, and the content items loaded from the data source will be rendered using the same template. However, if the view requirement is to use `Grid`, `StackLayout`, or `TableView`, each view item would have to be defined separately.

For instance, it might become quite cumbersome to create a settings view for Xamarin.Forms applications using the `TableView` control. In this implementation, if we cannot use the standard cell views, such as `EntryCell` or `SwitchCell`, because of requirements, the markup becomes even more redundant with each control having to declare similar fonts and colors that make up the theme of the application.

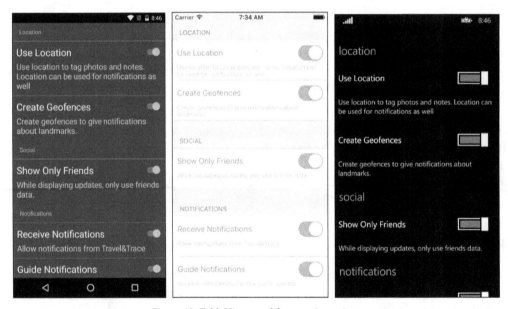

Figure 13: TableView used for a settings view

Custom cell views in this implementation were used to create a description element for each setting. If we look at the markup file, you can see the repeating styles for each text element:

```
<TableView Intent="Settings" HasUnevenRows="True">
  <TableRoot>
```

```xml
    <TableSection Title="Location">
      <ViewCell>
        <StackLayout Orientation="Vertical" Padding="10">
          <StackLayout Orientation="Horizontal">
            <Label TextColor="White" FontSize="24"
                VerticalTextAlignment="Center"
                HorizontalOptions="StartAndExpand"
                Text="Use Location" />
            <Switch IsToggled="True"></Switch>
          </StackLayout>
          <Label TextColor="Silver" FontSize="20"
              VerticalTextAlignment="Center"
              HorizontalOptions="StartAndExpand"
              Text="Use location to tag photos and notes.
              Location can be used for notifications as
              well">
          </Label>
        </StackLayout>
      </ViewCell>
      <ViewCell>
        <StackLayout Orientation="Vertical" Padding="10">
          <StackLayout Orientation="Horizontal">
            <Label TextColor="White" FontSize="24"
                VerticalTextAlignment="Center"
                HorizontalOptions="StartAndExpand"
                Text="Create Geofences" />
            <Switch IsToggled="True"></Switch>
          </StackLayout>
          <Label TextColor="Silver" FontSize="20"
              VerticalTextAlignment="Center"
              HorizontalOptions="StartAndExpand"
              Text="Create geofences to give notifications
              about landmarks.">
          </Label>
        </StackLayout>
      </ViewCell>
    </TableSection>
    <!-- Additional sections were removed for simplicity -->
  </TableRoot>
</TableView>
```

In this example, each label is defining at least `TextColor`, `FontSize`, `VerticalTextAlignment`, and `HorizontalOptions`. There is one pattern for setting labels and another one for description elements. Vertical and horizontal alignment options, however, apply to all text elements.

Initially, we can simplify the markup by creating an implicit style that will apply to all `Label` elements. Implicit styles do not define a resource key, hence they apply to all targeted controls, such as `TargetType`:

```
<ContentPage.Resources>
  <ResourceDictionary>
    <Style TargetType="Label">
      <Setter Property="HorizontalOptions"
        Value="StartAndExpand" />
      <Setter Property="VerticalTextAlignment" Value="Center" />
    </Style>
  </ResourceDictionary>
</ContentPage.Resources>
```

We can now create additional styles to set item labels and descriptions:

```
<Style x:Key="SettingLabel" TargetType="Label">
  <Setter Property="FontSize" Value="24"></Setter>
  <Setter Property="TextColor" Value="White"></Setter>
</Style>
<Style x:Key="SettingDescription" TargetType="Label">
  <Setter Property="FontSize" Value="20"></Setter>
  <Setter Property="TextColor" Value="Silver"></Setter>
</Style>
```

However, this does not work as we expected it to. The outcome demonstrates that the implicit styles were overridden by more specific style descriptions. It is important to realize that there is no implicit cascading between the styles defined for the same target controls. XAML is not HTML/CSS.

Figure 14: Implicit style is overridden with assigned styles

In order to create a cascading scheme, we need to base the `SettingLabel` and `SettingDescription` styles on the initial implicit style. For this purpose, we need to define a key for our base style and reference this base in the derived style declarations:

```
<ContentPage.Resources>
  <ResourceDictionary>
    <Style x:Key="BaseLabelStyle" TargetType="Label">
      <Setter Property="HorizontalOptions"
        Value="StartAndExpand" />
      <Setter Property="VerticalTextAlignment" Value="Center" />
    </Style>
    <Style x:Key="SettingLabel" BaseResourceKey="BaseLabelStyle"
      TargetType="Label">
      <Setter Property="FontSize" Value="24"></Setter>
      <Setter Property="TextColor" Value="White"></Setter>
    </Style>
    <Style x:Key="SettingDescription" BasedOn="{StaticResource
      BaseLabelStyle}" TargetType="Label">
      <Setter Property="FontSize" Value="20"></Setter>
      <Setter Property="TextColor" Value="Silver"></Setter>
    </Style>
  </ResourceDictionary>
</ContentPage.Resources>
```

Notice that the `SettingDescription` style uses the `BasedOn` declaration (similar to the WPF implementation), while `SettingLabel` uses the `BaseResourceKey` property. Both of these references can be used in Xamarin.Forms implementations.

Triggers and behaviors

At times, implementation requires style-related or behavioral changes of controls in accordance with changes of the same or any other control's properties or data, as well as certain events (for example, disabling a certain control according to the data input value changes). Under normal circumstances, implementations utilize data bindings where the data change event is routed to the presenter and the presenter changes the view, providing a trivial solution. However, if the UI event should trigger another UI change, the cost of data binding would be an overhead. Instead, the Xamarin.Forms markup offers triggers and behaviors that add complexity to intrinsic controls.

For instance, the settings view that we previously created for our application requires certain business rules. The first setting value, UserLocation, is a dependency of the UseGeofences setting. In other words, technically it is not possible to create geofences without using location services. For this specific scenario, we could create a data binding from the `IsToggled` value:

```
<Switch x:Name="SwitchUseGeofences" IsToggled="True"
            IsEnabled="{Binding Source={x:Reference
SwitchUserLocation}, Path=IsToggled}">
```

The preceding implementation works as expected since the `IsToggled` and `IsEnabled` values are both using `Boolean` as the value type. If we were to change any other property of the target UI element, we would have to implement a value converter. Moreover, multiple property changes would require multiple bindings.

Triggers provide an easy solution for this type of scenario. There are four types of trigger that can be used to initiate either a setter action or a custom implementation of a trigger action. Property triggers are used to create a visual state on a user control according to the value of a property of the same control. Data triggers are used in a similar fashion but in this case, the cause for the trigger is defined by data binding. Event triggers are bound to user control events and multi triggers can encompass and invoke an action that is dependent on multiple conditions.

The same scenario from the previous example can, in this case, be implemented with a `DataTrigger`. Iterating on the scenario, the implementation can set the enabled and text color properties on the associated description label:

```
<ViewCell>
  <StackLayout Orientation="Vertical" Padding="10">
    <StackLayout Orientation="Horizontal">
      <Label Text="Create Geofences" Style="{StaticResource
SettingLabel}" />
      <Switch x:Name="SwitchUseGeofences" IsToggled="True"
            IsEnabled="{Binding Source={x:Reference
SwitchUserLocation}, Path=IsToggled}">
        <Switch.Triggers>
          <DataTrigger TargetType="Switch" Binding="{Binding
Source={x:Reference SwitchUserLocation}, Path=IsToggled}"
Value="True">
            <Setter Property="IsEnabled" Value="False"></Setter>
          </DataTrigger>
        </Switch.Triggers>
      </Switch>
    </StackLayout>
```

```
        <Label Text="Create geofences to give notifications about
landmarks."
                 Style="{StaticResource SettingDescription}">
          <Label.Triggers>
            <DataTrigger TargetType="Label" Binding="{Binding
Source={x:Reference SwitchUserLocation}, Path=IsToggled}"
Value="False">
                <Setter Property="IsEnabled" Value="False"></Setter>
                <Setter Property="TextColor" Value="Transparent"></Setter>
            </DataTrigger>
          </Label.Triggers>
        </Label>
      </StackLayout>
</ViewCell>
```

Let us also implement a notification when the main control is disabled, warning the user about other settings being disabled. For this implementation, we will need an event trigger and a trigger action implementation. A trigger action implementation consists of implementing the `TriggerAction<T>` class and the virtual `Invoke` method: (see the *Dependency injection* section for the implementation of `INotificationService`)

```
public class WarningTriggerAction : TriggerAction<Switch>
{
    public string Message { get; set; }
    protected override void Invoke(Switch sender)
    {
        if(!sender.IsToggled)
            DependencyService.Get<INotificationService>()
                .Notify(Message);
    }
}
```

Then, we will need to declare the namespace containing the implementation in the root node of the page's markup:

```
xmlns:components="clr-namespace:Xamarin.Master.TravelTrace
    .Components;assembly=Xamarin.Master.TravelTrace"
```

And finally, we can add the event trigger to the main setting control:

```
<Switch x:Name="SwitchUserLocation" IsToggled="True">
  <Switch.Triggers>
    <EventTrigger Event="Toggled">
```

```
<components:WarningTriggerAction Message=
    "Disabling this setting will disable other values" />
  </EventTrigger>
 </Switch.Triggers>
</Switch>
```

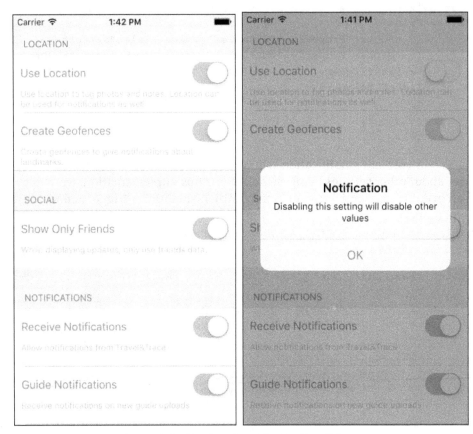

Figure 15: Notification triggered using EventTrigger

If we want this trigger to be applied to multiple controls (for example, the notification settings section in the example), we can create a new style for the main setting values and add the trigger to the style declaration:

```
<Style x:Key="SectionToggleSwitch" TargetType="Switch">
  <Style.Triggers>
    <EventTrigger Event="Toggled">
      <components:WarningTriggerAction Message=
        "Disabling this setting will disable other values" />
    </EventTrigger>
  </Style.Triggers>
</Style>
```

The same type of result could have been achieved with a behavior implementation for the Switch control. Behaviors are a more generic type of extension mechanism that allow developers to extend existing user controls without having to create derivatives of these controls.

For instance, if we were to use the same scenario (that is, when the switch control is toggled off, a notification window should be shown to the user), we would need to implement the base class, Behavior, with a type argument for Switch view:

```
public class SectionSwitchAlertBehavior : Behavior<Switch>
{
    public string Message { get; set; }

    protected override void OnAttachedTo(Switch control)
    {
        control.Toggled += ControlOnToggled;

        base.OnAttachedTo(control);
    }

    protected override void OnDetachingFrom(Switch control)
    {
        control.Toggled -= ControlOnToggled;

        base.OnDetachingFrom(control);
    }
    private void ControlOnToggled(object sender,
      ToggledEventArgs toggledEventArgs)
    {
        if (!toggledEventArgs.Value &&
          !string.IsNullOrWhiteSpace(Message))
        {
            DependencyService.Get<INotificationService>()
              .Notify(Message);
        }
    }
}
```

In a custom behavior implementation class, an OnAttachedTo method is used as the initialization function where the control can be customized. Similarly, OnDetachingFrom is used to clean up the customizations and any existing event handlers that might have been attached to the control. Even though it's technically possible, it is not advisable to modify the binding context using behaviors.

The custom behavior can be included either in styles targeting the same type of control or with in-place markup elements added to the specific control:

```
<Style x:Key="SectionToggleSwitch" TargetType="Switch">
  <Style.Behaviors>
    <components:SectionSwitchAlertBehavior Message=
      "Disabling this setting will disable other values" />
  </Style.Behaviors>
</Style>
```

Custom renderers

Xamarin.Forms provides the developers with a uniform markup and implementation framework to create native UI views for all Xamarin target platforms. The abstractions of provided UI elements are then used by the framework to render native controls. Similar to the Xamarin.Forms solution anatomy, each view/control in the Xamarin.Forms platform is a composite implementation. While the behaviors for the abstracted control logic are implemented and can be derived in portable class libraries, the renderers associated with each control for various platforms are implemented by platform-specific libraries.

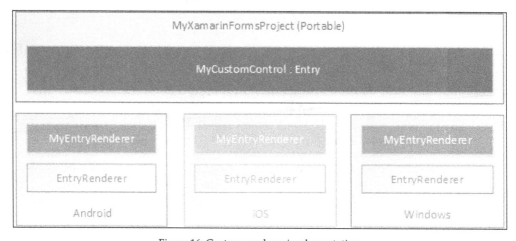

Figure 16: Custom renderer implementation

In order to customize a control, one must first create a derived class for the abstracted control. After this implementation, the custom control can be referenced with a `clr-namespace` declaration (similar to `TriggerAction` and `Behaviors`) and can be used in the view markup.

At this stage, the custom implementation of the control would use the default renderer for the base class. In order to change the way that native controls are rendered on a specific platform, we would need to provide a custom renderer implementation and register it using the `ExportRenderer` attribute on the same platform.

Custom renderers provide a powerful way to customize how the common view implementations with Xamarin.Forms should look on platform-specific views.

Patterns and best practices

In this section, we will discuss several implementation patterns and tools that developers generally resort to while developing Xamarin.Forms applications. Messaging and dependency injection features will be discussed further in *Chapter 9, Reusable UI Patterns*.

Messaging infrastructure

In an ideal implementation of the **Model-View-ViewModel (MVVM)** or **Model-View-Presenter (MVP)** pattern, each screen is self-contained; the screen modules for the view, model, and the mitigation components communicate with each other using various communication channels.

However, in complex applications, there is sometimes the need for a communication channel between these self-contained elements, since the result of an action on one of the screens should be propagated to other unrelated section(s) of the application with a shared interest in the result of this very action. As a solution to this problem, in MVVM frameworks such as MVVMCross, Prism, or MVVM Light, it is common to see an implementation of the Event Aggregator pattern providing a loosely coupled, multicast-enabled publisher/subscriber messaging infrastructure. Event Aggregator can be described as the eventing hub, which receives multiple types of strongly typed messages and delivers these messages to multiple subscribers.

In Xamarin.Forms, the Event Aggregator is called the `MessagingCenter`. It exposes three groups of methods: `Subscribe`, `Unsubscribe`, and `Send`. The `Subscribe` and `Unsubscribe` methods are used by the event observers, and the `Send` method is used by the publisher.

In this paradigm, the subscriber is responsible for providing the instance and/or the type of the sender together with the expected type of the message (that is, a simple text parameter defining the message). The message type or name is an identifier for the message and together with the message signature (the sender type and the arguments type), it makes up the decision criteria for the subscribers. Finally, the last provided parameter is the callback delegate, which can have the sender, and possibly the event arguments, as parameters:

```
MessagingCenter.Subscribe<MyViewModel, MyMessageContract>(this,
"MyMessageName",
    (sender, data) =>
    {
        // TODO: Use the provided data and the sender
    });

// or
//MessagingCenter.Subscribe(this, "MyMessageName", (sender) => { },
myViewModelInstance);
```

The publisher is responsible for providing the message with the same message name and signature. On the publisher's side, the message signature is made up of the message name and the message argument parameter:

```
MessagingCenter.Send(this, "MyMessageName", new MyMessageContract
{
    // TODO: Pass on the required data.
});
```

MessagingCenter can prove to be very utile, providing simple solutions/workarounds for architectural problems (especially scenarios where a Separation of Concerns is in question) in Xamarin.Forms applications, and creating a decoupled communication channel between components.

Dependency injection

As previously mentioned, one of the biggest drawbacks of using **Portable Class Libraries (PCLs)** to implement common cross-platform libraries is the fact that the platform-specific features cannot be accessed directly since the platform-dependent modules cannot be referenced by these libraries.

One of the most effective and elegant solutions to this problem is using dependency injection (aka IoC - Inversion of Control). Using dependency injection, platform-specific functionality should be abstracted into segregated interfaces, and these interfaces can later be used to access the implementation modules injected with the provided dependency containers.

`DependencyService` in Xamarin.Forms allows applications to use platform-specific implementation through the abstraction interfaces.

In a common scenario, the first step would be to define the abstraction (in the common portable forms library) that is going to be used by the common application layer.

For a demonstration, let us implement a module that uses the native messaging methods to display a notification for the user:

```
public interface INotificationService
{
    void Notify(string message);
}
```

Now we can implement this interface in platform-specific projects. In the Xamarin. Android project, we can implement this using a toast notification:

```
[assembly:Xamarin.Forms.Dependency(typeof(NotificationService))]
namespace Xamarin.Master.TravelTrace.Droid.Modules
{
    public class NotificationService : INotificationService
    {
        public void Notify(string message)
        {
            var toast = Toast.MakeText(Application.Context,
                message, ToastLength.Long);
            toast.Show();
        }
    }
}
```

For the iOS platform, we can create a local notification message and present it using the shared application infrastructure. However, local notifications for foreground applications are automatically dismissed (only at the UI level can one still implement an event delegate for a notification received event and display an alert instead). Hence, we will use the `UIAlertController` class and present it using the current window:

```
[assembly: Xamarin.Forms.Dependency(typeof(NotificationService))]
namespace Xamarin.Master.TravelTrace.iOS.Modules
{
    public class NotificationService : INotificationService
    {
        public void Notify(string message)
        {
            //
            // This will not fire for the foreground application
            //UILocalNotification localNotification = new
            // UILocalNotification();
            // localNotification.FireDate =
            // NSDate.Now.AddSeconds(2);
            //localNotification.AlertBody = message;
            //localNotification.TimeZone =
            // NSTimeZone.SystemTimeZone;
            // UIApplication.SharedApplication
            // .PresentLocalNotificationNow(localNotification);
            // UIApplication.SharedApplication
            // .ScheduleLocalNotification(localNotification);

            //Create Alert
            var okAlertController = UIAlertController.Create
              ("Notification", message,
              UIAlertControllerStyle.Alert);

            //Add Action
            okAlertController.AddAction(UIAlertAction.Create("OK",
              UIAlertActionStyle.Default, null));

            if (UIApplication.SharedApplication.KeyWindow != null)
                UIApplication.SharedApplication.KeyWindow
                .RootViewController.PresentViewController(
                  okAlertController, true, null);
        }
    }
}
```

And finally, for the Windows Phone platform, we can only use the local toast notifications with the currently running applications on Windows Phone 8.1 and Windows 10 mobile. For other versions, similar to the iOS scenario, local toast notifications are not allowed for foreground applications. For this reason, we can implement a simpler notification dialog using the `MessageBox` class:

```
[assembly: Xamarin.Forms.Dependency(typeof(NotificationService))]
namespace Xamarin.Master.TravelTrace.WinPhone.Modules
{
    public class NotificationService : INotificationService
    {
        public void Notify(string message)
        {
            MessageBox.Show(message);
        }
    }
}
```

In order to use the `INotificationService` interface in the portable class library that implements the Xamarin.Forms application, we need to resolve the interface to create an instance of one of the platform-appropriate implementations:

```
DependencyService.Get<INotificationService>().Notify("Hello Xamarin.
Forms!");
```

It is important to note that in this sample implementation, the `Dependency` assembly attribute was used to register the platform-dependent implementation classes. It is also possible to use the `Register` method of `DependencyService` to create dependency containers:

```
Xamarin.Forms.DependencyService.Register<INotificationService,
NotificationService>();
```

The `Register` method has to be invoked after the initialization of Xamarin.Forms (that is, the `Forms.Init` method) and before any dependent module is loaded.

Shared project versus portable project

Xamarin.Forms extensions introduce two types of multi-project solution templates. Each template contains platform-specific projects as well as a common project to implement platform-agnostic components for these native applications.

In the previous examples we were using the PCL project template, which creates three platform-specific projects, each referencing a cross-platform portable class library. Platform-specific projects delegate the application initialization to the portable class library that initializes Xamarin.Forms and renders the pages implemented using Xamarin.Forms.

The second project template creates a shared project that is included and compiled into the platform-specific projects. In this scenario, since we are technically not dealing with a platform-agnostic implementation (that is, implementations in the shared project are directly compiled into the referencing projects), developers are free to use platform-specific features, given that the compilation conditions are used for appropriate platforms.

The easiest way to demonstrate the difference between the two approaches would be to re-implement the notification service from the previous section without dependency injection. In the previous example, we needed to create an abstraction of the notification feature to be used in common views and inject the implementation from platform-specific projects in the runtime. In the case of a shared project, we can implement the same feature using conditional compilation:

```
public class NotificationService
{
    public void Notify(string message)
    {
        if (!string.IsNullOrWhiteSpace(message))
#if __IOS__
    var okAlertController = UIAlertController.Create("Notification",
message, UIAlertControllerStyle.Alert);

    okAlertController.AddAction(UIAlertAction.Create("OK",
UIAlertActionStyle.Default, null));

    if (UIApplication.SharedApplication.KeyWindow != null)
        UIApplication.SharedApplication.KeyWindow.RootViewController
            .PresentViewController(okAlertController, true, null);
#elif __ANDROID__
    var toast = Toast.MakeText(Application.Context, message,
ToastLength.Long);
    toast.Show();
#elif WINDOWS_PHONE
            MessageBox.Show(message);
#endif
    }
}
```

In this case, each platform compilation uses a specific section of the function. We can also use other types of abstraction and partial classes or methods to create elegant implementations according to the requirements of the scenario.

Platform-specific fine-tuning

In spite of, or even because of, the fact that Xamarin.Forms tries to provide a uniform implementation layer and then translates this layer into native controls, at times developers are faced with the challenge of implementing retouches for specific platforms. These modifications vary from small changes, such as font size (because of device- and platform-dependent pixel measures) or background color, to more systematic problems, such as not having the auto-layout implementation for `TableViews` on the iOS platform. There are various ways to deal with this type of situation, and the `Device` class is generally the access point to these solutions.

When dealing with common typographic controls, such as a `Label` or an `Entry` field, the simplest way to comply with the design or accessibility requirements of a specific device is to use the built-in styles available in the `Device.Styles` class. There are several style elements, such as `BodyStyle`, `SubtitleStyle`, and `CaptionStyle`, that can be used to solve common implementation problems. The style elements in this class are calculated for the current platform/device in the runtime, hence they have to be referenced by a `DynamicResource` XAML markup extension when dealing with markup rather than code.

A simple label using the `TitleStyle` can be implemented as follows:

```
var mylabel = new Label
{
    Text = "Text for my Title",
    Style = Device.Styles.TitleStyle
};
```

It can also be declared in the markup file as follows:

```
<Label x:Name="MyLabel" Text="Text for my Title"
Style="{DynamicResource TitleStyle}" />
```

Another useful platform-specific typography-related utility is the `NamedSize` enumeration. The `NamedSize` enumeration can be used with the `Device.GetNamedSize` method to choose the most suitable font size in the target platform for a text field. The enumeration provides four built-in options for different scenarios:

```
var mylabel = new Label {Text = "Text for my Title"};

// A Large font size, for titles or other important text elements
mylabel.FontSize = Device.GetNamedSize(NamedSize.Large, typeof
(Label));
```

A built-in converter can also be used to include the font size in XAML markup:

```
<Label x:Name="MyLabel" Text="Text for my Title" FontSize="Large" />
```

For more general implementation requirements, `Device.Idiom` and `Device.OS` provide valuable target platform information related to the type of device (desktop, phone, tablet, and so on) and the operating system of the device (Android, iOS, Windows, or Windows Phone) respectively.

 Currently, Windows Phone 8.1 and Windows Phone Silverlight versions cannot be differentiated using the `Device.OS` property. Conditional compilation can be used as a replacement for this distinction.

Additionally, the `Device.OnPlatform` function and its XAML extension counterpart can help developers implement platform-specific styles. The `OnPlatform` function uses three values for each platform and returns the appropriate value according to the `Device.OS` property.

Visualizing a label using the `OnPlatform` function would look similar to the following snippet:

```
var mylabel = new Label {Text = "Text for my Title"};
mylabel.FontSize = Device.OnPlatform<double>(
    Android: 24, WinPhone: 24, iOS: 18);
```

Or, using the XAML markup extension, it would look like this:

```
<Label x:Name="MyLabel" Text="Text for my Title">
  <Label.FontSize>
    <OnPlatform x:TypeArguments="x:Double" Android="24" WinPhone="24"
iOS="16"/>
  </Label.FontSize>
</Label>
```

The `Device.OnPlatform` function has another overload that can be used to execute certain actions according to current operating system.

Summary

Briefly, Xamarin.Forms provides the toolset to increase code-sharing between platform-specific projects and provide developers with a uniform experience when developing UI components for these projects. The Xamarin.Forms framework, in general, proves to be indispensable, especially for cross-platform implementation where platform-dependent feature requirements are minimal.

This uniform abstraction layer is responsible for rendering the platform-specific UI controls and creating native experience for the users. This layer can also be extended using various features and patterns, some of which were discussed in this chapter.

We will be focusing on more re-usable view elements and implementation patterns in the next chapter. Xamarin.Forms will again be referenced in this context.

9
Reusable UI Patterns

In this chapter, we will discuss strategies and patterns for reusing visual assets (that is, text and media resources) in cross platform projects. Furthermore, reusable assets will be iteratively explained from the localization perspective. Finally, some advanced software architectural topics about Model-View-Controller and Model-View-ViewModel patterns will be analyzed and demonstrated. This chapter is divided into the following sections:

- Visual assets
- Localization
- Architectural patterns

Visual assets

We can classify any resource included in the project at compile time and used by the user interface as a visual asset. Visual assets can vary from simple text elements to media items (for example images, animations, videos, and so on) to be used for creating the visual elements of the user interface. Each Xamarin target platform provides different mechanisms to store and dispatch these assets.

On Android and iOS, resources and their localized representations are kept in the designated `Resources` folder and substructures. On Windows Phone (both Silverlight and Windows Runtime), resources can be managed by using embedded resource files (that is, `resw` or `resx`).

Text resources

Each Xamarin target platform uses various strategies to filter out static text resources, such as the content of a message dialog or a label, from the **View** implementation. Doing this helps developers separate human readable resources from code base, creating a project structure in line with the separation of concerns principle.

Xamarin.Android

On the Android platform, text resources can be stored in the `strings.xml` file and retrieved through code or used in declarative markups (that is, AXML files). The XML file containing the string resources can be found or created in the `Resources\values` directory. There is no relevance between the filenames and how the resources are retrieved later on.

The resource XML file has a simple format, where each string is defined as an XML node with an associated name as an attribute:

```
<resources>
  <string name="ApplicationName">Fibonnaci Calculator</string>
  <string name="SingleCalculation">Single Calculation</string>
  <string name="RangeCalculation">Range Calculation</string>
  <string name="GCCollect">GC Collect</string>
</resources>
```

The string values can later be used in markup, and also in Android declarative attributes, using the `@string/<ResourceName>` notation:

```
<Button
    android:text="@string/SingleCalculation"
    android:layout_width="match_parent"
    android:layout_height="wrap_content"
    local:MvxBind="Click NavigateToSingleCalculationCommand" />
<Button
    android:text="@string/RangeCalculation"
    android:layout_width="match_parent"
    android:layout_height="wrap_content"
    local:MvxBind="Click NavigateToRangeCalculationCommand" />
```

In order to add an activity label for a view, the `ApplicationName` string can be included directly with the `@string` notation:

```
[Activity(Label = "@string/ApplicationName")]
```

On top of the classic string resources, a collection of string resources and quantity strings can also be included in the resource XML file(s). Quantity strings are resource strings with a definition for different countable references for various scenarios with the correct pluralization rule.

For instance, for an application with English as the default language, the plural quantity strings would look similar to the following (for example, a singular word for one, a plural form for others):

```
<plurals name="CalculationsCompleted">
  <item quantity="one">%d calculation was completed.</item>
  <item quantity="other">%d calculations were completed.</item>
</plurals>
```

Whereas for the Turkish language, it would look similar to the following (the same rule applies to all countable words):

```
<plurals name="CalculationsCompleted">
  <item quantity="other">%d islem tamamlandi.</item>
</plurals>
```

Examples of this usage can be extended to Slavic languages (for example Russian, Polish, and Czech), where languages have different use cases for a small number of items or for numbers ending with certain digits. Possible switch values for quantities are `zero`, `one`, `two`, `few`, `many`, and `other`. The application of these switches follows the rules defined for language plurals in the unicode common locale data repository (see `http://unicode.org/repos/cldr-tmp/trunk/diff/supplemental/language_plural_rules.html` for more information). For instance, English does not require a specific handling for few items or zero items, so any rule defined for these cases will be ignored by the runtime.

Once the resource XML file(s) are modified, you can see that the `Resource.Designer.cs` file is (re)generated with each compilation. This file contains the associated ID values for different types of resources and can be used for retrieving the resource items with the `Resources` utility class.

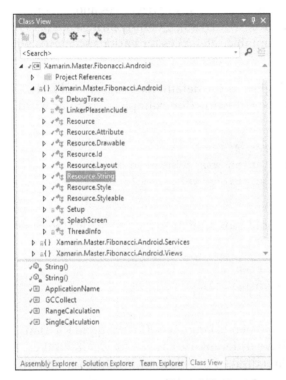

Figure 1: Generated resource constants

Using the `Resources` utility, text resources can be retrieved in the following ways:

```
// Getting a single text value
var singleStringValue =
  Resources.GetText(Resource.String.ApplicationName);
// Getting a string array
var stringArrayValue =
  Resources.GetTextArray(Resource.Array.MyStringArray);
// Getting a pluralized version for 2 items
var quantity =
  Resources.GetQuantityString
  (Resource.Plurals.CalculationsCompleted, 2, 2);
```

Additionally, other primitive data types (for example, integers, Booleans, and so on), as well as units or `structs` used in style definitions (for example, dimension and color) can be included in resource XML files.

Xamarin.iOS

On the iOS platform, the simplest way to separate the text resources from the rest of the project would be to create `.strings` files (for example, `Localizable.strings`), which follow a simple JSON-like pattern with key/value pairs:

```
"GCCollect" = "GC Collect";
"RangeCalculation" = "Range Calculation";
"SingleCalculation"= "Single Calculation";
```

These string values, compiled into bundle resources, can, later on, be accessed using the `NSBundle.MainBundle.LocalizedString` method:

```
var localizedString = NSBundle.MainBundle.LocalizedString
    ("RangeCalculation", "");
```

Localized string values can be used as labels for UI controls, creating a loosely-coupled relationship between the static text content and the actual runtime components. This process is referred to as internationalization in the iOS ecosystem. Internationalized controls and elements can easily be localized for different languages. `strings` files can be created in the `Resources` folder or can be placed in the `Base.lproj` folder inside the `Resources` directory, which constitutes the base localization project folder for iOS projects (the default/fallback resources).

For storyboards, the internationalization process can be a little more complicated. Each UI element in a storyboard is assigned a unique identifier called the **Object ID** in Xcode, while it is referred to as the **Localization ID** in Xamarin Storyboard Designer. In order to assign text content to a specific item on the storyboard, developers are required to create string files for each storyboard (for example, for a storyboard called `Main.storyboard`, you will need to create a `Main.strings` file) and use the localization ID of the specific control and the name of the text attribute:

```
/* Class = "UIViewController"; title = "Single Calculation";
ObjectID = "138"; */
"138.title" = "Single Calculation";
/* Class = "UILabel"; text = "Ordinal"; ObjectID = "153"; */
"153.text" = "Ordinal";
/* Class = "UIButton"; normalTitle = "Calculate"; ObjectID =
"156"; */
"156.normalTitle" = "Calculate";
```

As one can see, the attribute names and casings are clearly different from the actual type properties of UI controls (for example, `text` for `UILabel`, `normalTitle` for `UIButton`). The iOS internationalization guidelines can provide details on the storyboard attributes.

Another way to create the base internationalization file for a storyboard is to use Xcode to generate the `string` file. In order to modify the Xamarin.iOS project with Xcode, the **Open With** context menu item can be used to select **Xcode Interface Builder** for a storyboard and the main project window to access the project properties.

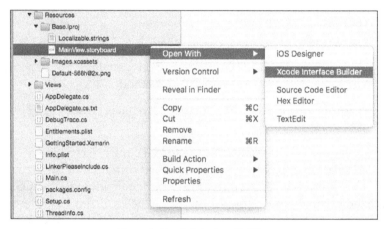

Figure 2: Xcode Interface Builder

In the Xcode interface, the localization settings are located on the project settings page. If the base localization folder was created beforehand, the **Base Localization** option will already be checked in the project settings localization section.

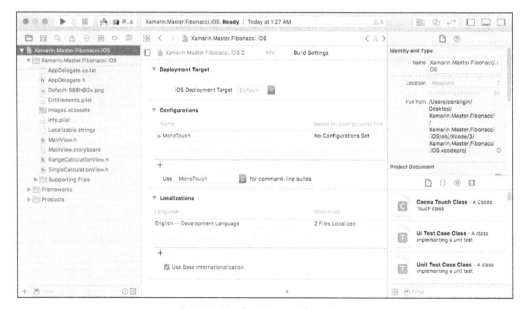

Figure 3: Xcode project configuration

Any additional language selection generates a language specific .lproj folder and the .strings file for the targeted storyboards and strings files. Once the Xcode window is closed, these changes will be reflected in the Xamarin.iOS project structure.

Windows Phone

In Windows Phone (Silverlight) projects, resources are managed through traditional resx files (a legacy of the .NET framework). The default language resources are generated with the project template and stored in the AppResources.resx file, located under the Resources folder.

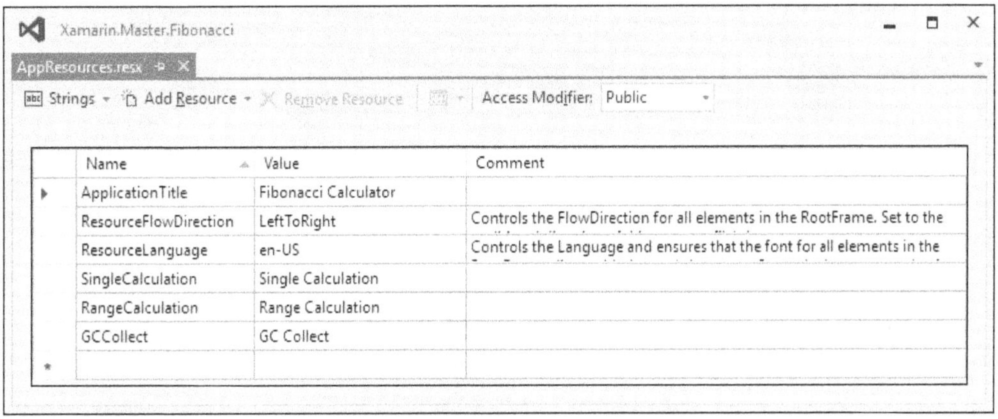

Name	Value	Comment
ApplicationTitle	Fibonacci Calculator	
ResourceFlowDirection	LeftToRight	Controls the FlowDirection for all elements in the RootFrame. Set to the
ResourceLanguage	en-US	Controls the Language and ensures that the font for all elements in the
SingleCalculation	Single Calculation	
RangeCalculation	Range Calculation	
GCCollect	GC Collect	

Figure 4: Windows Phone resources

Additional types of content that can be embedded in the resources file are images, icons, audio, and other types of files. These files can be accessed through code and also in markup, using the generated AppResources class. Another generated class, LocalizedStrings, provides access to the resources stored in the embedded resource file(s):

```
<StackPanel>
    <Button x:Name="SingleCalculation"
            Content="{Binding LocalizedResources.
                SingleCalculation, Source={StaticResource
                LocalizedStrings}}"
            Style="{StaticResource NavigationButtons}"></Button>
    <Button x:Name="RangeCalculation"
            Content="{Binding LocalizedResources.RangeCalculation,
                Source={StaticResource LocalizedStrings}}"
            Style="{StaticResource NavigationButtons}"></Button>
    <Button x:Name="GCCollect"
```

```
                Content="{Binding LocalizedResources.GCCollect,
                    Source={StaticResource LocalizedStrings}}"
                Style="{StaticResource NavigationButtons}"></Button>
    </StackPanel>
```

In Windows Phone 8.1 (that is, Windows Runtime) and Windows 10, the applications use a `resw` file (called `PRIResource`, referring to the compilation method). Even though the format of `resx` and `resw` files is identical, `resw` files can only contain primitive values (that is, string values or values that can be expressed as strings). Using `resw` files, developers can assign style or other attribute values directly to user controls using the `Uid` value of the controls, similar to the internationalization of storyboards on iOS.

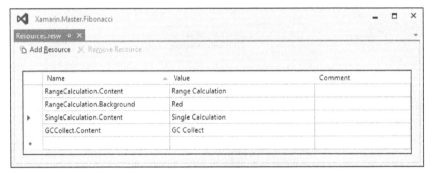

Figure 5: Windows Runtime PRI resources

In addition to the targeted resources, developers are still free to use simple resource strings. These resources can be accessed using the `ResourceLoader` class and the `GetString` method.

Image resources

Mobile application projects can contain media assets from external sources as well as the application bundle. In each target platform, media assets can be included in different ways.

While iOS and Windows Phone do not dictate a certain location in the project tree for media assets, in Android projects, developers are obliged to include image documents in the drawable folder of the Resources directory.

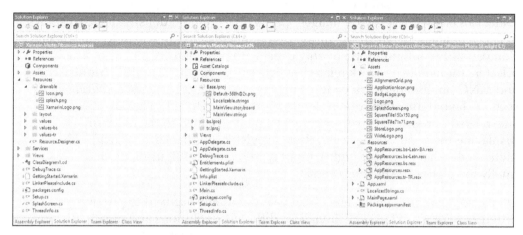

Figure 6: Project structures

Similar to the text resource structure on the iOS platform, it is advisable to place language-neutral image elements (for the default language) in the Base.lproj location if you are planning to localize them in later iterations. Also, asset catalogs can be employed to simplify the management of images and their pixel-perfect alternatives for different resolutions (see the *Adaptive visual assets* section).

Adaptive visual assets

Adaptive UI patterns for applications targeting Xamarin platforms force developers, at times, to include variations of media assets for different resolutions and pixel densities. Even though the image resources are scaled according to the aforementioned adaptive UI metrics, the scaled images do not always result in visually pleasing displays (for example, an image resized to double the original size, to have the same physical screen dimensions on different devices, does not appear as it should).

The Android platform uses the device compatibility configuration qualifiers for both image and text resource folders (that is, `drawables` and `values`), as well as other types of resources, such as layouts. In such projects, compatibility qualifiers are concatenated to the resource folder as a suffix (for example, the `drawables-xhdpi` folder can be used to provide images specific to extra high density device displays of approximately 320 dpi) and various default resources are added to this folder. Compatibility configuration not only deals with pixel density, but also provides selectors for mobile network related switches (that is, **MCC (mobile country code)** and **MNC (mobile network code)**), language, and region (see the *Localization* section), layout direction (that is, left to right or right to left), various screen size-related options, screen orientation, UI mode (related to the platform displaying the application—a car, desk, television, appliance, or watch), night mode (that is, day or night), input type-related configurations, and finally the platform API level/version.

On the iOS platform, image assets can be individually suffixed to provide different versions of the same image for different resolutions and device idioms (that is, iPhone, iPod, and iPad). Device idiom values (that is, device modifiers) are used with the tilde (~) character and can identify resources for iPhone and iPod using the `~iphone` suffix and resources for iPad using the `~ipad` suffix. The `@2x` suffix, which should appear before the device modifier, is used to identify high resolution image variants.

Before the introduction of Windows Phone 8.1, the Windows Phone operating system only supported four variations: WVGA (480 x 800, only used by WP 7.1), WXGA (768 x 1280), 720p (720 x 1280), and 1080p (1080 x 1920). The only way to differentiate between these resolutions was to use the `App.Current.Host.ScaleFactor` device configuration property (for example, a scale factor of 100 refers to WVGA and 150 refers to HD). Windows Store apps (including Windows Phone 8.1) provide an automated scaling mechanism similar to that of iOS and Android. On the Windows Phone 8.1 platform, each resource file and/or folder can be suffixed with various qualifiers to support multiple display scales, languages and regions, contrasts, and similar, to tailor a customized look and feel for different device configurations. If the qualifiers are applied to a specific file, each qualifier/value pair should be separated by an underscore and added between the filename and the extension (that is, `filename.qualifiername-value_otherqualifier-value.fileextension`). If the qualifiers are applied to complete folders, for each qualifier/value, a subfolder should be created (that is, `resourcefolder/qualifier-value/otherqualifier-value/`).

For instance, see the following project path:

```
Images/en-US/config-designer/myImage.scale-140_layoutdir-LTR.png
```

This can be accessed with the `Images/myImage.png` resource path.

Reusable assets

Managing media assets in cross platform projects, especially if you are providing variations for different device configurations, can become quite a hurdle. In order to reuse these assets for multiple platforms, linked file references can be utilized (**Add | Existing Item | Add as Link**).

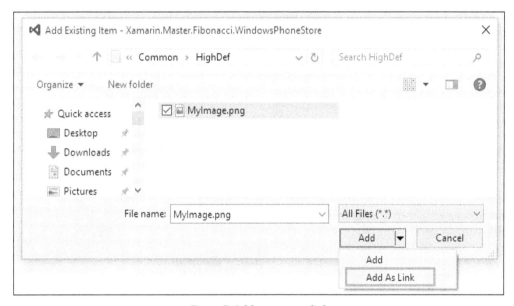

Figure 7: Add resource as link

Using this strategy, image documents can be included in a common location for all platform-specific projects (for example, the common portable library), and only linked file references can be added to platform-specific projects.

This way, image documents are not copied to multiple locations, but only compiled into different platform-specific projects.

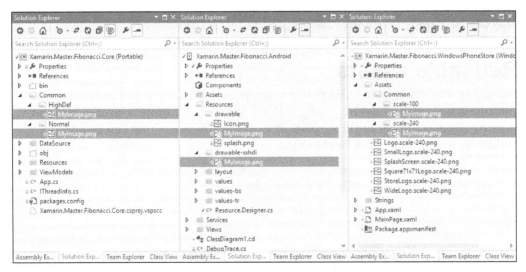

Figure 8: Linked resources for normal and high definition in Windows Phone and Android projects

Text resources in a cross-platform project do not differ greatly between platforms, especially if the resources in question are simple string values, rather than targeted attributes for UI controls (for example, text content specified for a label or a button on a storyboard). Another observation is that most of the text resource values are handled as key/value pairs in XML format (for Windows Phone and Android) or with simple JavaScript-like notation (in iOS). Elaborating on these assumptions, we can create an automated process that evaluates a common resource file and creates/generates the resource strings for the target platforms.

Considering the fact that we will use either a shared project library or a portable class library that will contain the shared code for the platform specific projects, this common project would be the most appropriate location to store the common resource strings. We can use this project to create the common resource package in the resx format.

These embedded resource files, as previously mentioned, are simple XML files in which the string resources pairs are stored in `<data>` nodes with the `name` attribute as the key and the `<value>` text node as the value (the rest of the file contains the XSD schema and metadata values for code generation).

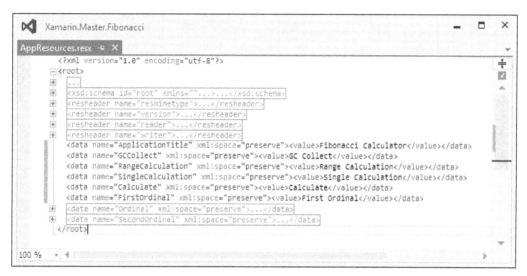

Figure 9: Resx file XML structure

Android string resources have a similar structure with less complexity and different node names (that is, resource values are represented with `<string>` text nodes with the attribute `name`). Conversion between the two XML files is fairly simple with an XSL transformation in Visual Studio.

XSL is an abbreviation for Extensible Stylesheet Language and is used for transforming XML documents from one format to another. XSLT files may utilize templates, XPath queries, and other XSL functions to process XML document content. More information can be found at http://www.w3schools.com/xsl/default.asp.

To transform the resource file into the Android format, we will create an XSLT file in the same folder as the `AppResources.resx` file in the common project. In order to create the Android XML resource file, we need to select each `<data>` element from the `<root>` node and create `<string>` nodes with appropriate text content and attributes inside the `<resources>` root node:

```
<?xml version="1.0" encoding="utf-8"?>
<xsl:stylesheet version="1.0"
  xmlns:xsl="http://www.w3.org/1999/XSL/Transform"
    xmlns:msxsl="urn:schemas-microsoft-com:xslt" exclude-result-
      prefixes="msxsl">
  <xsl:output method="xml" indent="yes"/>
  <xsl:template match="/">
    <resources>
      <xsl:for-each select="/root/data">
        <string>
          <xsl:attribute name="name">
            <xsl:value-of select="@name"/>
          </xsl:attribute>
          <xsl:value-of select="value"/>
        </string>
      </xsl:for-each>
    </resources>
  </xsl:template>
</xsl:stylesheet>
```

Now, after this step, we can use the XML menu to debug the XSLT file using the `resx` file:

Figure 10: XSL Transformation debug session in Visual Studio

After confirming that the transformation works as expected, we can now automate this process to regenerate the strings file every time the common project is rebuilt. For this automation, we can use a third-party XML transformation command line application and add the console command as a pre-build event command line argument using the project settings. Another option would be to use the out-of-box MSBuild task XslTransformation to add a BeforeBuild target.

> In order to add new build targets, the csproj file needs to be modified in Visual Studio. For this purpose, the common project first needs to be unloaded using **Unload Project** from the project context menu, and the project file can be edited using the **Edit <Project File Name>** option from the same context menu.

The XslTransformation task is a simple build task with three basic parameters for the XML file that needs to be transformed (that is, XmlInputPath), the XSL file to be used for the transformation (that is, XslInputPath), and finally the output path (that is, OutputPaths):

```
<Target Name="BeforeBuild">
  <XslTransformation
    XslInputPath="Resources\AndroidTransform.xslt"
    XmlInputPaths="Resources\AppResources.resx"
    OutputPaths="..\Xamarin.Master.Fibonacci.
      Android\Resources\values\strings.xml" />
</Target>
```

With this modification, every time the common project is built (with a default setup, the common project should be built before the Android project), the strings.xml file will be generated and placed into the values folder in the Android project.

The same transformation approach is applicable to the iOS localized strings files. In an iOS-specific transformation, the output should be set to text and the transformation style sheet should create the key/value pairs. In order to create the lines of text for each data element in the embedded resource file, the concat function can be utilized:

```
<?xml version="1.0" encoding="utf-8"?>
<xsl:stylesheet version="1.0" xmlns:xsl="http://www.w3.org/1999/XSL/
Transform"
  xmlns:msxsl="urn:schemas-microsoft-com:xslt" exclude-result-
  prefixes="msxsl">
  <xsl:output method="text" encoding="utf-8" indent="no" omit-xml-
    declaration="no"/>
```

```
<xsl:template match="/">
  <xsl:for-each select="/root/data">
    <xsl:value-of select="concat('&quot;', @name, '&quot; =
        &quot;', value, '&quot;;', '&#xA;')" />
  </xsl:for-each>
</xsl:template>
</xsl:stylesheet>
```

In this stylesheet, it is important to note that text elements (symbols), such as double quotes and carriage return (that is, line feed and end of line), are HTML encoded.

Once the transformation result is confirmed, we can add another `XslTransformation` task to the project file as a `BeforeBuild` target to create the localized `strings` file:

```
<XslTransformation
  XslInputPath="Resources\IOSTransform.xslt"
  XmlInputPaths="Resources\AppResources.resx"
  OutputPaths="..\Xamarin.Master.Fibonacci
    .iOS\Resources\Base.lproj\Localizable.strings" />
```

Using the same implementation, the translation values containing the `resx` files can be transformed and used to generate localized resources for the target platforms. In addition to XSL transformations, T4 templates can also be used to generate the text resource files. Since certain build tasks (including `XslTransformation`) are not yet supported by xBuild and Xamarin Studio, T4 templates can provide an alternative if your main development environment is Mac OS and main development IDE is Xamarin Studio. With T4 templates, it is also possible to iterate through each file in the common resources and generate matching localization files in platform-specific projects.

The next section will summarize the localization strategies on Xamarin target platforms.

Localization

Localization and globalization are the two fundamental concepts of mobile applications. In the previous sections, we discussed different ways of separating visual content from the rest of the application. This process, in essence, prepares the mobile application to be localized and is generally a part of the globalization phase. Globalized applications should function the same way, independent of the culture or locale they are being executed on. During localization, developers are supposed to create language-specific resources and integrate them into the globalized applications.

Locale and culture

Locale can be defined as the umbrella term that includes all regional configurations on a specific device (or a specific application in some cases). The locale not only represents the user interface language, but also the formats used to display dates, times, numbers, and currency values.

As part of the globalization effort, in Xamarin target platforms, developers first need to identify which languages are going to be supported as part of the localization effort. A mobile application, after it is published and installed by the user, should manifest the supported languages so that the user interface can be rendered either with the locale that is dictated by the operating system (if supported) or the default/fallback language of the application.

The supported languages manifest is a calculated value according to the resources provided (Android) or a pre-declared manifest or project entry (iOS and Windows Phone).

Windows Phone

In Windows Phone Silverlight application projects, resources for different languages can be provided using resource packages according to the naming conventions. The provided packages should then be referenced in the WMAppManifest.xml file. The easiest way to include additional language support for a Windows Phone application is to use the project properties to identify the supported cultures.

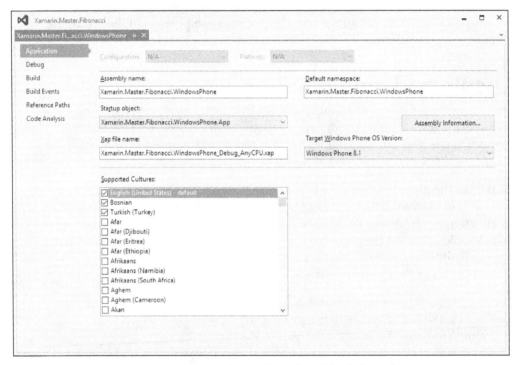

Figure 11: Project Properties for Windows Phone Silverlight application

Once the project configuration modifications are saved, Visual Studio automatically creates the associated resx files (for example, AppResources.bs.resx for Bosnian, AppResources.tr-TR.resx for Turkish) and updates the application manifest. The default language can be modified from the package manifest (that is, package.appxmanifest) or the application manifest (WMAppManifest.xml) designers.

Windows Store applications (that is, Windows Phone 8.1) are globalized using folders named after the supported languages containing the `resw` resource files. For instance, in order to create an application that targets the same cultures as the previous example, we would need to create a folder structure and culture-specific resource files similar to the following:

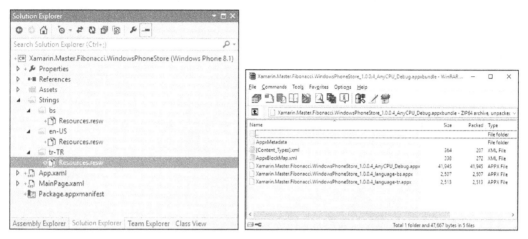

Figure 12: Windows Store apps supported cultures and app bundle

Once the application package is created, you will notice that instead of a single application package, an application bundle is created and each supported culture has an associated store app package in the bundle.

> Application bundles are used in Windows Store applications to reduce the size of the application packages that users are going to download for specific CPU architecture (ARM, x86, or x64), display hardware (image and other media assets, optimized for different resolutions), or locale. The packaging strategy can be selected while creating application packages, but if bundling is declined, developers are required to create a different upload package for each CPU architecture they are planning to support with their applications.

Xamarin.iOS

As previously explained, for Xamarin.iOS, once the additional languages are selected for the project in the Xcode development environment, generated localization folders and files are automatically added to the Xamarin.iOS project. The generated storyboard string files initially contain the possible localizable fields and the assigned values from the storyboard. Other string bundle resource files are copied with the same values from the `Base.lproj` folder.

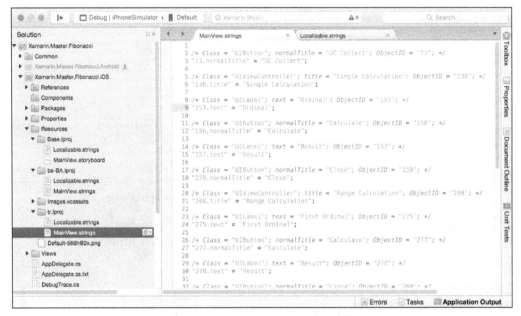

Figure 13: Localized Xamarin.iOS project

When using text resource files for localization, the `LocalizedString` function for the `MainBundle` property either returns the value that matches the current user language selection or the default value defined in the `Base.lproj` directory.

When using Visual Studio for creating and editing the `strings` files, it is a good idea to map the `strings` extension to JavaScript editor using the **Options** dialog and the **Text Editor | File Extension** section.

In order to load a language-specific resource that does not match the current preferred language(s) configuration, you will need to use the localization bundle path and retrieve the localized resources using the same function on this bundle:

```
var path = NSBundle.MainBundle.PathForResource("tr", "lproj");
NSBundle languageBundle = NSBundle.FromPath(path);
var localizedString = languageBundle.LocalizedString
  ("RangeCalculation", "");
```

The native development language directory (that is, `Base.lproj`), as well as the language-specific folders, can also be used to store other types of bundle resources, such as image resources, storyboards, XIB files, or even language-specific `Info.plist` files. (The `InfoPlist.strings` file in a language directory can be used to override values from the application's `Info.plist` file, such as the application name.)

It is crucial to add the supported languages to the info manifest. For localization, there are two relevant keys. The first relevant item is the *Localization* native development region (that is, `CFBundleDevelopmentRegion`) and the second key is the *Localizations* (that is, `CFBundleLocalizations`). While the native development region defines the language associated with the `Base.lproj` location, the localizations entries provide information about the other supported localizations.

Xamarin.Android

Localization in Xamarin.Android projects, similar to the folder structure of Windows Phone 8.1 projects, is achieved using a specific folder structure with the language code suffixed into the localized resource items (for example, `drawable-tr` or `values-en`).

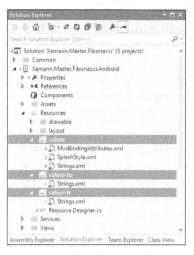

Figure 14: Android localization folder structure

An appropriate resource is selected in the runtime using a simple elimination algorithm that selects the correct resource file according to the locale, display density, display size, touch support, and other criteria.

Xamarin.Forms

The Xamarin.Forms portable class library project template provides the ideal environment for text resource sharing. In this setup, with a process similar to Windows Phone Silverlight projects, resx files can be used to create resource bundles that can be used to localize the cross-platform views created with Xamarin.Forms framework.

Figure 15: Localized Xamarin.Forms resources

Once the embedded resource files and their translation counterparts are added to the common PCL project, the resource entries can be accessed using the generated static class. In order for the generated class to be accessible from the platform specific implementations, the **Custom Tool** property of the resource file must be set to PublicResXFileCodeGenerator and the **Build Action** property to Embedded Resource.

With Xamarin Studio or Visual Studio, the file properties window can be used to set to the correct access modifier for the resource accessors. In Visual Studio, the resource editor can also be used to correct the access modifier of resource items (that is, select **Access Modifier | Public** using the resource designer).

In the Windows Phone runtime, the correct resource files are loaded according to the current thread culture, so the preceding implementation would automatically choose the appropriate embedded resource. However, supported languages should still be configured using the application manifest. In Xamarin.iOS, the correct resources are loaded according to the users' language preferences (not the current UI language) and supported languages should be included in the `Info.plist` file using the `CFLocalizations` entry. For the Android platform, UI language selection is taken as the identifier for the resources.

The following implementation would localize the tabbed page implementation from the previous chapter:

```
var tabbedPage = new TabbedPage();

tabbedPage.Children.Add(new ContentPage
{
    Title = TextResources.TabItemRecent,
    Content = new StackLayout
    {
        // Omitted for clarity
    },
    Icon = "social.png"
});
```

In the preceding example, the highlighted line of code sets the accessor properties to specific resource elements. When using XAML for the same implementation, we can resort to statically bound properties using the `TextResources` generated class:

```
<TabbedPage
    xmlns="http://xamarin.com/schemas/2014/forms"
    xmlns:x="http://schemas.microsoft.com/winfx/2009/xaml"
    x:Class="Xamarin.Master.TravelTrace.Views.MainTabView"
    xmlns:resources="clr-namespace:Xamarin.Master.
        TravelTrace.Resources;assembly=Xamarin.Master.TravelTrace">
    <ContentPage
        Title="{x:Static resources:TextResources.TabItemRecent}"
        Icon="social.png">
```

It is important to include the CLR namespace containing the generated resource accessor.

Architectural patterns

The user interface of an application can be described as the packaging over the sum of all the moving parts underneath. As applications get more complex, the responsibilities of the user interface increase and it gets harder to package the product underneath. Leaving aside the static parts of the UI (that is, assets described in the previous sections of this chapter), it is the most volatile part of an application. In order to counteract the entropy that builds up throughout the application's lifetime, solve recurring problem patterns, and re-use modules, developers often utilize certain design patterns in their development efforts. Especially in cross-platform projects, the importance of these architectural design patterns have been proven to be irrefutable.

For demonstration purposes, let's use a simple form-submit scenario. In this implementation, the users will be greeted with a form they will have to fill in. Once all the required text fields are populated by the user, he/she will submit the content using the submit button. The data is then validated and stored. The user should then be informed about the submission with a read-only screen where he/she can see the submitted and stored data.

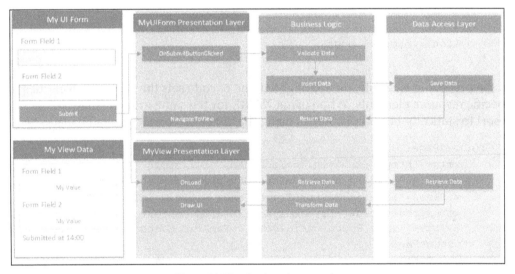

Figure 16: The classic *n*-tier scenario

In an *n*-tier implementation, the presentation tier would be responsible for visualizing the data and would hold an instance of the API façade. The API façade would implement the business logic to validate the information and submit it to the data tier instance. The data tier would be solely responsible for communicating with the persistence store (possibly through the service layer).

The event subscriptions (that is, text field changed or submit button clicked) would be implemented in the presentation layer. On successful submission, the presentation layer would pass on the current API object to a new presentation container and visualize the submitted data. Even though this approach provides a clear separation between the tiers, there are still strong ties between the layers in the hierarchy (that is, the presentation layer holds a strongly typed reference of the API and the API either reuses or creates a new instance of the data model). The application tier also creates an unnecessarily large and complex structure that should provide the required methods for all the containers and related scenarios in the presentation layer. The presentation layer still has the most responsibility in terms of event-driven implementation. If we transpose this implementation onto a Xamarin cross-platform project, we would be able to reuse the complete application tier and the data tier across platforms. However, it would still require quite a bit of re-implementation for the presentation layer for other platform projects, as this layer is responsible for using the API. Another downside of this pattern is the fact that, other than the façade, it isn't easy to unit test the implementation (that is, there are multiple event subscriptions on the presentation layer).

MVP (model-view-presenter) and **MVVM (model-view-viewmodel)**, both derivatives of **MVC (model-view-controller)**, try to answer some of these issues for classic *n*-tier implementations. Both of these patterns inherently use a passive presentation layer and delegate the main responsibility to the supervising or mediating component; the main reason for this is the fact that unit testing the view is generally impractical, hence it should be devoid of logic as much as possible. The presenter communicates with the data tier actively and is responsible for how the view should be visualized. In this paradigm, the only way the view communicates with the mediator is through routed events (separation of concerns). It is also important to note that in these architectural implementations, the application is divided into self-sufficient triads (that is, model, view, and presenter) which make up different use-cases and views in the application. Façades are generally used only in the model component.

MVC

The MVC pattern was initially introduced into Smalltalk, and later on popularized with its (excessive) use in web applications and frameworks. In classic MVC implementation, the **Model** not only provides access to a data store but also implements any required business logic. The **Model** can be described as the core implementation of the problem domain, independent of the user interface.

The **Controller** generally represents the logic stripped out of the **View**; it can send commands to the **Model** as well as the **View**, and receive the routed events from the **View**. Changes in state (that is, in the **Model**), are reflected on the **View** with or without the intervention of the **Controller** (classic MVC allows active or implicit interactions between the **Model** and the **View**).

iOS app architecture

In iOS applications, the main development language hitherto has been Objective-C. The Cocoa and Cocoa Touch frameworks used for Mac OS and iOS application development, respectively, were also developed mainly in Objective-C. Considering the strong ties between Objective-C and SmallTalk, it is no surprise the main development pattern adopted and enforced by the iOS development kit is MVC.

In the Cocoa version of MVC implementation, direct communication between the **View** and **Model** is completely abandoned (and prohibited) because of the technical requirements of the mobile application development environment, and in order to increase the reusability of model and view components. In this pattern, the **Controller** (also called the mediator at times) is given the main responsibility to control the flow of data between the **View** and the **Model**. From this aspect, Cocoa's implementation of MVC undeniably resembles the MVP pattern:

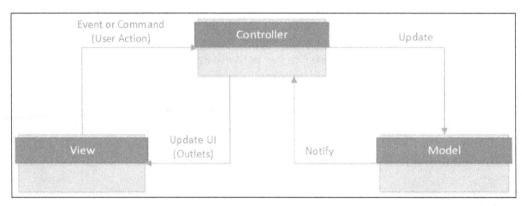

Figure 17: Cocoa MVC

In this implementation schema, developers are encouraged to decouple the components of the triad from each other and implement the communication between them only through the defined abstractions.

The separation between the **View** and the **Controller** is generally achieved with commands, outlets, and bindings. Commands provide actionable composites that can be passed from one layer to another, and outlets are extensions of certain UI elements so that the controller can subscribe to events and control how the UI is presented according to state.

When view elements are designed using XIBs or storyboards (that is, storyboards are used to generate the XIBs at compile time), the outlets are defined as access points for the **View-Controller**. **View-Controllers** do not have a direct dependency on the **View**, nor does the **View** have any knowledge of the **Controller**. This setup complies with the separation of concerns principle and provides a loosely coupled structure as advised.

If we were to implement the scenario from the previous example, we would be exposing two outlets for the text input fields in the submit form and an outlet for the submit button. These outlets would, in return, be used by the Controller assigned to the **View** for subscribing to certain events, to validate and submit the data. The **View-Controller** (that is, **UIController**) is also responsible for changing how the controls are displayed (for example, validation can change the color of the text input field) and communicating user actions such as the submission of data to the **Model**. Navigating to another view is also the responsibility of the **Controller** in this case.

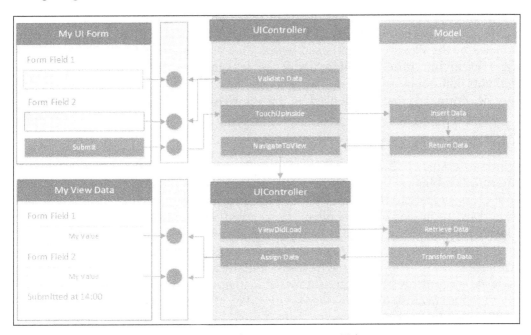

Figure 18: MVC demonstration on an iOS form

Segue navigation between views is another possible navigation strategy when the Controller for the new **View** exists in the calling **Controller**, or the same UI controller is used for both of the views (that is, the same **Controller** could have been used for both submit and read-only views in the preceding example).

MVVM

MVVM (Model-View-ViewModel), a derivative of the MVP pattern, provides well-established boundaries between the UI, business logic, and data. After its emergence, it almost immediately became the main implementation pattern for **WPF (Windows Presentation Foundation)** applications. The data binding features provided by the WPF framework make up the foundation of this mediation pattern.

> Data binding is the terminology used to describe the mechanism which connects data visualization elements from the UI layer (that is, the controls) to other controls or data objects from other tiers. The synchronization between the two actors of the binding is maintained through various events (for example, the `INotifyPropertyChanged` interface is used to propagate value change events).

In this pattern, the ViewModel is the main actor, whose responsibility is to control the data flow between the **View** and the **Model**. The outlets, in this architecture, are exposed by the ViewModel and used by the View implementation (as opposed to the iOS MVC architecture). The ViewModel provides these outlets in the form of data elements that can be associated to attributes or states of the UI controls, and also as generic commands that can be used by the **View** controls to respond to user input.

Windows Runtime

Windows Phone applications, as well as Windows Store applications, natively support data binding for UI controls. This feature makes Windows Phone applications ideal candidates for this architecture. However, architectural elements should still be implemented by developers according to the requirements of specific projects. There are multiple (open-source or commercial) libraries that can be included as NuGet packages in development projects, including Prism (a cross-platform MVVM library, which was initially a pet project of the Microsoft patterns and practices team, but is now being maintained by the community) and MVVMCross (a cross-platform open source MVVM framework).

At the core of the MVVM pattern and data binding, we can locate the implementation of a bindable base class. A bindable base provides the implementation of the INotifyPropertyChanged interface and makes it easier to identify and implement the data elements that will take part in data binding. This interface is used to route value changed events from data items and their properties to UI elements.

A simple bindable base implementation would look similar to:

```
public abstract class BindableBase : INotifyPropertyChanged
{
    protected virtual void SetProperty<T>(ref T property, T value,
      [CallerMemberName] string propertyName = null)
    {
        if (Equals(property, value)) return;

        property = value;

        OnPropertyChanged(propertyName);
    }

    public event PropertyChangedEventHandler PropertyChanged;

    protected virtual void OnPropertyChanged([CallerMemberName]
      string propertyName = null)
    {
        var handler = PropertyChanged;
        if (handler != null) handler(this, new
          PropertyChangedEventArgs(propertyName));
    }
}
```

The implementation of this class can be used with model data items so that any change can be reflected on the UI:

```
public class ModelData : BindableBase
{
    private string m_Property1BackingField = string.Empty;

    public string Property1
    {
        get
        {
```

```
                return m_Property1BackingField;
        }
        set
        {
            SetProperty(ref m_Property1BackingField, value);
        }
    }
}
```

Now the `ModelData` class can already be used as the ViewModel and its bindings provided to `Property1`:

```
public MainPage()
{
    this.InitializeComponent();

    this.DataContext = new ModelData {Property1 = "Hello MVVM"};
}
```

The data binding to an input control on the main page would look similar to this:

```
<TextBox Text="{Binding Property1, Mode=TwoWay}">
```

In this binding scenario, we set the binding mode to `TwoWay`. This binding type means that any change on this property value, either on the ViewModel or on the user interface (that is, on user input), would be propagated to the UI element, or vice versa.

Data bindings can be maintained using different modes. The **OneTime** binding is used to update the target property using the source property when the data source changes. This type of binding is generally used by read-only controls. The **OneWay** binding is used only to update the target property when the source property value changes, whereas the **TwoWay** mode is for duplex synchronization. Finally, **OneWayToSource** is used only to update the source property if there are any changes on the target property.

Data bindings are not limited to values from and to ViewModel properties. Bindable properties of user controls can also be bridged in this pattern. Moreover, bindable properties of user controls include behavioral and style attributes (for example, the `IsEnabled` property of a `TextBox` user controls). Additional bindable properties can be provided to intrinsic or derived user controls using attached and/or dependency properties.

Command binding is another concept which provides a decoupled way to associate user action controls (for example, Button) with executable elements on the data context (that is, the ViewModel). In order for a user control to be bound to a command, the user control should implement a bindable command attribute and the ViewModel should provide an ICommand implementation of a specific action. The ICommand interface is a simple interface containing a CanExecute property, an associated CanExecuteChanged event (which is generally bound to the IsEnabled property of the user control), and the Execute method.

A simple command implementation that will validate the data model from the previous example and then execute would look similar to the following implementation (note that MVVM frameworks generally provide a generic Command class, which accepts delegates and/or lambdas for Execute and CanExecute methods):

```
public class SubmitCommand : ICommand
{
    private readonly ModelData m_DataContext;

    public SubmitCommand(ModelData dataContext)
    {
        m_DataContext = dataContext;

        m_DataContext.PropertyChanged += (sender, args) =>
        {
            if(args.PropertyName == "Property1" &&
                CanExecuteChanged !=null)
                CanExecuteChanged(this, null);
        };
    }

    public bool CanExecute(object parameter)
    {
        return m_DataContext.Property1.Length > 5;
    }

    public void Execute(object parameter) {
        // TODO:
    }

    public event EventHandler CanExecuteChanged;
}
```

With this implementation (either public or a nested class of the data model defined previously), we can initialize and expose the command when a new `ModelData` class is initialized:

```
public ModelData()
{
    Submit = new SubmitCommand(this);
}

public ICommand Submit { get; set; }
```

Finally, the binding for this command in XAML markup would look similar to:

```
<Button Content="Submit" Command="{Binding Submit}"></Button>
```

If we were to use the MVVM pattern to implement the previous form submission scenario, we can observe the implementation of both data and command bindings. We could implement a ViewModel class that is responsible for loading and submitting a bindable data item. The view would have the bindings to the ViewModel properties and commands, as well as bindings to the data item itself.

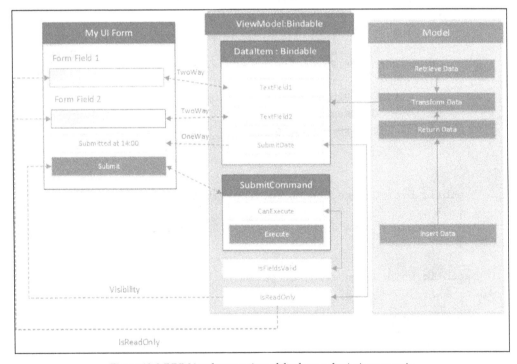

Figure 19: MVVM implementation of the form submission scenario

In this design, SubmitCommand is used both to submit the user input to the **Model** and to validate the form itself (using the CanExecute method). The IsReadOnly property of the ViewModel is bound to the IsReadOnly properties of the text fields and the Visibility property of the submit button (in read-only mode, instead of the submit button, the submitted label should be displayed), possibly with an IValueConverter (an interface used in two-way conversions between bound properties in data-binding scenarios).

Value converters implement the IValueConverter interface to apply custom logic to the binding process. They are generally used as adapters for the CLR type of the target property and the source property (for example, if the data model property type was a string defining a certain color, we would need to convert/parse this value to SolidColorBrush or similar to assign it to visual elements' properties).

Besides the loose coupling and modularity achieved by using MVVM, the pseudo-finite automaton provided by the ViewModel allows developers to easily recreate different data states used by the view and implement unit tests without much hassle.

MVVM on Xamarin.iOS and Xamarin.Android

In Xamarin projects, in order to create a uniform structure between the applications for different platforms and maximize code sharing, it is a widely accepted implementation principle to use the MVVM pattern solution-wide. Since data bindings and commanding pattern implementations are not natively supported on iOS and Android, using an MVVM framework that supports cross-platform development with Xamarin can be a solution.

It is important to mention that iOS and Cocoa have the concept of key-value observing, and a binding-like implementation can be applied to some extent.

On Xamarin.iOS and Xamarin.Android, bindings are generally provided through the extensions to UIViewController (on iOS) and Activities (on Android). In iOS, this implementation strategy transforms the **View** and **Controller** from MVC architecture into mere **View** implementations, while the ViewModel, conceptually, replaces the **Model** implementation. Bindings to the ViewModel are initialized in the application lifecycle events of the UIViewControllers and Activities.

MVVM with Xamarin.Forms

The data binding feature of Xamarin.Forms is an implementation/port of the WPF data bindings, so XAML bindings are supported for both data and commands. The main difference between Xamarin.Forms and Windows Runtime is that in Windows Store applications, binding context for a user control or a container is configured using the `DataContext` property, whereas in Xamarin.Forms, the `BindingContext` property is used for the same purpose. Xamarin.Forms additionally provides generic command implementation classes (namely, `Command` and `Command<T>`) which allow developers to expose commands without having to implement the `ICommand` interface in nested classes for the ViewModels.

Summary

In cross-platform projects, with or without Xamarin.Forms, it is advisable to maintain the View elements as thin and devoid of static and/or sharable elements as possible. As discussed in this chapter, each Xamarin target platform supports resource and asset management in particular ways. These methodologies can be expanded to share static resources between the platform-specific projects by using linked resources and/or using special build techniques.

Architectural patterns, imposed by the platform or otherwise, can also be employed either at the beginning of the project or as the project matures through iterations. MVC and MVVM, as well as MVP, patterns help reduce the sharable logic components on the View, creating a more loosely-coupled project structure (see quality identifiers in *Chapter 1, Developing with Xamarin*).

After having covered different aspects of the Xamarin framework and UI-related concepts, in the next part of the book, we will discuss **Application Lifecycle Management** (**ALM**)-related topics to create an efficient development pipeline for individuals or teams dealing with Xamarin projects.

10
ALM – Developers and QA

This chapter provides an introduction to **Application Lifecycle Management (ALM)** and continuous integration methodologies on Xamarin cross-platform applications. As the part of the ALM process that is most relevant for developers, unit test strategies will be discussed and demonstrated, as well as automated UI testing. This chapter is divided into the following sections:

- Development pipeline
- Troubleshooting
- Unit testing
- UI testing

Development pipeline

The development pipeline can be described as the virtual production line that steers a project from a mere bundle of business requirements to the consumers. Stakeholders that are part of this pipeline include, but are not limited to, business proxies, developers, the QA team, the release and configuration team, and finally the consumers themselves. Each stakeholder in this production line assumes different responsibilities, and they should all function in harmony. Hence, having an efficient, healthy, and preferably automated pipeline that is going to provide the communication and transfer of deliverables between units is vital for the success of a project.

In the Agile project management framework, the development pipeline is cyclical rather than a linear delivery queue. In the application life cycle, requirements are inserted continuously into a backlog. The backlog leads to a planning and development phase, which is followed by testing and QA. Once the production-ready application is released, consumers can be made part of this cycle using live application telemetry instrumentation.

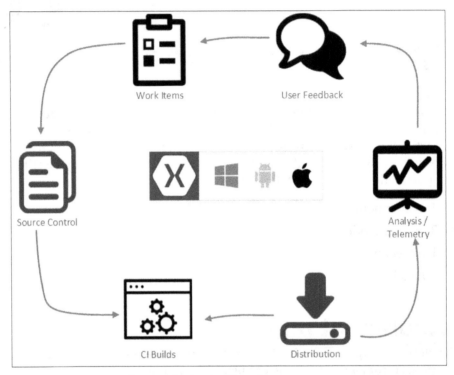

Figure 1: Application life cycle management

In Xamarin cross-platform application projects, development teams are blessed with various tools and frameworks that can ease the execution of ALM strategies. From sketching and mock-up tools available for early prototyping and design to source control and project management tools that make up the backbone of ALM, Xamarin projects can utilize various tools to automate and systematically analyze project timeline.

The following sections of this chapter concentrate mainly on the lines of defense that protect the health and stability of a Xamarin cross-platform project in the timeline between the assignment of tasks to developers to the point at which the task or bug is completed/resolved and checked into a source control repository.

Troubleshooting and diagnostics

SDKs associated with Xamarin target platforms and development IDEs are equipped with comprehensive analytic tools. Utilizing these tools, developers can identify issues causing app freezes, crashes, slow response time, and other resource-related problems (for example, excessive battery usage).

Xamarin.iOS applications are analyzed using the XCode Instruments toolset. In this toolset, there are a number of profiling templates, each used to analyze a certain perspective of application execution (such as the allocations template that was used in *Chapter 2*, *Memory Management*, for memory profiling). Instrument templates can be executed on an application running on the iOS simulator or on an actual device.

Figure 2: XCode Instruments

Similarly, Android applications can be analyzed using the device monitor provided by the Android SDK. Using Android Monitor, memory profile, CPU/GPU utilization, and network usage can also be analyzed, and application-provided diagnostic information can be gathered. **Android Debug Bridge** (**ADB**) is a command-line tool that allows various manual or automated device-related operations.

For Windows Phone applications, Visual Studio provides a number of analysis tools for profiling CPU usage, energy consumption, memory usage, and XAML UI responsiveness. XAML diagnostic sessions in particular can provide valuable information on problematic sections of view implementation and pinpoint possible visual and performance issues:

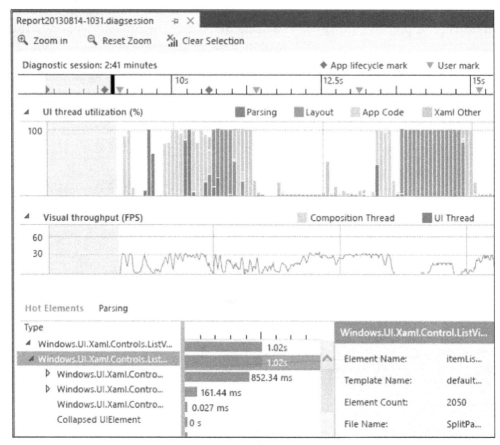

Figure 3: Visual Studio XAML analyses

Finally, Xamarin Profiler, as a maturing application (currently in preview release), can help analyze memory allocations and execution time. Xamarin Profiler can be used with iOS and Android applications.

Unit testing

The **test-driven development (TDD)** pattern dictates that the business requirements and the granular use-cases defined by these requirements should be initially reflected on unit test fixtures. This allows a mobile application to grow/evolve within the defined borders of these assertive unit test models. Whether following a TDD strategy or implementing tests to ensure the stability of the development pipeline, unit tests are fundamental components of a development project.

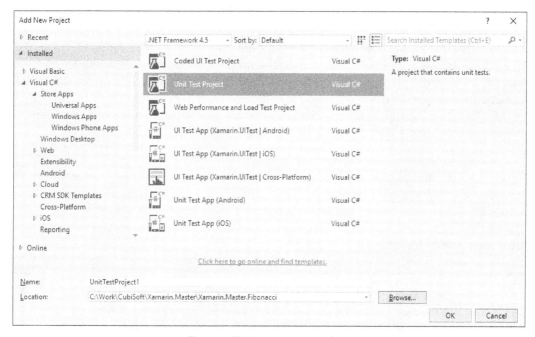

Figure 4: Unit test project templates

Xamarin Studio and Visual Studio both provide a number of test project templates targeting different areas of a cross-platform project. In Xamarin cross-platform projects, unit tests can be categorized into two groups: platform-agnostic and platform-specific testing.

Platform-agnostic unit tests

Platform-agnostic components, such as portable class libraries containing shared logic for Xamarin applications, can be tested using the common unit test projects targeting the .NET framework. Visual Studio Test Tools or the NUnit test framework can be used according to the development environment of choice. It is also important to note that shared projects used to create shared logic containers for Xamarin projects cannot be tested with .NET unit test fixtures. For shared projects and the referencing platform-specific projects, platform-specific unit test fixtures should be prepared.

When following an MVVM pattern, view models are the focus of unit test fixtures since, as previously explained, view models can be perceived as a finite state machine where the bindable properties are used to create a certain state on which the commands are executed, simulating a specific use-case to be tested. This approach is the most convenient way to test the UI behavior of a Xamarin application without having to implement and configure automated UI tests.

While implementing unit tests for such projects, a mocking framework is generally used to replace the platform-dependent sections of the business logic. Loosely coupling these dependent components (see *Chapter 8, Xamarin.Forms*) makes it easier for developers to inject mocked interface implementations and increases the testability of these modules. The most popular mocking frameworks for unit testing are Moq and RhinoMocks.

Both Moq and RhinoMocks utilize reflection and, more specifically, the Reflection.Emit namespace, which is used to generate types, methods, events, and other artifacts in the runtime. Aforementioned iOS restrictions on code generation make these libraries inapplicable for platform-specific testing, but they can still be included in unit test fixtures targeting the .NET framework. For platform-specific implementation, the True Fakes library provides compile time code generation and mocking features.

Depending on the implementation specifics (such as namespaces used, network communication, multithreading, and so on), in some scenarios it is imperative to test the common logic implementation on specific platforms as well. For instance, some multithreading and parallel task implementations give different results on Windows Runtime, Xamarin.Android, and Xamarin.iOS. These variations generally occur because of the underlying platform's mechanism or slight differences between the .NET and Mono implementation logic. In order to ensure the integrity of these components, common unit test fixtures can be added as linked/referenced files to platform-specific test projects and executed on the test harness.

Platform-specific unit tests

In a Xamarin project, platform-dependent features cannot be unit tested using the conventional unit test runners available in Visual Studio Test Suite and NUnit frameworks. Platform-dependent tests are executed on empty platform-specific projects that serve as a harness for unit tests for that specific platform.

Windows Runtime application projects can be tested using the Visual Studio Test Suite. However, for Android and iOS, the NUnit testing framework should be used, since Visual Studio Test Tools are not available for the Xamarin.Android and Xamarin.iOS platforms.

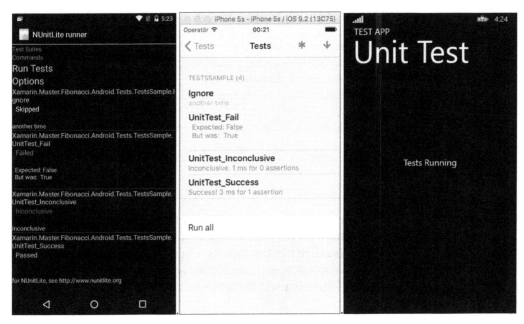

Figure 5: Test harnesses

The unit test runner for Windows Phone (Silverlight) and Windows Phone 8.1 applications uses a test harness integrated with the Visual Studio test explorer. The unit tests can be executed and debugged from within Visual Studio.

Xamarin.Android and Xamarin.iOS test project templates use NUnitLite implementation for the respective platforms. In order to run these tests, the test application should be deployed on the simulator (or the testing device) and the application has to be manually executed.

It is possible to automate the unit tests on Android and iOS platforms through instrumentation; however, these methods will be discussed in the next chapter.

In each Xamarin target platform, the initial application lifetime event is used to add the necessary unit tests:

```
[Activity(Label = "Xamarin.Master.Fibonacci.Android.Tests",
MainLauncher = true, Icon = "@drawable/icon")]
public class MainActivity : TestSuiteActivity
{
    protected override void OnCreate(Bundle bundle)
    {
        // tests can be inside the main assembly
        //AddTest(Assembly.GetExecutingAssembly());
        // or in any reference assemblies
        AddTest(typeof(Fibonacci.Android.Tests.TestsSample).Assembly);

        // Once you called base.OnCreate(), you cannot add more
assemblies.
        base.OnCreate(bundle);
    }
}
```

In the Xamarin.Android implementation, the `MainActivity` class derives from the `TestSuiteActivity`, which implements the necessary infrastructure to run the unit tests and the UI elements to visualize the test results. On the Xamarin.iOS platform, the test application uses the default `UIApplicationDelegate`, and generally, the `FinishedLaunching` event delegate is used to create the `ViewController` for the unit test run fixture:

```
public override bool FinishedLaunching(UIApplication application,
NSDictionary launchOptions)
{
    // Override point for customization after application launch.
    // If not required for your application you can safely delete this
method

    var window = new UIWindow(UIScreen.MainScreen.Bounds);
    var touchRunner = new TouchRunner(window);

    touchRunner.Add(System.Reflection.Assembly.
GetExecutingAssembly());
```

```
    window.RootViewController = new UINavigationController(touchRunn
er.GetViewController());

    window.MakeKeyAndVisible();

    return true;
}
```

The main shortcoming of executing unit tests this way is the fact that it is not easy to generate a code coverage report and archive the test results.

Neither of these testing methods provide the ability to test the UI layer. They are simply used to test platform-dependent implementations. In order to test the interactive layer, platform-specific or cross-platform (Xamarin.Forms) coded UI tests need to be implemented.

UI testing

In general terms, the code coverage of the unit tests directly correlates with the amount of shared code which amounts to, at the very least, 70-80 percent of the code base in a mundane Xamarin project. As explained in the previous chapters, one of the main driving factors of architectural patterns was to decrease the amount of logic and code in the view layer so that the testability of the project utilizing conventional unit tests reaches a satisfactory level. Coded UI (or automated UI acceptance) tests are used to test the uppermost layer of the cross-platform solution: the views.

Xamarin.UITests and Xamarin Test Cloud

The main UI testing framework used for Xamarin projects is the Xamarin.UITests testing framework. This testing component can be used on various platform-specific projects, varying from native mobile applications to Xamarin.Forms implementations, except for the Windows Phone platform and applications. Xamarin.UITests is an implementation based on the Calabash framework, which is an automated UI acceptance testing framework targeting mobile applications.

Xamarin.UITests is introduced to the Xamarin.iOS or Xamarin.Android applications using the publicly available NuGet packages. The included framework components are used to provide an entry point to the native applications. The entry point is the Xamarin Test Cloud Agent, which is embedded into the native application during the compilation. The cloud agent is similar to a local server that allows either the Xamarin Test Cloud or the test runner to communicate with the app infrastructure and simulate user interaction with the application.

Xamarin Test Cloud is a subscription-based service allowing Xamarin applications to be tested on real mobile devices using UI tests implemented via Xamarin.UITests. Xamarin Test Cloud not only provides a powerful testing infrastructure for Xamarin.iOS and Xamarin.Android applications with an abundant amount of mobile devices but can also be integrated into Continuous Integration workflows.

After installing the appropriate NuGet package, the UI tests can be initialized for a specific application on a specific device. In order to initialize the interaction adapter for the application, the app package and the device should be configured. On Android, the APK package path and the device serial can be used for the initialization:

```
IApp app = ConfigureApp.Android.ApkFile("<APK Path>/MyApplication.
apk")
                .DeviceSerial("<DeviceID>")
                .StartApp();
```

For an iOS application, the procedure is similar:

```
IApp app = ConfigureApp.iOS.AppBundle("<App Bundle Path>/
MyApplication.app")
    .DeviceIdentifier("<DeviceID of Simulator")
    .StartApp();
```

Once the App handle has been created, each test written using NUnit should first create the pre-conditions for the tests, simulate the interaction, and finally test the outcome.

The IApp interface provides a set of methods to select elements on the visual tree and simulate certain interactions, such as text entry and tapping. On top of the main testing functionality, screenshots can be taken to document test steps and possible bugs.

Both Visual Studio and Xamarin Studio provide project templates for Xamarin.
UITests.

Xamarin Test Recorder

Xamarin Test Recorder is an application that can ease the creation of automated
UI tests. It is currently in its preview version and is only available for the
Mac OS platform.

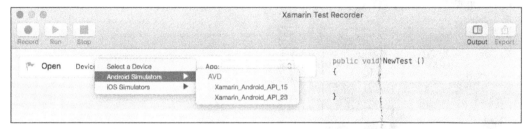

Figure 6: Xamarin Test Recorder

Using this application, developers can select the application in need of testing and
the device/simulator that is going to run the application. Once the recording session
starts, each interaction on the screen is recorded as execution steps on a separate
screen, and these steps can be used to generate the preparation or testing steps for
the Xamarin.UITests implementation.

Coded UI tests (Windows Phone)

Coded UI tests are used for automated UI testing on the Windows Phone platform.
Coded UI Tests for Windows Phone and Windows Store applications are not any
different than their counterparts for other .NET platforms such as Windows Forms,
WPF, or ASP.Net. It is also important to note that only XAML applications support
Coded UI tests.

Coded UI tests are generated on a simulator and written on an Automation ID premise. The Automation ID property is an automatically generated or manually configured identifier for Windows Phone applications (only in XAML) and the UI controls used in the application. Coded UI tests depend on the UIMap created for each control on a specific screen using the Automation IDs. While creating the UIMap, a crosshair tool can be used to select the application and the controls on the simulator screen to define the interactive elements:

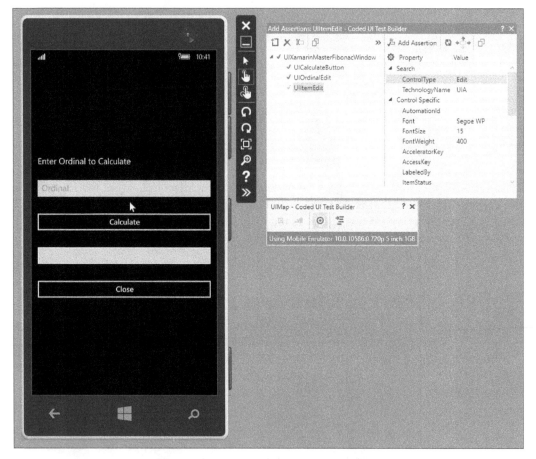

Figure 7:- Generating coded UI accessors and tests

Once the UIMap has been created and the designer files have been generated, gestures and the generated XAML accessors can be used to create testing pre-conditions and assertions.

For Coded UI tests, multiple scenario-specific input values can be used and tested on a single assertion. Using the `DataRow` attribute, unit tests can be expanded to test multiple data-driven scenarios. The code snippet below uses multiple input values to test different incorrect input values:

```
[DataRow(0,"Zero Value")]
[DataRow(-2, "Negative Value")]
[TestMethod]
public void FibonnaciCalculateTest_IncorrectOrdinal(int ordinalInput)
{
    // TODO: Check if bad values are handled correctly
}
```

Automated tests can run on available simulators and/or a real device. They can also be included in CI build workflows and made part of the automated development pipeline.

Calabash

Calabash is an automated UI acceptance testing framework used to execute Cucumber tests. Cucumber tests provide an assertion strategy similar to coded UI tests, only broader and behavior oriented. The Cucumber test framework supports tests written in the Gherkin language (a human-readable programming grammar description for behavior definitions). Calabash makes up the necessary infrastructure to execute these tests on various platforms and application runtimes.

A simple declaration of the feature and the scenario that is previously tested on Coded UI using the data-driven model would look similar to the excerpt below. Only two of the possible test scenarios are declared in this feature for demonstration; the feature can be extended:

```
Feature: Calculate Single Fibonacci number.
Ordinal entry should greater than 0.

Scenario: Ordinal is lower than 0.
    Given I use the native keyboard to enter "-2" into text field
Ordinal
    And I touch the "Calculate" button
    Then I see the text "Ordinal cannot be a negative number."

Scenario: Ordinal is 0.
    Given I use the native keyboard to enter "0" into text field
Ordinal
    And I touch the "Calculate" button
    Then I see the text "Cannot calculate the number for the 0th
ordinal."
```

Calabash test execution is possible on Xamarin target platforms since the Ruby API exposed by the Calabash framework has a bidirectional communication line with the Xamarin Test Cloud Agent embedded in Xamarin applications with NuGet packages.

Calabash/Cucumber tests can be executed on Xamarin Test Cloud on real devices since the communication between the application runtime and Calabash framework is maintained by Xamarin Test Cloud Agent, the same as Xamarin.UI tests.

Summary

Xamarin projects can benefit from a properly established development pipeline and the use of ALM principles. This type of approach makes it easier for teams to share responsibilities and work out business requirements in an iterative manner.

In the ALM timeline, the development phase is the main domain in which most of the concrete implementation takes place. In order for the development team to provide quality code that can survive the ALM cycle, it is highly advised to analyze and test native applications using the available tooling in Xamarin development IDEs.

While the common codebase for a target platform in a Xamarin project can be treated and tested as a .NET implementation using the conventional unit tests, platform-specific implementations require more particular handling. Platform-specific parts of the application need to be tested on empty shell applications, called test harnesses, on the respective platform simulators or devices.

To test views, available frameworks such as Coded UI tests (for Windows Phone) and Xamarin.UITests (for Xamarin.Android and Xamarin.iOS) can be utilized to increase the test code coverage and create a stable foundation for the delivery pipeline.

Most tests and analysis tools discussed in this chapter can be integrated into automated continuous integration processes. The infrastructure used for source control and continuous integration build and testing processes will be the topic of the next chapter.

11
ALM – Project and Release Management

This chapter explains the essentials of version control and automated continuous integration workflows. Source control options, as well as automated build strategies, will be demonstrated for Xamarin projects. Additional topics such as live telemetry collection and beta application distribution hubs will also be covered. This chapter is divided into the following sections:

- Source control
- Continuous integration
- Automated testing
- Beta deployment
- Live telemetry

Source control

Regardless of working as a team or as an individual, source control or version control remains a fundamental element of a software project development pipeline. Source code repository is the term used to describe the code management storage that deals with the versioning and consolidation of the code base. Additional features of source code repositories may include, but are not limited to, branching, reviews, shelves, and similar productivity-related capabilities. However, these items apply to any type of software development project and are out of the scope of this book.

For Xamarin projects, developers can utilize several types of repositories. The selection of a repository generally depends on the environment setup of choice (that is, operating system, development IDE, and so on).

TFVC

Team Foundation Version Control (**TFVC**) is the name given to the native repository provided by Team Foundation Server and its cloud-based counterpart Visual Studio Team Services (formerly, Visual Studio Online). TFVC is a centralized version control system where the version history is kept in a centralized server repository and the clients have only one version (that is, the workspace version) of each file.

TFVC provides a very familiar source code management toolset for Xamarin developers accustomed to the Microsoft development stack. For Xamarin developers using Windows and Visual Studio, TFVC is an ideal choice since it has native integration to Visual Studio. Source code management is implemented on the premise of "check-in" and "check-out" actions. Each code check-in can additionally include references to project metadata artifacts such as tasks, features, and bugs. Associating change sets (that is, a bundle of source code files to be checked-in) and project metadata provides an ideal development pipeline for developers working in a team.

For developers using Xamarin Studio on Windows or Mac OS, the only available option to use TFVC is to install Team Explorer Everywhere. Team Explorer Everywhere is an Eclipse plugin, which can be installed on Mac OS and employed to check in and check out source code items. Developers using Xamarin Studio on Windows can still install and use the free editions of Visual Studio to access TFS servers.

Git

Git, unlike TFVC, is a distributed version control system where each developer has a clone of the entire source repository, and each clone is managed locally until the changes are published to the central server. Developers are also free to create private local branches and switch from one branch to another without much hassle. Branches can be merged, published, or closed according to the requirements.

Xamarin Studio has native support for Git and developer commands such as `pull`, `clone`, `commit`, and `push` can be executed within the IDE. This native support makes Git repositories ideal candidates for developers using a Mac-based development environment.

Visual Studio also supports Git repositories and the classic Pull-Commit-Push flow. In addition to Visual Studio support, with recent updates to Visual Studio Team Services it is possible to create team projects using a Git repository. The selection of the Version Control type does not interfere with other project related options or the build setup. However, it is currently not possible to use the project management related features (for example, associating change sets with task items) using a Git repository.

Figure 1: Team Foundation Server with Git

It is also possible to set up a team project that utilizes multiple types of repositories. These repositories can be accessed using only the latest version of Visual Studio (that is, Visual Studio 2015 Update 1) at the moment.

The next section provides additional integration options for scenarios involving TFS and Git repositories.

TFS/Git scenarios

In certain scenarios, developers can choose, or are obliged to use, Git repositories together with a centralized TFVC repository (for example, developers with a Mac OS development setup do not have direct integration with TFVC). In this kind of a situation, there are several available utilities and implementation patterns that can help teams prepare their development infrastructure.

Git bridge

One of the integration paths that can be employed is the Git-TF tool maintained on CodePlex by Microsoft. The Git-TF tool is a platform agnostic tool written in Java. It utilizes TFVC APIs to enable developers to use a TFS repository together with a local Git repository.

In this integration path, either a single member or several members of a Xamarin development team can use a local or shared Git repository synchronized with the central repository using the Git-TF tool.

For a setup in which the individual developer uses a local Git repository in sync with TFVC, the TFS repository first needs to be cloned to the local machine:

```
git tf clone http://myserver:8080/tfs $/TeamProjectA/Main
```

After cloning, development can continue on the local machine using the Git repository. Local commit executions will not be reflected on the central repository. In the meantime, the central repository can be merged with the local repository using the `pull` command of Git-TF:

```
git tf pull --rebase
```

Once the development task is complete, the code can be checked in to TFS using the `checkin` command (instead of `git push`):

```
git tf checkin --associate=123,124 --message="Additional items for Task 123"
```

Git-TF provides the option to associate/resolve work items on TFS and include check-in comments similar to a standard code check-in.

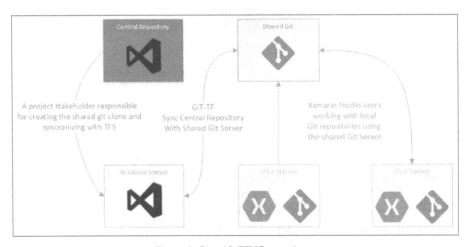

Figure 2: Git with TFVC repository

Another possibility would be to configure a shared Git repository for several team members so that each developer can clone it to their local environment and use it as a branch. In this setup, code merging and synchronization between the central repository (TFVC) and the shared Git repository would have to be handled by an administrator.

Similarly, the Git-TFS tool maintained on GitHub is an open-source project written in .NET and provides a bidirectional integration between TFS and Git repositories. However, this tool currently does not have a version available for Mac OS. Git-TFS provides support for some advanced TFS scenarios related to workspace handling and shelvesets.

NuGet packages

As previously discussed, NuGet packages are one of the code sharing strategies in cross-platform projects using Xamarin. NuGet packages can also be utilized to create the bridge between TFVC and Git, possibly by providing PCL libraries for Xamarin target platforms.

For instance, we can consider a scenario where shared projects between Windows Store applications and Xamarin.iOS are implemented on a Windows-based development environment, whereas Xamarin.iOS development team members use a Mac OS development setup with Xamarin Studio. The team project in this example can include a TFVC repository (for shared code and Windows Store app implementation) and a Git repository (for Xamarin.iOS development). The synchronization between the two servers can be handled through NuGet packages.

NuGet packages can be built and deployed with **Continuous Integration (CI)** build processes using out-of-the-box TFS build task definitions, making the NuGet process part of the development pipeline and continuous integration.

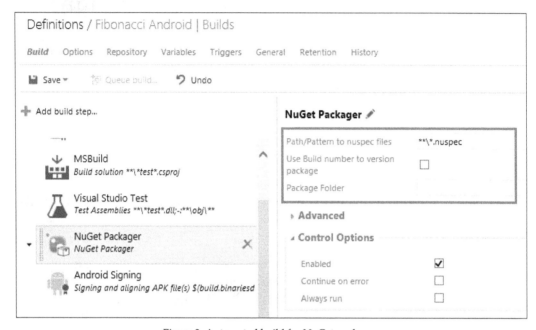

Figure 3: Automated build for NuGet packages

For NuGet package distribution, on top of the commercially available products (for example, the Artifactory server), Visual Studio Team Services can also be used to create NuGet source feeds and publish them privately for members of the development team.

Subversion (SVN)

Subversion is another source control repository type, generally referred to as SVN or Apache Subversion. Subversion repositories can be readily created in Mac OS developer environments using XCode development tools. Xamarin Studio has native support for SVN (version 1.6 or higher). Subversion can be an easy solution for individual Xamarin developers who prefer a Mac-based development environment. Even though there are publicly available Visual Studio extensions and integration tools for the Windows environment enabling the use of SVN, natively supported Git and TFVC are generally preferred over SVN.

Continuous integration

Continuous integration (CI) is the name for the software practice involving the aforementioned source control management strategies, together with automated build/deploy and testing phases. Nowadays, CI generally refers to the automated build/deploy and testing phases of **Application Lifecycle Management** (**ALM**).

For Xamarin projects, software engineers are free to use a vast number of CI management tools, available both commercially and with freemium licensing (that is, limited features for free usage).

Visual Studio Team Services

Visual Studio Team Services (**VSTS**) is the cloud-based version of Team Foundation Server and provides convenient features for Xamarin developers. Currently available as a freemium subscription-based service, teams are free to manage a limited number projects with a limited number of team members.

In VSTS team projects, both Git and TFVC development repositories can be managed, planned, automatically built, tested, and possibly deployed (see the Beta deployment section for VSTS integration).

Figure 4: TFS automated Xamarin builds

Out-of-the-box build templates that include Xamarin.iOS and Xamarin.Android projects can be executed on hosted build agents. While the latter build template can be executed with a shared hosted build agent, Xamarin.iOS needs a specialized build host with Xamarin.iOS capabilities to be associated with the team project.

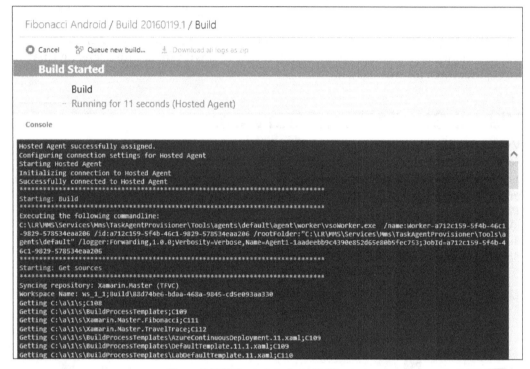

Figure 5: VSTS hosted Android build agent

For the Xamarin.Android build template, developers are required to insert Xamarin license details. However the build agent does not occupy a license seat except for the duration of the build. The build definition template includes an activation step where the build agent is registered as an occupant of the Xamarin license, and another step after the build is complete to remove the license.

In VSTS, Xamarin Test Cloud can also be integrated to execute automated acceptance tests using the default build template.

TeamCity

TeamCity (JetBrains) is another CI server, which provides automated builds and a great number of integration scenarios for various platforms. TeamCity can be downloaded and installed locally on multiple operating systems (including OS X and Windows) and is available as a freemium product (with limited free build agent installations and build configurations).

For Xamarin development teams, the biggest advantage of TeamCity is the fact that it can be installed on Mac OS. Once the build server is configured (it can be on the same machine as the server running the TeamCity server), builds for Xamarin. Android and Xamarin.iOS can be triggered on various actions, such as repository changes and schedules.

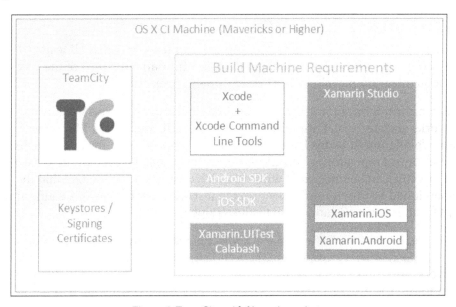

Figure 6: TeamCity with Xamarin projects

Additional possible integration scenarios and build steps in terms of Xamarin projects involve the Calabash instrumentation of application packages and Xamarin Test Cloud submission.

Other

Xamarin development teams have the luxury to be able to use many other online/cloud-based SaaS (Software-as-a-Service) providers, available for both internal and open source development. The most popular of these services is GitHub, which provides both private and public repositories as a subscription-based service. CI build providers such as AppVeyor and Travis CI have native integration with GitHub and can be readily used for various platform-specific build configurations.

Finally, Jenkins is another CI server which is available for free and commercial installations. Jenkins can be integrated with various repositories and can be configured to build and test Xamarin projects.

Automated testing

Automated testing, in other words running the unit tests or coded UI tests established as part of the development effort, is a fundamental part of the continuous integration cycle in most development projects.

To prepare a test fixture for a Xamarin project, developers can use various frameworks such as Visual Studio testing suite, nUnit, and xUnit. Moreover, Xamarin development teams have the freedom to choose from the available list of source control repositories and CI platforms. Fortunately, each of these aspects of a CI pipeline can be integrated without much hassle, due to the fact that the aforementioned testing frameworks provide test adapters for various configurations (except for the native Visual Studio testing framework).

For instance, let us consider a Xamarin project hosted on the TFVC repository on Visual Studio Team Services, where the unit test fixture is written utilizing the xUnit framework. As a first step, in order for the TFS build agent to facilitate the xUnit adapter to run the unit test fixture, the test adapter has to be installed as a NuGet package for the solution.

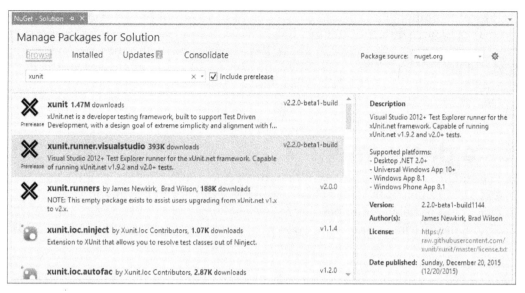

Figure 7: xUnit test adapter

After the adapter package is deployed to the source control repository, the team build can now include the testing step using the custom adapter.

In Visual Studio team builds, if the custom adapter is not defined, the tests are run using the default adapter. The build step, in this case, would report that no tests could be found.

Figure 8: xUnit test adapter setup

In this configuration, the `packages` folder of the solution for NuGet packages was used as the source directory (for example, `$(Build.SourcesDirectory)\Xamarin.Master.Fibonacci\packages\<path>`). It is also possible to use the `binaries` folder of the test project to access the adapter binary. It is also important to note that the MSBuild task prior to the Visual Studio Test task for the test projects is essential before executing the actual test fixture.

Beta deployment

Beta testing is an essential part of a Xamarin development pipeline. Using beta testing distribution hubs such as HockeyApp, Crashlytics, or Testflight, application packages can be delivered to beta users/testers. For Windows Phone 8.1 and Android, the distribution of application packages using simple networking methods is also possible (for example, using shared network locations, download links, and so on).

HockeyApp

HockeyApp stands out as the only beta distribution hub that supports all Xamarin target platforms, including Windows Runtime, and has integration capabilities for various CI configurations.

Initially a beta testing platform for iOS and Android, the Stuttgart-based company expanded their SDK to support Microsoft mobile development platforms. HockeyApp was ultimately acquired by Microsoft. However, it continues to support various mobile platforms, including Mac OS.

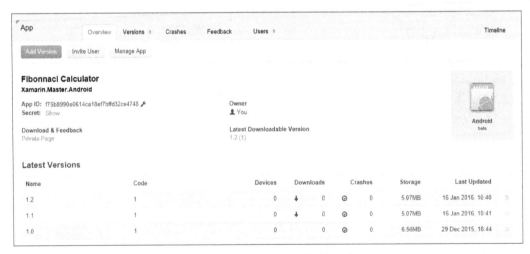

Figure 9: HockeyApp app dashboard

Application packages for the HockeyApp distribution hub can be uploaded directly from the web interface. Team members and/or beta testers should download the HockeyApp application to their mobile devices to be able to download the latest packages from the server.

In addition to manual release, HockeyApp provides two public APIs: one for clients and one for developers. The Client API is used to communicate with the server to deliver application runtime-related analytics, while the Developer API provides developers with the necessary functionality to upload and distribute application packages.

For Visual Studio Team Services (Visual Studio Online) and Jenkins, there are integration modules that make it possible to publish applications as part of CI builds.

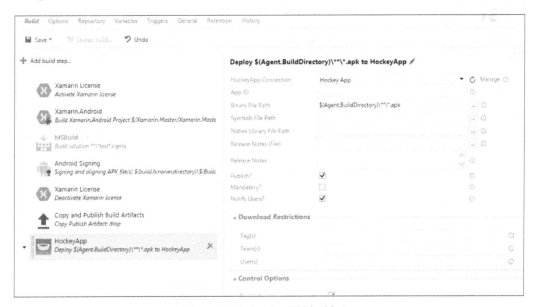

Figure 10: HockeyApp TFS build step

HockeyApp suite also includes crash analytics features that can be integrated into bug tracking systems such as Visual Studio Team Services, Assembla, BaseCamp, BitBucket, and so on.

HockeyApp offers free and enterprise licensing options.

Crashlytics

Crashlytics is another beta analysis platform, which provides distribution and crash reporting features for Xamarin.iOS and Xamarin.Android applications.

Crashlytics provides integration with other collaboration tools such as PivotalTracker, JIRA, GitHub, and BitBucket. It also offers a public API, providing service hooks for various integration scenarios.

Crashlytics was recently purchased by Twitter and continues to support the two Xamarin target platform applications. Crashlytics is currently part of the Twitter fabric development platform and is offered as a free service.

TestFlight

TestFlight, started as a beta testing platform for iOS and Android applications, immediately cancelled support for Android applications after their acquisition by Apple. It is now part of the Apple Developer Program and is only accessible through iTunes Connect.

Submissions to TestFlight are no different from actual Apple Store application packages. The final distributable package (`.ipa`) should be prepared for submission and uploaded using the Application Loader to Apple servers (see *Chapter 12, ALM – App Stores and Publishing,* for further information).

Unfortunately, this process cannot currently be automated as there are no build integration options and no public API.

Package distribution

In contrast to iOS devices, both Android and Windows Phone devices can install and run application packages that are distributed via the Internet or mobile storage.

For Windows Phone 8 and 8.1, the testing device should be configured as a developer device using the Windows Phone SDK. In order for a developer to unlock Windows Phone devices, a Windows developer account is necessary (this is a free subscription):

Figure 11: Windows Phone developer unlock

After the registration step, developers can install application packages either using the SDK tools or, if there is hardware support, using an SD card and the default store application.

For Android platform, there are available freeware tools that can be used to install `.apk` packages. The default package manager can also be used to install custom application packages shared as a network resource.

Live telemetry

Live telemetry is the term used to define the analytical information collected from applications being used by their target audience or beta testers. These analytic values are invaluable for feature rich mobile applications to identify how the customers are actually engaging with these applications on different hardware configurations, since Xamarin applications may be targeting devices running iOS, Android, or Windows Phone with various hardware configurations and peripherals.

With telemetry, development teams can gather information about user input patterns in different scenarios, application utilization flows, and platform impediments/strengths. While statistical information such as this is essential for UX design, values such as crash/exception details, network connectivity, memory consumption, and other diagnostic data on real-world usage scenarios can be useful as health indicators for the application.

There are numerous telemetry providers and frameworks for Xamarin target platforms. These frameworks can be included in Xamarin applications through binding packages (for example, Google Analytics for Android applications), and telemetry platforms targeting Xamarin applications, such as Xamarin Insights and/or Microsoft Application Insights, can be included in Xamarin implementations.

Xamarin Insights

Xamarin Insights is the analytics and crash reporting platform built specifically for Xamarin target platforms. Xamarin Insights implementations can be used in each Xamarin platform project including Xamarin.Forms applications and Windows Runtime. This is a subscription-based service and live telemetry can be seen on the web-based dashboard.

In order to start using Xamarin Insights in a cross-platform application solution, Xamarin Insights NuGet package(s) should be included in platform-specific projects. After the framework client assemblies are introduced, Xamarin.Insights runtime can be initialized using the subscription key.

For instance, if we were to include and initialize the Xamarin Insights module in a Xamarin.Android application using MVVMCross implementation, the initialization can be included in the application setup:

```
public class Setup : MvxAndroidSetup
{
    public Setup(Context applicationContext) :
base(applicationContext)
    {
        Insights.Initialize("<API Key>", applicationContext);

        // Identifying the specific user, and follow the usage pattern
in the rest of the execution
        var traits = new Dictionary<string, string> {
            {Insights.Traits.Email, "john.smith@contoso.com"},
            {Insights.Traits.Name, "John Smith"}
        };
        Insights.Identify("john.smith@contoso.com ", traits);
    }
}
```

In this implementation, the `Identify` method is an optional call. It is used to identify user-specific traits rather than general usage patterns.

 No matter which platform is running the Xamarin Insights content, the application should be enabled to use the Internet connection (that is, application manifest). It is also advised to enable permissions such as BATTERY_STATS, READ_LOGS, ACCESS_WIFI_STATE, and so on, on a Xamarin.Android application to collect additional information. Similarly, on Windows Phone 8, ID_CAP_IDENTIFY_DEVICE capability must be added to identify the specific device while recording telemetry.

Once the Xamarin Insights context is initialized, additional reporting calls can be executed on shared libraries (for example, ViewModel implementations).

Application Insights

Application Insights is another subscription based service/platform that can be used with Xamarin applications. This cloud-based suite was initially released by Microsoft for web applications, but it slowly made its way into mobile applications. The application insights NuGet package(s) can be used with Xamarin.Android (API level 15 and higher) and Xamarin.iOS (version 6 and higher) applications. Application Insights, with a limited feature set, can be used on an unlimited number of devices with a limited amount of data processing for free.

Application Insights usage scenarios are, in essence, very similar to Xamarin Insights. The initial step is to use the platform-specific initializer to start the telemetry session. Once the telemetry context is created, an instance of a `TelemetryClient` can be used to either start automatic diagnostic recording or send manual data to the insights server:

```
var telemetryClient = new TelemetryClient();

// User Action Event
telemetryClient.TrackEvent("Calculation Completed");

// Send a metric:
telemetryClient.TrackMetric("Calculation Range", (ordinal2 -
ordinal1));

// Nominal values by which you can filter events:
var nominalValues = new Dictionary<string,string> { {"calculation",
"rangeCalculation"}};
```

```
// Metrics associated with an event:
var metrics = new Dictionary<string,int>
        {
            {"ordinal1", ordinal1},
             {"ordinal2", ordinal2}
        };

    telemetryClient.TrackEvent("Calculation Completed", nominalValues,
    metrics);
```

Together with crash analytics provided by HockeyApp, usage statics and server-side data (if any) with Application Insights for mobile application, live telemetry can provide valuable insights about Xamarin applications.

 Application Insights is slowly being transitioned out in favor of HockeyApp. This transition was first announced in November 2015 during the Connect() conference. As of April 2016, Microsoft will stop accepting new submissions for Xamarin applications as well as Windows Store and Windows Phone apps. In June 2016, the application insights data for mobile apps is completely being migrated to the HockeyApp.

Summary

Overall, tools available for the .NET platform can be easily utilized to manage and streamline the development pipeline tasks. On top of the Microsoft-based offerings, there are a number of service providers with the freemium subscription model. This can create great opportunities for individual/independent developers.

For source control, the most logical choices are Git and TFVC. While TFVC is an ideal solution for developers with a Windows-based development environment setup, Git provide native integration to Xamarin Studio on both Windows and Mac OS environments.

Independent from the repository choice, Visual Studio Team Services or other CI platforms such as TeamCity can be employed to create automated testing and build workflows.

Finally, beta testing and collected telemetry are fundamental elements for Xamarin projects. With real use-cases and analytical data on usage patterns, developers can fine-tune their applications and avoid problems before the actual release.

In the final chapter, we will be discussing the preparation steps for store submission and distribution options for Xamarin applications.

12
ALM – App Stores and Publishing

This chapter explains the processes related to app package preparation and release, which constitutes the last step of the application lifecycle. General information about application packages and bundles is followed by information about different release channels and release management tools. The chapter is divided into the following sections:

- Release packages
- Distribution options
- Line of business apps

Release packages

On each Xamarin target platform, release packages differ in several ways from the development packages prepared during the development and testing phases. Release packages are optimized to take up less space and consume less resources in the runtime (both processing time and memory resources). They also do not contain symbol files or inter-process communication channels (such as **Java Debug Wire Protocol (JDWP)**) required for **just-in-time (JIT)** debugging. It is also important to mention that Xamarin.iOS and Xamarin.Android projects, once built for release, are virtually no different from applications built with native development tools.

In order to prepare the application for release, developers need to take several preparation steps before actually building the application. These steps differ slightly on each platform.

Xamarin.Android app package (.apk)

Developers preparing Xamarin.Android application release packages should follow a certain checklist to create an optimized package for release.

Disabling debugging

The initial step of preparing a Xamarin.Android application for release is to disable the debugging channel, called Java Debug Wire Protocol, used by Xamarin tools or adb to communicate with the **Java Virtual Machine (JVM)**. If not disabled, this channel can pose a security risk.

JDWP can be disabled by using either the application manifest or the AssemblyInfo. cs file. In order to disable debugging using the application manifest, the android:debuggable attribute needs to be set to false on the application node:

```
<application android:label="Fibonnaci Calculator"
             android:debuggable="false"
             android:icon="@drawable/Icon">
</application>
```

The entry in the AssemblyInfo.cs looks similar:

```
[assembly: Application(Debuggable = false, BackupAgent = typeof(Prefer
encesBackupService))]
```

> Note that debug builds contain certain permissions, such as storage access and Internet usage, automatically enabled. Once the application is built with a release configuration, it is a good idea to run the application through another round of regression testing and, if necessary, modify the explicit permission declarations in the application manifest.

Linking

During the development phase, application deployments generally contain the whole set of Xamarin.Android runtime assemblies (no linking). Linking is the process where only the required components are introduced into the application package to reduce the application package's size. A static analysis algorithm (that is, ahead-of-time compilation) is used during the linking process, in which the dependencies are identified and included in the bundle.

There are three available options that define which assemblies will be put through the process of linking:

- **None**: This is the default configuration value for debug builds. No linking is performed.

- **Sdk Assemblies Only**: Only Xamarin.Android runtime assemblies are linked.

- **Sdk and User Assemblies**: Both Xamarin.Android runtime assemblies and the application libraries are statically analyzed for code reach.

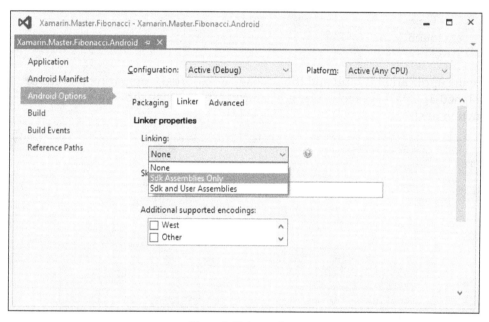

Figure 1: Linker options

In order to ensure that certain types and namespaces are included in the final package, even though they are not statically reachable, a simple public class declaration with public methods using the required types as parameters can create the necessary code reachability (see `LinkerPleaseInclude.cs`):

```
public class LinkerPleaseInclude
{
    public void Include(Activity act)
    {
        act.Title = act.Title + "";
    }
}
```

Linking certain types and methods can also be achieved using a link description file. In order to create a link description file, an XML file with the build action set to `LinkDescription` should be created in the Xamarin.Android project. The file schema for `LinkDescription` uses a simple declarative structure:

```xml
<?xml version="1.0" encoding="utf-8" ?>
<linker>
  <assembly fullname="Mono.Android">
    <type fullname="Android.App.Activity" >
      <method name="get_Title" />
      <method name="set_Title" />
    </type>
  </assembly>
</linker>
```

Once the application is built and the package is exported, comparing the size of the signed `apk` packages for `None`, `Sdk`, and `All` assemblies shows a noticeable reduction in size:

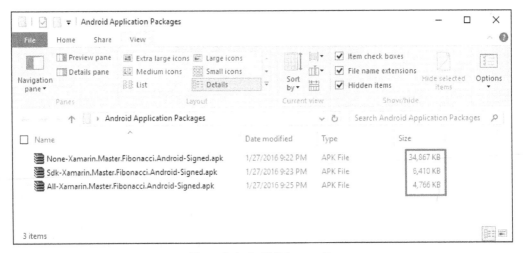

Figure 2: Android linker results

Just like the release build, after the linking step, it is highly advised to run another setup regression test to see if the application features are functioning as expected.

Packing options

Important application package-related configuration values can be found in the **Packaging** section of the **Android Options** tab of the **Project Properties** page. In spite of the fact that most of the configuration values are disabled by default in a normal release build, they might be used for optimizing the release package in certain scenarios. **Use Shared Runtime** and **Use Fast Deployment** are, under normal circumstances, intended for debug builds and are used to increase the productivity of developers.

- **Bundle assemblies into native code**: This option instructs the mono compiler to bundle the application assemblies into a native shared library as a security measure (only available with an Enterprise license).

- **Generate one package (.apk) per selected ABI**: Each selected **Application Binary Interface** (**ABI**) will cause the compiler to generate a separate package. For instance, if armeabi-v7a and x86 CPU architectures are selected, two application packages will be generated.

- **AOT Compilation** (experimental): Ahead-of-time compilation converts the application assemblies into native code to decrease the initialization time for the application while increasing the application package size (only available with Business or Enterprise licenses).

- **Enable Multi-Dex**: In order to work around the DEX method count limit, the Multi-Dex feature was introduced in the Android Lollipop (API 21) release and a retroactive support library was released for API levels 4 through 20. This option enables the use of multiple DEX files.

> Android application packages contain an executable bytecode file called the Dalvik Executable file (DEX). This file contains the compiled code used in the application runtime and has a limit of $64*2^{10}$ (65536) methods referenced (including Android framework methods, library methods, and custom code introduced by the application).

- **Enable ProGuard**: ProGuard is another option that can help reduce the size of the application and the DEX declarations. For applications developed with a native toolset, ProGuard can also obfuscate the application code, but this option is currently not available for Xamarin.Android applications.

Packaging

Once the preparation steps are complete, Xamarin.Android application packages can be created either with Visual Studio or Xamarin Studio. Xamarin Studio offers the option of archiving the builds so that they can be easily signed and pushed to available channels.

The application package can be archived using the **Archive for Publishing** option in the project context menu. (Similarly, the **View Archives** button can be used to access previous archives.) In the archives view, the selected application package can be signed and ready for store submission or ad-hoc (see *Distribution options*) distribution.

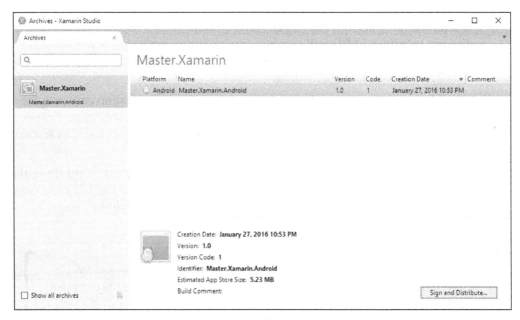

Figure 3: Xamarin Studio package archives

Packages created with the `Export Android Package` option using Visual Studio are signed with the debug key. These packages should not, and in most cases cannot, be distributed through normal channels. In order to create the release-ready package, the unsigned package from the build directory should be located and the package should be signed using the `jarsigner` utility from Java SDK.

Xamarin.iOS app bundle (.ipa)

Before any iOS application can be published to the App Store, there are several configuration values that need to be configured and revised. More importantly, the build process should be configured as a release build and the package should be signed with a proper identity before it can be submitted through iTunes Connect.

Build options

For a release build (ad-hoc or app-store), once the active build configuration is set, some of the values are automatically adjusted to the developers' convenience. For instance, options related to debugging such as **Enable Profiling** and **Enable incremental builds** are automatically disabled. These options, together with the **Enable Debugging** option, produce larger application packages that are not valid for store submission.

Other than the debugging options, the supported CPU architectures must be carefully configured. While it is possible to combine the selections (such as ARMv7 + ARM64, as seen in the figure below), each architecture targets a certain iPhone or iPad model. ARMv6 was the initial CPU architecture that was used in iPhone 3G. This architecture is no longer supported by iOS compilers. Starting with iPhone 3GS, up until iPhone 5, including iPads, the CPU architecture used was ARMv7. ARMv7s and ARM64 were used in iPhone 5 and iPhone 5s respectively. iPhone 6 uses ARMv8, which is another 64-bit processor (that is, the build requirement would be ARM64).

Figure 4: iOS build configuration

Low Level Virtual Machine (LLVM) is the name of the set of tools/libraries designed for the compile-time optimization of programs written in various programming languages. It was released under an open source license. During the development phase, Xamarin tools only utilize mono compiler (mtouch). Mono compiler produces less optimized but more "accessible" binaries that make them possible to debug and diagnose. However, for release builds using LLVM, it can generate much more optimized results.

While LLVM provides both package size and runtime enhancements, the Thumb-2 instruction set is simply an executable size improvement. ARMv7 and ARMv7s processors use this compact instruction set. It can provide a significant reduction in the package size at the expense of slower execution time.

Linking

Linking works in a similar way as in Xamarin.Android platform. In addition to arbitrary class creation with public methods to avoid certain classes being linked out, on Xamarin.iOS, Preserve attribute can be used on class declarations to inform the compiler about the necessity of a certain class and its members (such as [Preserve(AllMembers = true)]).

Provisioning profile

Provisioning profiles are used to set up the entitlements and package signing information for iOS applications. In order to create a publishing-ready iOS package, users first need to create the application metadata on Apple's iOS provisioning portal.

On the provisioning portal, developers should first choose a unique application name and a bundle ID. These will be used to identify the application once it is published. Additionally, the App Services that are required by the application should be selected.

Other than the App ID, a distribution profile should be created for the application. In order to create the distribution profile, one would need to select the Provision->Distribution node on the application portal navigation tree. Using the + button, a new distribution profile can be created. In the distribution profile wizard, the user need to select the distribution type (that is, **App Store** or **Ad Hoc**), select the App ID that was previously created, possible deployment devices, and a signing certificate (a signing certificate can be requested from Apple's Members Center).

Once the App ID and provisioning profile are created, the application metadata should be set up in the Xamarin.iOS project settings in the iOS **Application Settings** section (`Info.plist` and `Entitlements.plist` files can also be directly configured).

Finally, the **Archive for Publishing** button can be used to create the release package. Once the build is complete, the new package will be shown in the archives window. Selecting the correct application and using the **Sign and Distribute** option will open the publishing wizard where the previously configured provisioning profile can be selected and applied to the current build package.

Windows Phone app package (.appx)

Windows Phone and Windows Store application packages are prepared using the available toolset for Windows app developers in Visual Studio. In the release preparation phase, Windows Phone applications do not require or interact with any Xamarin components.

Distribution options

Just like the beta builds, there are different distribution options for the release versions of Xamarin applications. Public app stores are the easiest and the most convenient way to distribute mobile applications, targeting the general public. On the other hand, private application distribution channels may be needed for enterprise application distribution scenarios.

App store(s)

For Xamarin.iOS and Windows Phone applications, the only official distribution stores are application stores maintained by Apple and Microsoft respectively. Each of these application stores has a well-defined submission flow involving both content validation (that is, whether the application meet the content guidelines) and technical validation (that is, does the application meets the quality criteria). It is highly advisable to read the appropriate application certification guidelines before submitting the release-ready package to either of these stores. In order to distribute applications using iTunes Connect tools and Apple App Store, developers need to apply for a developer account and pay an annual subscription fee. Windows App Store requires a developer account subscription, which at the moment is free of charge.

On the other hand, Android developers have a big pool of options as public app distribution channels. The most popular stores are the Google Play and Amazon App stores. Both of these stores allow developers to publish both paid and free applications.

The Google Play store serves as the official app store for the Android operating system. It was originally called the Android Market and later on merged with two other Google products, namely Google Music and Google eBookstore. The Google Play store requires developers to sign up with a small subscription fee before they can distribute applications. Security and quality testing is one of the most essential steps of the app certification process, which makes this store the most trusted among Android users.

On the other hand, the Amazon App store was initially created for Amazon Kindle Fire devices specifically, and yet it became the second biggest store for Android applications. Developers can sign up for a free developer account, and the revenue share model is the same as other popular stores (that is, 70% developer/30% store).

Other than the two biggest stores, there are other application stores for Android applications. The most intriguing app store provider is the F-Droid store, which focuses on free and open source software (FOSS) for the Android operating system. This store attracts many users since the store policy dictates that there is no tracking, advertising, or dependencies in distributed applications.

Ad-hoc

Ad-hoc distribution is the name given to the process by which application packages are distributed to users for testing or private use through various communication channels (such as shared storage, online sharing, e-mail, and so on).

This type of distribution was mentioned in the beta testing part of the previous chapter, but at times, applications built only for internal use can be distributed in this manner.

The ad-hoc distribution concept can be divided into two categories: signed and unsigned distribution. The official way of distributing application packages over the air is to digitally sign the application packages with a trusted certificate (that is, the signing identity should be created using the official channels such as signing certificate providers). Once the application package is digitally signed with a certificate from a trusted provider, the app can be sideloaded to mobile devices. Sideloading is the process of installing an app without using a public or private store.

If the application is signed by a self-signed certificate, the application publisher would simply be unidentifiable. In this type of scenario, either the owner of the device should allow applications to be installed from unknown sources (on Android and Windows 10 mobile devices) or the device should be developer unlocked (on Windows Phone) or jailbroken (on iOS). While unlocking a device is an official process on Windows Phone devices, jailbreaking violates the end-user license agreement for iOS.

Line of Business apps

Line of Business applications, or LOB apps, is a term generally used synonymously with enterprise applications. These applications are either developed in-house, or outsourced for the specific needs of a company. In other words, LOB apps can be categorized as business rather than consumer applications. They are generally domain-specific and target a small group with a specific need.

Private channel distribution (Android)

One way of distributing LOB applications built for Android platform is to use the Google Play private channels. Applications distributed through these channels are restricted to users of a specific domain. In order to use private channels, one needs to have a subscription to either Google Play for Work, Google Apps for Business, Education, or Government.

While app pricing and other distribution settings may still apply to these private apps, the testing and validation steps are skipped in the store submission process. App submissions can either be done by the owner of the channel or the permissions can be delegated to another user in the same domain.

Apple Developer Enterprise Program

The Apple Developer Enterprise Program is Apple's initiative to support companies to develop and distribute in-house applications. This program is only available for companies that exist as a legal entity (the D-U-N-S number is required). Once the organization is enrolled in the Enterprise Program, development and release management team members can be assigned roles, as well as digital certificates and provisioning profiles. However, these provisioning profiles cannot contain the App Store distribution method (that is, the only available provisioning profiles are in-house and ad-hoc).

Create iOS Distribution Provisioning Profile
Generate provisioning profiles here. To learn more, visit the How To section.

Distribution Method	⦿ In House	◯ Ad Hoc
Profile Name	Enter a profile name	

Figure 5: Provisioning profile for Apple Developer Enterprise Program

The applications built under the enterprise program can be distributed through native or third-party **Mobile Device Management (MDM)** solutions, as well as ad-hoc packages.

Windows Phone private distribution

Windows Phone applications can be developed and distributed for in-house utilization, using the application signing certificate purchased from Symantec (Symantec is currently the only provider of this type of certificate). Using the mobile signing certificate, application packages can signed and distributed through MDMs or sideloaded into company devices.

Most MDM providers, such as Microsoft Intune, come equipped with a company store application that can be used to provide applications for company devices. Device management systems also make it possible to install the company applications directly for domain users.

It is also possible to install the signing certificate on devices, which will benefit from in-house applications and distribute applications through custom company hub applications.

Summary

In this chapter, we briefly went over the package preparation process for Xamarin. Android and Xamarin.iOS applications (and also Windows Phone). As you can see, preparing the release package is a little more complicated then pressing the **Debug** button on the development IDE of choice. However, each of these platforms have well-defined application certification guidelines and online resources.

Once the release packages are prepared, it is up to the developer to choose between different distribution options, including but not limited to, the public and private stores that can be used to publish the release packages. Public store applications can be delivered to the general public, while private distribution channels or ad-hoc deployments, involving sideloading and MDMs, can be used for LOB applications.

Index

Monotouch Profiler (iOS only) 38
multithreading, on Xamarin
  about 53
  concurrency model, on iOS 56
  single thread model 54, 55
  Task-based Asynchronous
      Pattern (TAP) 55

N

native libraries
  about 193
  linking, versus binding (iOS) 196-198
  managed callable wrappers
      (Android) 193-195
navigation
  about 207
  horizontal navigation 208-212
  jump navigation 214
  vertical navigation 212, 213
Near Field Communication (NFC)
      protocol 178
NuGet packages
  about 21
  reference 22

O

OAuth 134, 135
OData 133, 134

P

package distribution 344, 345
packing options
  AOT Compilation 353
  Bundle assemblies into native code 353
  Enable Multi-Dex 353
  Enable ProGuard 353
  Generate one package (.apk) per
      selected ABI 353
pages, Xamarin.Forms
  CarouselPage 252
  ContentPage 253
  MasterDetail page 249-252
  NavigationPage 252
  Tabbed page 247-249
parallel execution 62-64

patterns
  best practices 39, 64
peer-to-peer (P2P) networks 178
peripherals
  about 176
  Bluetooth 177
  Near Field Communication (NFC) 178
  Wi-Fi Direct 178
permission levels, of file
  Append 95
  EnableWriteAheadLogging 95
  MultiProcess 95
  Private 95
  WorldReadable/WorldWritable 95
platform-specific concepts
  about 33
  Automatic Reference Counting (ARC) 33
  object reference types 33
Portable Class Libraries (PCLs) 274

Q

quality, in cross-development
  about 23
  abstraction 23
  loose-coupling 24
  nativity 24
  reusability 23

R

release packages
  about 349
  Windows Phone app package (.appx) 357
  Xamarin.Android app package (.apk) 350
  Xamarin.iOS app bundle (.ipa) 355
Representational State Transfer (REST) 129

S

services (Android only)
  about 84, 85
  bound service 84
  started service 84
SGen garbage collector 32
Shared Preferences 93
SignalR
  defining 136-138

messaging 123, 124
OAuth 134, 135
OData 133, 134
RESTful services 129-133
SOAP/XML services 124-128
transport 123
Windows Communication Foundation (WCF) 124
Windows Notification Services (WNS) 156
Windows Phone app package (.appx) 357
Windows Presentation Foundation (WPF) 310
Windows Runtime
design metrics 204

X

Xamarin
about 1
cross-platform projects, with 1
Xamarin.Android app package (.apk)
about 350
debugging, disabling 350
linking 350-352
packaging 354
packing options 353
Xamarin Component Store
reference 23
Xamarin.Forms
about 241
anatomy 242, 243
components 247
defining 241, 242
project structure 243-246

Xamarin Insights 346, 347
Xamarin.iOS app bundle (.ipa)
about 355
build options 355, 356
linking 356
provisioning profile 356
Xamarin platforms
background downloads 151-155
defining 148
NSUrlConnection/NSUrlSession (iOS Only) 149-151
permissions 148, 149
push notifications 155-157
Xamarin Profiler
about 34, 35
allocations instrument 35
Time Profiler 35
Xamarin solution structure
about 15
components 23
NuGet packages 21
portable class libraries 16, 17
shared projects 18, 19
Xamarin.Forms 20
Xamarin Test Cloud 326
Xamarin Test Recorder 327
Xamarin.UITests 325
Xcode Instruments 38
XSL
about 295
reference link 295

www.ingramcontent.com/pod-product-compliance
Lightning Source LLC
Chambersburg PA
CBHW062041050326
40690CB00016B/2982